The Right Pathway

Ethical & Moral values for all ages in the light of Quranic Verses

Prof. Muhammad Rafi

Paramount Books (Pvt) Ltd.
Karachi | Lahore | Islamabad | Hyderabad | Faisalabad | Peshawar | Abbottabad

The Right Pathway
by
Prof. Muhammad Rafi

First Edition 2015

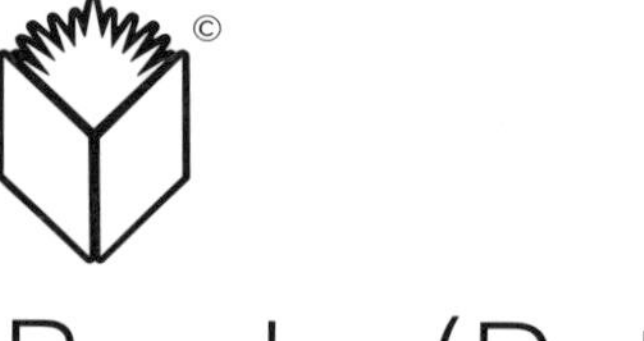

Paramount Books (Pvt) Ltd.
152/O, Block-2, P.E.C.H.S., Karachi-75400. Tel: 34310030
Fax: 34553772, E-mail: info@paramountbooks.com.pk
www.paramountbooks.com.pk

ISBN: 978-969-637-051-2
Printed in Pakistan

PUBLISHER'S NOTE

Dear Readers,

Publishers who are innately loyal to their profession are naturally inclined to treat the books that they publish nearly the same way as they would their children. It is only natural, therefore, that weaknesses are also the same when some books come closer to their heart than others. *The Right Pathway* is one such book for me. I sincerely hope that the following lines will enable you to understand my justification for writing this Publisher's Note, as well as appreciate the need and importance of publishing such a book in relevance to the modern day life context.

It seems that today's fast paced life has deprived most youngsters from being beneficiaries of moral and ethical guidance which used to be instilled into growing minds by parents and elders at home. Adults who lacked this advantage while young, and children who are now growing up while devoid of the benefits of this grace and character refinement, have unfortunately been affected, and all these factors have got combined to retard the social progress of humanity, resulting in a scenario which is not at all agreeable.

Fortunately, things are not as damaging as they seem because there still are many sections of human societies around the world, which are contributing in their own way to arrest and avert societal decadence as described above. This book is a humble input to augment the efforts and sacrifices being made by these noble souls. Moreover, this universal problem does not exist with the same intensity and acuteness everywhere. Its severity differs from situation to situation, place to place, parent to parent, and teacher to teacher.

It will not be fair if this book *The Right Pathway (Ethical & Moral Values for all Ages in the Light of Quranic Verses)* and its precursors, *Moral Pathways for All Ages, Moral Compass for Young People*, are not dedicated to those who inspired these two books in the first place. The author of these titles, my very good friend Professor Muhammad Rafi, and I have decided to dedicate this book, with true humility, to each and every individual in the world who lives his or her life within the ambit of universally accepted human values.

With best wishes,

Iqbal Saleh Muhammad
Managing Director
Paramount Books (Pvt) Ltd.

THE AUTHOR

Prof. Muhammad Rafi has a law degree and a Master's in English Literature both from the University of Karachi. After a distinguished teaching career for more than 38 years he retired as Head of the Department of English and Principal of Government Islamia Science College in 2004. He was the Principal of Institute of Business Management (IoBM) College of Economics and Social Development from 2005 to 2007.

He has also taught at the University of Karachi, NIPA (National Institute of Public Administration), Executive Development Academy. A widely travelled man, he has been a member of the Karachi University Senate, Karachi University's Board of Studies (English Department), various sports, academic, curricular and examining bodies of the Government of Sindh, Karachi Board of Intermediate Education, Karachi University, Pakistan Banking and Finance Services Commission. He is on the Board of Governors of the Board of Secondary Education. He has also written Friday feature for Daily Dawn regularly from 1998 to 2012.

CONTENTS

THE STRAIGHT PATH OF LIFE

'(Allah) guide us on the straight path' (1:6)

I expect to pass through this world once. Any good therefore that I can do, or any kindness that I can show to any fellow creature, let me do it now. Let me not defer or neglect it. I shall not pass this way again.(Anonymous)

The history of mankind tells us that the fate of a nation rests on its younger generation and its future is tied with the training of its youth. This goal is neither decided in the political arena, nor on the battlefield. It is decided in the system of education and its imparting institutions. This system, if rightly planned and sincerely executed, provides nurseries where future generations are nurtured, leading to prosperity, peace and happiness. This system enables the youth to subdue the forces and resources of nature by acquisition of adequate knowledge through a well-balanced and elaborate system capable of harnessing human potential in consonance with permanent social, ethical and moral values.

HUMAN VALUES

Human values can be viewed objectively as universal determinants in all human decision making. All decisions ultimately lead to a choice among alternatives of what is most valued, for whatever reasons and are determined by a particular value system that is in vogue. These values are limited to a particular period of time and space and are relative in nature. Islam, on the other hand asserts that its teachings are not confined to any particular tribe, nation or country. It boldly asserts that Messengers were sent amongst different nations in different times. They were Divinely ordained to impart the same guiding system. But, as these messages were, one by one, muddled by human interpolation, the same 'Heavenly Elixir' has, for all times, been bottled in the Quran and hermetically sealed against all possible human influence, interference and distortions.

'Undoubtedly We have sent down the Message, and it is Our responsibility to guard it from any sort of corruption' (15:9)

QURANIC GUIDANCE

The Quran demands that every Muslim must submit to the Divine commands and seek guidance and enlightenment from it. All the actions of a Muslim are disciplined by the laws of the Quran through ceaseless endeavour, righteous deeds, creative thinking, common sense, discernment, deep mental discipline and balanced judgment. In the Quranic terminology this is called 'Furqan' – the fundamental principle on which we should base our whole edifice of purposeful activity. The greatness of the Quran is that it lays bare a principle and its relevant values are based on that principle. Those who submit to these values are called Muslims. The objective of highlighting these values in this book is to provide guidance to everyone in general and the youth in particular.

Allah, the Creator and the Sustainer, has declared that the Quran is His last and final Book revealed to mankind for guidance (6:114). As such, it contains a complete code of life and permanent values which remain unalterable even with the passage of time and provide guidance regarding all the problems which mankind would face till the end of time. Allah says, 'It is up to Us to collect it, have it memorized and preserve it – so when We collect it/preserve it, you should follow it.' (75:17,18)

ETERNAL QUALITIES OF QURAN

The Quran itself explains its eternal qualities:

1. It is a guidance for all and removes all doubts (2:2)
2. Muslims are ordained to obey and follow the Quran and not anything else (7:3)
3. The Messenger (Nabi) ﷺ was also ordained to follow and obey the Quran (10:109)
4. Those who do not decide their affairs according to the Quran are the ones who are unbelievers (Kafireen) (5:44)
5. No one is authorized to make any changes in it (6:34)
6. The Quran confirms and preserves the earlier Revelations (5:48)
7. There is nothing contradictory in it (4:82)
8. All differences can be resolved by following the guidance contained in this Book (42:10)
9. Whatever is revealed in the Quran, has also been explained in it (75:19)
10. It ordains mankind to think, ponder and do research (47:24)
11. It is easy to get guidance and advice from the Quran (54:17), but at the same time it

is necessary that the one seeking guidance should keep one's mind clear, clean and unprejudiced (56:79)

12. Allah, the Almighty, has taken upon Himself the responsibility of keeping it preserved in all respects (15:9)

FINAL AUTHORITY

The Holy Quran, according to Islamic principles, is the final authority in all matters of life and death. The injunctions, principles, laws and values enshrined in it form the corner-stone of the Islamic polity and the limits laid down by it provide the framework within which the laws of the Islamic state may be formulated.

The Quran is the last and final of the Divine Books. No subsequent human opinion or pronouncement in matters of religion, therefore, can be recognized as authoritative; nor can any man made laws repugnant to the Quran and no subsequent human opinion or pronouncement in matters of religion be regarded as binding upon Muslims. The Quran transcends the barriers of time and space and its laid down principles evolve in accordance with the needs of time.

EDUCATION SYSTEM

An all embracing comprehensive education system will ultimately enable the youth to conquer and subdue the forces and resources of nature. The outer world is a true image of man's inner self. As long as there is no change in man's inner self, there can be no change in the outer world either. The Quran considers the change in human beings absolutely necessary to bring about an external revolution.

'Verily Allah does not change the state of a people till they change themselves.' (13:11)

When nation stops thinking, reflecting and searching; words and concepts lose their meaning. This process of semantics distorts a nation's vision and world-view. Consequently the people continue to wade through the mire of glaring contradictions, smug in self-deception. Education per se is such a construct today not only in Pakistan alone, but also in the whole world.

If we live and work giving preference to the guidance of the Divine Revelation; then the flow of information and knowledge will ultimately find its own level in the minds of the potential users and the most honourable and beneficial for the whole humanity will survive.

'The negative forces, as a result of the conflict between truth and falsehood pass away like scum and that which is beneficial for mankind remains on the earth.' (13:17)

'The system of the universe is a clear proof that Allah's plan is to produce positive results. Anything that does not produce such results is eliminated and replaced by another capable of producing constructive results.'o (14:19)

PROPER EDUCATION SYSTEM

An efficient and rightly guided education system is all-embracing and develops the character and personality of the students. Students stepping into their teens have a dynamic, impressionable mind hungry for information, knowledge and answers to happenings, common and unusual. In order to be useful citizens and better human beings their curiosity and thirst for knowledge has to be satisfied keeping in view the primary objective of developing their personality, character and outlook of life. This will ultimately make them better human beings through identification and transformation of values into behavioural activities.

Many believe that things are morally right or wrong independently of whatever we might happen to suppose, while others claim that right and wrong amounts to nothing more than subjective preference. Undoubtedly, if education is goal-oriented and has a proper positive direction, it acts intelligently and helps in positive and meaningful upbringing of children, who can achieve their highest degree of individual and collective social excellence.

'Allah will raise the ranks of those who believe and those who have acquired knowledge.' (58:11)

'Avoid those who are ignorant and cultivate the spirit of forgiveness and tolerance.' (7:199)

'The Quran lays down the basic principle of respecting and honouring all human beings irrespective of their religion , beliefs, colour, language, status, birth etc.' (17:70)

MORALITY

Morality relates not only to practical situations but to ideas about human nature and how 'moral values' fit into our conception of the world. Morality applies to all and moral values do not change whatever the situation. Moral education - the training of heart and mind towards the good–involves many things. It involves rules and percepts of human relationship. It must provide training in good habits. Most of us fail to realize that good habits formed at an early age make all the difference. There is nothing more influential, more determinant, in a child's life than the moral power of quiet example. Parents, teachers and adult family members must take morality seriously and justify moral values by example.

MORAL VALUES AND VIRTUES

Values are those qualities that are regarded by a person or a group as important and desirable. As compared to the prevailing relative values in the world, the Divine guidance has given permanent values as the basic source of the highest values on which character development is based. These values act as leaven in the life of people.

The basic purpose of this book is to show what virtues and moral values look like, what they are in practice, how to recognize them, and how they work. If society wants the youth to possess the tracts of character we most admire, we need to teach what those traits are and why they deserve both admiration and allegiance. This book may not be equipped with a stereophonic sound system, but its inward method of sending purposeful message, coded in the hue of established permanent values, is like a worldwide web that reaches out to those who are willing to listen, understand, imbibe and apply these values in their lives. Moral values have to be identified in form and content of those traits. Young people in particular, and others in general, must achieve a minimal level of understanding these moral values to enable them to make sense of what these values really mean and how these values can help them to live a good life. The Quran guides all human beings in understanding these moral and ethical values. It also emphasizes the importance of applying these values in life.

'Help one another in good deeds and piety, and do not assist in crime and rebellion, and fear Allah. Surely Allah is severe in punishment' (5:2)

SELF AWARENESS

Some of the current world problems involving nuclear war, creationism and evolution, have not been taken up in this book. It must be realized that formation of character in people is educationally and socially a different task which has to precede the difficult ethical controversies of the day. This book deals with the basic moral values that will enable those who acquire them to reach a positive and successful position on all issues of life. All moral values in this book have been substantiated by stories and poems. Ayats (verses) from the Holy Quran have been given to further guide those who are interested in knowing what the Divine directives are in relation to these values. It is for everybody, especially all young people of all political, social and religious backgrounds, and it speaks to them on a more fundamental level than race, gender and religion. It addresses them as human beings. Everyone can benefit and enjoy the contents of this book. It will re-open their minds to a better self-awareness in light of the directives and principles of the Quran.

The Quran envisages a society in which the potentialities, the latent abilities of all individuals are developed, and no one in such a society is deprived of the necessities of life.

'And We have provided therein (in the land) sustenance for you, and for those for whom you do not provide.'(15:20)

'Spend in the cause of Allah from your sustenance and do not make your own hands contribute to your destruction. Do all things gracefully, for Allah loves those who do things with excellence.'(2:195)

'And the earth He has created for the benefit of all living beings.' (55:10)

The subsequent results are always positive and this is the promise of Allah to all those who follow His guidance.

'They shall have the good news of happiness in this present worldly life as well as in the life hereafter.'(10:64)

The stories, in this book, are there to show that moral values, ethics and virtues are not only to be possessed, but are the pivotal part of human nature. Some of the stories illustrate a moral value in reverse only to emphasize its importance by being aware about its opposite.

RESPONSIBILITY OF PARENTS, RELATIVES AND TEACHERS

How can children imbibe virtues and values? This is the primary responsibility of parents, family members and teachers. These values are sown in childhood and nurtured as children grow up. After all, nobody is born a criminal. Children are like plants. You sow the seeds and also reap the benefit of its growth and development. The fact that young people need to be taught moral values suggests that there are moral 'truths' that can be learned in the same way as other facts. Similarly all age groups can benefit from the contents of this book.

QURANIC VALUES

Philosophers, thinkers and great minds throughout centuries have given much thought to the solution of problems faced by man. But human efforts and judgment, while providing temporary panacea, can be biased, self-centred and relative. On the other hand, Divine Guidance is balanced, just, objective and eternal. Allah has prescribed a system, which is equally beneficial to all, and excludes no one. This Guide eliminates the prevailing method whereby one party or group advances and progresses at the cost of others. In essence, it is a set of permanent values an individual or nation should follow to ensure the welfare and progress of mankind.

These values act as a guide as to how a person should live and act.

1. Respect and honour all human beings irrespective of their religion, colour, race, sex, language, status, property, birth, profession/job and so on [17:70]
2. Talk straight, to the point, without any ambiguity or deception [33:70]
3. Choose best words to speak and say them in the best possible way [17:53, 2:83]
4. Do not shout. Speak politely keeping your voice low. [31:19]
5. Always speak the truth. Shun words that are deceitful [4:9]
6. Do not confound truth with falsehood [2:42]
7. Say with your mouth what is in your heart [3:167]
8. Speak in a civilized manner in a language that is recognized by the society and is commonly used [4:63, 2:83]
9. When you voice an opinion, be just, even if it is against a relative [6:152]
10. And turn not your face away from men with pride, nor walk in insolence through the earth. [31:18]
11. Do not talk, listen or do anything vain [23:3, 28:55]
12. Do not participate or witness any falsehood and if you pass evil talk or play, pass by it in dignity [25:72]
13. Do not come near any immodesty or lewdness whether openly or secretly [6:151]
14. If, unintentionally, any misconduct occurs by you, then correct yourself expeditiously [3:135]
15. Do not be contemptuous or arrogant with people [31:18]
16. Do not walk haughtily or with conceit for you cannot split the earth [17:37)
17. And be moderate (or show no insolence) in your walking, and lower your voice. Verily, the harshest of all voices is the voice (braying) of the ass. [31:19]
18. Walk with humility and sedateness [25:63]

19. Keep your gazes lowered devoid of any lustful looks and obscene and indecent (salacious) stares [24:30-31, 40:19]
20. If you do not have complete knowledge about anything, better keep your mouth shut. You might think that speaking about something without full knowledge is a trivial matter. But it might have grave consequences [24:15-16]
21. When you hear something malicious about someone, keep a favourable view about him/her until you attain full knowledge about the matter. Consider others innocent until they are proven guilty with solid and truthful evidence [24:12-13]
22. Ascertain the truth of any news, lest you accuse and blame someone in ignorance and afterwards repent of what you did [49:6]
23. Do not follow blindly any information of which you have no direct knowledge. (Using your faculties of perception and conception) you must verify it for yourself. In the Court of Allah, you will be held accountable for your hearing, sight, and the faculty of reasoning [17:36]
24. Never think that you have reached the final stage of knowledge and nobody knows more than yourself. Remember! Above everyone endowed with knowledge is another endowed with more knowledge [12:76]. Even the Messenger ﷺ was asked to keep praying, "O my Sustainer! Advance me in knowledge." [20:114]
25. The believers are but a single Brotherhood. Live like members of one family, brothers and sisters unto one another [49:10]
26. Do not make mockery of others or ridicule others [49:11]
27. Do not defame others [49:11]
28. Do not insult others by nicknames [49:11]
29. Avoid suspicion and guesswork. Suspicion and guesswork might deplete your communal energy [49:12]
30. Spy not upon one another [49:12]
31. Do not backbite one another [49:12]
32. When you meet each other, offer good wishes and blessings for safety. When a courteous greeting is offered to you, meet it with a greeting still more courteous or (at least) of equal courtesy [4:86]
33. When you enter your own home or the home of somebody else, compliment the inmates [24:61]
34. Do not enter houses other than your own until you have sought permission; and then greet the inmates and wish them a life of blessing, purity and pleasure [24:27]
35. Treat kindly -Your parents-relatives-the orphans- and those who have been left alone in the society [4:36]

36. Take care of -the needy,-the disabled- Those whose hard earned income is insufficient to meet their needs- And those whose businesses have stalled – And those who have lost their jobs. [4:36]
37. Treat kindly-Your related neighbours, and unrelated neighbours-wayfarers (Companions by your side in public gatherings, or public transport). [4:36]
38. Be generous to the needy wayfarer, the homeless , and the one who reaches you in a destitute condition [4:36]
39. Be nice to people who work under your care [4:36]
40. Do not follow up your gifts with reminders of your generosity [2:262]
41. Do not expect a return for your good behaviour, not even thanks [76:9]
42. Cooperate with one another in good deeds and do not cooperate with others in evil and bad matters [5:2]
43. Do not try to impress people on account of self-proclaimed virtues [53:32]
44. You should enjoin right conduct on others but mend your own ways first. Actions speak louder than words. You must first practise good deeds yourself, then preach [2:44]
45. Correct yourself and your families first [before trying to correct others] [66:6]
46. Pardon gracefully if anyone among you commits a bad deed out of ignorance, and then repents and amends [6:54]
47. Divert and sublimate your anger and potentially virulent emotions to creative energy, and become a source of tranquillity and comfort to people [3:134]
48. Call people to the Way of your Lord with wisdom and beautiful exhortation. Reason with them most decently [16:125]
49. Leave to themselves those who do not give any importance to the Divine code and have adopted and consider it as mere play and amusement [6:70]
50. Sit not in the company of those who ridicule Divine Law unless they engage in some other conversation [4:140]
51. Do not be jealous of those who are blessed with more than what you have [4:54]
52. In your collective life, make rooms for others [58:11]
53. When invited to dine, Go at the appointed time. Do not arrive too early to wait for the preparation of meal or linger after eating to engage in useless conversation. Such things may cause inconvenience to the host [33:53]
54. Eat and drink [what is lawful] in moderation [7:31]
55. Do not waste your wealth senselessly [17:26]
56. Fulfil your promises and commitments [17:35]
57. Keep yourself clean, pure [9:108, 4:43, 5:6]

58. Dress-up in agreeable attire and adorn yourself with exquisite character from inside out [7:26]
59. And eat up not one another's property unjustly (in any illegal way e.g. stealing, robbing, deceiving, etc.), nor give bribery to the rulers (judges before presenting your cases) that you may knowingly deprive others of their possessions sinfully. (Seek your provision only by fair effort) [2:188]
60. Be patient (2:153, 74:7)

May Allah keep us all under His protection and guidance and enable us to read, understand and follow the Quran.

All these values are achievable. Preservation of these values elevates the level of life from the animal to the human. The concept of values does not exist among the animals, but it forms the line of demarcation between animal and man. In line with the Quranic values we can understand the purpose of our existence and model our lives accordingly.

A Muslim reflects these values in his character and personality. Some of these qualities that he professes and practices are:

Positive Attitude:
- Is aware of own potential.
- Makes an effort to improve character and behaviour.
- Inculcates positive thoughts and feelings.
- Gives preference/priority to good manners, habits and tastes.

Justice:
- Accords equality to all human beings.
- Works with dedication.
- Does not conceal the truth whatsoever be the reason.
- Confounds not the truth with falsehood.

Constructive Approach:
- Is beneficial to the humanity in affairs that are constructive and based on values.
- Has a vision.
- Is willing to serve and improve.

Helpful:
- Assures a favourable and beneficial environment.
- Assists others who are in need.
- Treats his helpful attitude as a responsibility.

Forgiving:
- Takes initiative in forgiving others.
- Accepts margin for error or shortcomings.
- Grants pardon without harbouring resentment.

Kind and Loving:
- Shows sympathy, understanding, consideration and warm hearted nature.
- Is gentle and well natured and easy to get along with.
- Avoids aggression and violence.

Considerate and Accommodating:
- Is kind, thoughtful and obliging.
- Always prefers the needs of others over his own.
- Has regard for the needs and feelings of others.

Tolerance:
- Respects beliefs, opinions and practices of others.
- Manifests feeling of tolerance towards others.
- Is patient, good tempered and emotionally stable.
- Is capable of enduring hardship and pain.

Cooperation:
- Is always willing to work together for a common end or purpose.
- Facilitates positive efforts.

Trustworthy:
- Returns the deposits and entrusted wealth to rightful owners.
- Is reliable and capable of being depended upon and worthy to be believed.

Hardworking:
- Has capacity for prolonged and laborious effort.
- Is industrious and hard-working.
- Has untiring energy and unflagging pursuit of excellence.

Discipline and Courage:
- Has self-control, self-direction and sense of caring.
- Is disciplined and never shirks responsibilities.
- Is courageous and brave due to his positive character.
- Is capable of facing danger and fear with confidence and resolution.

Respect for Humanity:
- Knows that all human beings are equal by birth and are worthy of respect without discrimination of colour, cast, religion and gender.
- Initiates respect for all in society.
- Is not in conflict with societal norms of decency, peace, honesty and respect
- of law.

Honest and Positive Attitude:
- Is fair, equitable, incorruptible, righteous and candid.
- Applies honesty and positive attitude towards others, his work and duties.
- Displays integrity and upright behaviour in all matters.

God Conscious:

- Practically follows the Divine directives in serving humanity.
- Lives with a constant realization of God's divine presence and withstands the power of temptation boldly.
- Has a heart mercifully blessed with abiding humility.
- Is aware of the moral and ethical aspect of one's conduct and behaviour.

MORAL VALUES AND OUR SOCIETY

Moral values organize our society-both the way we actually apply them, and the way we might do them better. The key concepts are familiar to all. The challenge is to discover what they really mean, and how we can make them work together.

There are two types of people in the world - those who create dissensions and disharmony and chaos, who separate man from man, and those who bring about peace, harmony, love and togetherness.

'Those who are happy and contented with this worldly life without giving any importance to the Divine Guidance, they will certainly have hell as their home because of their bad deeds; and those who do acts of righteousness, their Sustainer shall guide them on the right path, and they will lead a blissful life of heaven where streams flow (10:7,8,9) and their lives will be a living testimony that Allah has not created the universe in vain or for destructive purposes (3:189-191). In such a society each person will desire the welfare of all others. This is how they will proclaim the 'Hamd'(Praise) of Allah-the Nourisher of all humanity (1:1)

You have to decide which group you would join. The Moral Pathways will always point towards the latter.

'And to Allah belongs all that is in the heavens and all that is on earth. And so He will reward those who do good with what is best' (53:31)

'Allah has designed the universe such that no action goes without consequence' (11:7, 45:22)

SCISSORS AND NEEDLE

A tailor was at work. He took a piece of cloth and a pair of shining, costly scissors and cut the cloth into pieces and bits. Then he put the scissors down at his feet. Then be took a small needle and thread and started to sew the pieces of cloth into a fine shirt. When be had finished, he stuck the needle on to his turban. The tailor's son was watching and asked, "Father, the scissors are costly and look beautiful; but you throw them down at your feet.

This needle is worth almost nothing, yet you place it carefully on your head. Is there any reason for this illogical behaviour?"

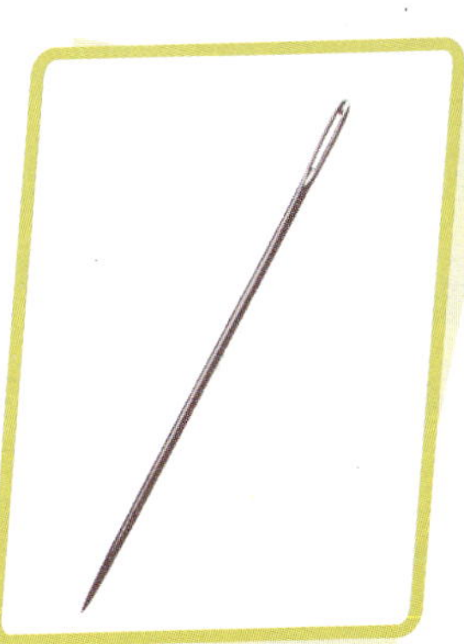

"Yes my son. The scissors have their function, no doubt, but they only cut the cloth into pieces. The needle, on the contrary, unites the pieces and enhances the value of the cloth. Therefore, the needle to me is more precious and valuable. The value of a thing depends upon its utility, son, not on its cost-price or appearance."

WALK THE TALK

Courage, ethics, morals, integrity, truth, honesty are words, important words; but they are nothing more than words unless we actually live by them. This is a great challenge which we must all face with determination, commitment and perseverance. We must walk the talk.

ROLE OF YOUNGER GENERATION

The book deals with values that can be transcribed into reality. Parents, teachers and elders should be helpful in guiding the children towards an improvement in their inner-self. Only then there can be a change in the outer world as the outer world is a true image of man's inner-self or character.

Our younger generation is quite capable of understanding the true worth of these values and imbibing them in their character. This would certainly enhance their personality for their own benefit and the general well-being of the society they live in.

REMINDER

This book reminds us of what is important and it should help all readers to lift their eyes. Someone rightly said, "Whatever is true, whatever is honourable, whatever is right, whatever is pure, whatever is lovely, whatever is good repute, if there is any excellence and anything worthy of praise, let your mind dwell on these things."

'Remember those who do not pay any heed to the Divine Guidance, Allah will never guide them to the right path and a severe punishment awaits them' (16:104)

Allah ordains that those who do evil can never be treated on the same pedestal as equals to those who are righteous

'Do those who do evil expect that We will hold them and the righteous people on the same pedestal as equals, so that their lives and deaths are alike ?How bad is the judgment that they make ! (45:21)

The highway of life may be full of thorny obstacles, but all impediments fall like nine pins once we decide to adopt the Divine Guidance in our lives. It all depends upon the degree of conviction that we have in the moral and ethical Quranic value system. It is the only guide left for mankind that confidently proclaims its ability to lead to its goal.

'Allah Who has created all the objects in the universe has also undertaken to make them aware of their goal and guide them towards it' (20:50)

Human intellect is gradually advancing towards a better comprehension of the Divine Guidance. Notwithstanding the forces of exploitation, the eternal truth is ultimately bound to prevail; the sooner the better for the emancipation of mankind.

1 CHARACTER AND PERSONALITY

'Surely in the Messenger of Allàh you have indeed a noble pattern and example for those who look forward to Allah and the Day of Judgement and frequently remember Allah' (33:21)

When wealth is lost, nothing is lost :
When health is lost, something is lost;
When character is lost, everything is lost (Anonymous)

There are different shades to the meaning of 'character'. The dictionary would tell you that it is basically an attitude or a quality that defines a person. This means that you are defined by a certain act of habits, qualities or attitudes and these form the basis upon which character is judged.

While the evolution of nature proceeds under the direct control and supervision of Allah, man is an active participant in his own evolution. Man develops as a result of his own free choice and deliberate voluntary efforts. He has the freedom of choice and can either accept or reject the Divine Guidance. The results are obvious when the choice is made.

The outward signs of a weak character are commonly believed to be corruption, injustice, intolerance, cruelty, hypocrisy and exploitation; but these signs do not reflect the true nature and significance of the term. Ultimately a person's character is judged in terms of his moral behaviour which for a Muslim must be based on the permanent values of the Quran.

HONOUR

Honour is an important ingredient of character, but its standard varies from society to society. For example, there is a tribe in an island of the Pacific Ocean where dishonesty is the best conduct and the cleverest cheat is held in the highest esteem. Another example is that of nationalism which is recognized the world over as a political and social creed and those who serve their nation by exploiting other nations are regarded as patriots. On the contrary the Quran says that the positive human values are the same everywhere and unchangeable. It provides a universal standard of good character called 'Taqwa', which is usually translated as 'God consciousness' and 'piety'.

POSITIVE QUALITIES

A positive character and personality can only develop if the Divine Guidance is followed in letter and spirit. Such an attitude leads to the development and growth of one's personality and character. The Quran's message is that this development is not based on what you receive, but on what you give. Generosity, kindness and helpfulness promote this growth, while selfishness and meanness retard it. If this truth is clearly perceived, men will rush to help those who are needy. Pride in possession will give way to munificence. The acquisition impulse will be weakened and the urge to give will gain strength. The Quran extols those who put the interest of others above their own.

'They prefer others before themselves although they themselves may be poor and needy. Whoever guards himself from his own greed shall prosper' (59:9)

RIGHT CHOICE

People who deny the Divine Guidance take their own emotions as authority and believe that life is only this worldly existence. In this concept people are born, grow and die. Those who believe in this concept speculate on the basis of their superficial knowledge. On the other hand, the Quran considers such a life as that of an animal.

'Surely Allah will admit all who attain to faith and do righteous deeds into gardens through which running waters flow, whereas those who are bent upon denying the truth shall have – even though they may enjoy their worldly life and eat as cattle eat – the fire of the Hereafter for their deeds' (47:12).

That is why Divine Guidance is needed to develop character and personality.

Struggle between human values and material gain appears at all cross-roads in life and the test of one's character is the choice one makes. Riches, a life of comfort, a good name, high office and status, the charm of authority are all full of attraction and very tempting. Should one give them up for the sake of preserving moral and human values ? This is a very difficult question to answer. Self interest is ingrained in all of us. We would not sacrifice self-interest unless and until we are convinced that in doing so we stand to gain.

Think of a person who has had no food for several days and due to hunger is unable to sit up. If a dish full of the most delicious food is brought, will he not sit up and advance impatiently towards the dish, pick up a morsel to eat ? While in the process of eating if he hears that the food is laced with deadly poison, would he put the morsel in his mouth or would he throw it back into the dish and bang the dish on the floor ? He would undoubtedly do the latter since eating the stuff would mean certain death. He would prefer pangs of hunger rather than risk his life. Now suppose the dish, instead of poison, has been prepared from ill-gotten money. How will the hungry person react? Ten to one he would snatch the dish and swallow the contents. He will have a thousand reasons and excuses against the plea of ill-gotten money because he sees the gain in consuming the dish, but none in rejecting it. Were he convinced that the dish was as deadly as the one with poison; he would certainly throw it away. The truth is that in the case of a tie between a physical urge or a material gain and a moral human value of a person, a person will assess his options and if he is convinced that he stands to gain more by safeguarding his moral values, he will certainly sacrifice the physical urge. How is this conviction inculcated in the personality or character of a human being is the main objective of this book. This objective can only be achieved if one is fully convinced of the true worth of the Divine Quranic values. The strength of a positive character does not come from coercion or duress; it has to be voluntary and with sincere devotion (98:5).

'There is no compulsion in religion. Truth stands out clear from falsehood. He who turns away from the forces of evil and believes in Allah, has firmly grasped the handhold which never gives way, and Allah, whose support he takes, hears and knows everything'(2:256)

Allah has pointed out certain human instincts and traits which are necessary for human life; but if they are not kept in check or misused, can lead to trouble. Allah has cautioned against them:

'And who is more erring than he who follows the evil inclinations without guidance from Allah ? Verily, Allah does not guide the unjust' (28:50)

'"Quite often man invokes evil when he intends to pray for good, for he is prone to be hasty and impatient in his action' (17:11).

CHARACTER BUILDING

Character can have both positive and negative associations. For instance, when someone is called a man of character it means that he has positive qualities. He could be humorous, awkward, interesting or ridiculous, but he has a strong distinctive personality that sets him apart from others.

Every attitude of yours goes into the building of your character. If someone were to describe your character, they would take with consideration all aspects of your personality including your reactions and what others consider your strengths. In fact, the last aspect of other people's perceptions of your character is what goes into giving you a reputation, whether positive or negative.

Building of a character requires belief in Allah with conviction; because an absolute moral character cannot exist in material things, it can exist only in a mind from which all reality is derived. The Quran tells us that faith (Eeman) and character are inseparable. The Quran never misses to precede 'Aamelus Salaehat' (Do good deeds) with 'Al Lazeena Aamanu' (Those who have faith).

Here is another parable: Take the example of two persons working in a government office. They are there in self interest, working for a salary. If a businessman comes along asking for some concessions against the rules in return for a handsome bribe; the official to whom human character and personality is a nonentity will accept the amount provided he is assured of non-apprehension by the police. This is because the bribe brings him monetary gain. The other official who has faith in moral values will not accept the bribe because he values more the gain in being honest. He realizes that the acceptance of bribe will bring him physical gain but will harm his character. The refusal of bribe will, no doubt, mean a material loss but it would be a gain for his personality. In making this choice he does nothing against self-interest, he only opts for a greater gain. The choice avoids harm to his character and personality in the same manner in which harm to life made the hungry man reject the poisoned food.

The Quranic verse given below conveys this message aptly:

'I ask for no reward from you. My reward rests with Allah alone. I have been commanded to be one of those who totally submit themselves to Him' (10:72)

INTELLECT AND INSIGHT

Character and personality also depends upon how a person develops his insight to differentiate between immediate and long lasting gain. The poet philosopher Allama Iqbal draws a distinction between the two phases of intellect. When it cares only for the satisfaction of physical urges, he calls it 'Aql-e-Khud Been' (self seeking intellect) and when it cares for the satisfaction of the urges of both body and character, he calls it 'Aql-e-Jehan Been' (All seeing intellect). Thus anything done under the influence of 'self-seeking intellect' would be an act of wisdom; but what is done in pursuance of the 'all seeing intellect' would be wisdom cum intellect. A human being, through improvement in his character and attitude, has the potential of reaching a state higher than the angels; but at the same time he also possesses the power to deny God and become the lowliest of the low.

'O you who believe !If you follow the path shown by Allah, He will give you the faculty of moral evaluation and endow you with a standard by which to discern the true from the false and will cleanse you of your evil thoughts and deeds and will forgive your shortcomings for Allah is limitless in His favours' (8:29).

'We have indeed created man in the best and noble of forms; but then We reduce him to the lowest of the low (when he rejects and rebels against Us and pursues the evil way of life) (95:4,5)

RIGHT APPROACH

Moral character is an evaluation of an individual's moral qualities. The concept of character can imply a variety of attributes including the existence or lack of virtues such as integrity, courage, fortitude, honesty, loyalty, goodness, etc.

Youngsters spend a great deal of their time with their peers. At times they do not have any choice and may do things because everyone else does them. You might end up reading what they read, watch what they watch, eat what they eat and use the same language that they use because otherwise, you feel left out. The best way to counter this pressure is to select your friends carefully. Your friends should be a mixed group of people capable of tolerance, respect, decency, integrity and adaptability.

You should be courageous enough to tell others to mind their own business, when they interfere too much in your life. You must remember that you are an individual with a unique personality and your decision to eat, to dress and to talk is your own. If your friends cannot catch up with you, find new ones.

GREATNESS OF CHARACTER

History tells us that greatness of character comes not only from power or money, but from intelligence, tolerance, good behaviour and respect for culture. We learn that even the most hated characters will have some redeeming virtues that helped them to rise.

Character encompasses all aspects of a man's life. It is true that to expect a flawless character is a near impossibility. Some individual flaws or shortcomings in our character do not affect others like, for example, drinking too much tea. So it is better to focus on flaws that affect others.

According to the Quran, man is presented with the unique opportunity by being born in the human state and it is a tragedy for him to fret away and waste his life in pursuits which distract him from the essential goals of life.

'Life is like unto a shell and the self is the pearl-drop therein;
What is the shell worth if it cannot transform the pearl drop into a pearl?
Through self-knowledge, self-control and self-development,
The self can even conquer death'
(Iqbal 'Zarb-e-Kaleem')

Morals are principles and beliefs that determine right and wrong behaviour. Someone who is moral, behaves in a way that he believes is right. Morality is the code of conduct that is shown in our attitude, behaviour and actions. Our conscience, religion, family and society create morals and behavioural rules that we follow. Every country, people and society has its own moral standards. Something morally bad such as drinking alcohol or not respecting elders is not considered morally bad in the European societies. In most of the systems the lack of morality can be a sufficient cause for punishment.

The most dangerous person is the one who has intelligence and education, but no morals or character. That is why character is considered to be the sum of those qualities of moral excellence that stimulate a person to do the right thing.

One of the elementary principles of morality is universality; that is, if something is right for me, it is right for you. If it is wrong for you, it is wrong for me.

'When you voice an opinion, be just even though it be against your relative' (6:152)

PERSONALTY

Personality does not only show your character, but your whole nature. Sometimes we refer to a famous television or sports personality which means his overall character and nature. The development of a personality is also based on the family upbringing. Parents influence their children in many ways. Their attitude and behaviour, warmth and discipline, kindness and love are a source of inspiration for the children.

Moral development is also a lifelong process as new situations arise every day. Youngsters acquire the source of right and wrong not only through parental discipline but also in everyday conversations and dealings. Another resource for moral growth is the ability to share the feelings of others as if they were your own. Everyone should be treated as equal and at the same level.

'Let not the hatred of a people deviate you from justice. Deal justly for it is closest to being Allah-conscious (5:8)

VALUE SYSTEM

Morals and ethics are based on a value system and are also guided by religion, tradition and culture. For example, cheating, adulteration, vain pride, greed, hatred, violence, injustice and indecency are considered morally wrong by all religions and societies. Cultural practices such as the manner of greeting, the dress code and family life, etc. are all part of the moral value system.

All religions lay down a list of do's and don'ts. Those who follow them claim to be of good character. The best way is to be aware of these values and follow them as they were followed by those who are respected as religious leaders. All messengers of Allah brought the same message and their objective was to facilitate human beings in leading a good life by following the Divine guidance. They led not only by their lectures and sermons, but by setting personal examples through their behaviour, attitude and character.

'We have ordained for you (Muhammad) the same religion which We enjoined on Noah and which We have revealed to you, as well as Abraham, Moses and Jesus, advising them to observe to remain steadfast in faith and not get disunited' (42:13)

For those who believe in the Quran, the role model should be Muhammad ﷺ:

'In the Messenger of Allah, you have indeed a noble pattern and example for those who look forward to Allah and the Day of Judgment and frequently remember Allah' (33:21)

'The hand of the Momin is the hand of Allah
Dominant, resourceful, creative, ensuring success.
His heart and mind born of clay, he has the nature of light,
A creature with the attributes of the creator,
His heart is different to the riches of the two worlds;
His desires are few, but his purposes are great;
His ways are graceful, his glance fascinating;
He is soft in speech, but warm in quest,
In war and in peace his heart and mind are pure'
He is a flashing sword against untruth
And a protecting shield for truth;
His affirmation and negation,
Are the criteria for good and evil,
Great is his forgiveness, his justice, his generosity and his grace,
Even in anger he knows how to be kind
(Iqbal 'Baal-e-Jibreel (Wings of Gabriel)

Commitment in resisting temptation to compromise on values and beliefs will make a person stronger. We should hold ourselves to high standards and continually evaluate the image we see in the mirror. It will build our character and will also help us to be a person of quality.

STRONG BACKS

There is a story about a sea captain who in his retirement skippered a boat taking day-trippers to Shetland Islands. On one trip, the boat was full of young people. They laughed at the old captain when they saw him say a prayer before sailing out, because the day was fine and the sea was calm.

However they weren't long at sea when a storm suddenly blew up and the boat began to pitch violently. The terrified passengers came to the captain and asked him to join them in prayer.

But he replied, "I say my prayers when it's calm. When it's rough I attend to my ship."

Here is a lesson ... pray, not for lighter burdens, but for stronger backs.

A GOOD DEED

This is a true story that had happened in 1892 at Stanford University. Its moral will always be relevant.

A young, 18 year old student was struggling to pay his fees. He was an orphan, and not knowing where to turn for money, he came up with a bright idea. A friend and he decided to host a musical concert on campus to raise money for their education.

They reached out to the great pianist Ignacy J. Paderewski. His manager demanded a guaranteed fee of $2000 for the piano recital. A deal was struck. And the boys began to work to make the concert a success.

The big day arrived. Paderewski performed at Stanford. But unfortunately, they had not managed to sell enough tickets. The total collection was only $1600.

Disappointed, they went to Paderewski and explained their plight. They gave him the entire $1600, plus a cheque for the balance $400. They promised to honour the cheque as soon as possible.

"No." said Paderewski. "This is not acceptable." He tore up the cheque, returned the $1600, and told the two boys, "Here's the $1600. Please deduct whatever expenses you have incurred. Keep the money you need for your fees. And just give me whatever is left." The boys were surprised, and thanked him profusely.

It was a small act of kindness, but it clearly marked out Paderewski as a great human being. Why should he help two people he did not even know? We all come across situations like these in our lives. And most of us only think, "If I help them, what would happen to me?" The truly great people think, "If I don't help them, what will happen to them?" They don't do it expecting something in return. They do it because they feel it's the right thing to do.

Paderewski later went on to become the Prime Minister of Poland. He was a great leader, but unfortunately when the World War began, Poland was ravaged. There were over 1.5 million people starving in his country, and no money to feed them. Paderewski did not know where to turn for help. He reached out to the US Food and Relief Administration for help.

The head there was a man called Herbert Hoover— who later went on to become the US President. Hoover agreed to help and quickly shipped tons of food grains to feed the starving Polish people. A calamity was averted.

Paderewski was relieved. He decided to go across to meet Hoover and personally thank him. When Paderewski began to thank Hoover for his noble gesture, Hoover quickly interjected and said, "You shouldn't be thanking me Mr. Prime Minister. You may not remember this, but several years ago, you helped two young students go through college in the US. I was one of them."

The world is a wonderful place. What goes around comes around! Sometimes we notice it, sometimes we don't.

Most of the universal virtues that contribute to the good of the individual and society and affirm your dignity as a human being are derived from moral and ethical values.

ONLY HUMAN BEINGS HAVE VALUES AND CHARACTER

It is only among human beings that you have moral values and character because you have a personality. Animals, birds, fishes, etc. have no character or personality and hence have no moral values. If a lion kills a human being, it is not arrested for murder; while it is morally a crime for a human to take another human's life.

It is possible that the scrupulously honest man may not grow rich as quickly as some others who are unscrupulous and dishonest; but his ultimate success will be of a truer nature and without fraud and injustice. This will truly reflect his character . Even reputation takes a back seat when it confronts character, because character is what you really are, while your reputation is merely what others think about you.

Young people, at times, do not like to be repeatedly reminded of moral values and their importance in life. They feel that leading such a life means to abstain from enjoying the numerous sources of happiness and joy that Allah has given. This is a wrong concept and everyone must realize that Allah wants us to be happy and satisfied; however, this does not mean that you get busy in accumulating wealth and exploiting others.

PHYSICAL FITNESS

Youngsters should keep themselves physically well in order to fulfil their responsibilities as students and important members of the society they live in. You must have seen the glow of happiness on the faces of students who secure top positions in the class. It is the fruit of their labour that is reflected on their faces. Your hard work and even your relationship with animals and birds, and the environment shows your character. That is why it is good to be considerate and kind to animals, birds, trees and plants and everything else in Nature.

Personal leadership is not a singular experience; it is rather the ongoing process of keeping your vision before you and aligning your life with moral values. The life of a Muslim is one of a trial:

'Do men imagine that they will be left at ease because they say 'we believe', and will not be tested with affliction' (29:2)

In the dynamic universe, Allah keeps everything moving forward, actualizing its latent capabilities. In the universe, man is the most dynamic being. It is up to him to rise up or descend into an abyss of darkness:

'Had We so willed, We would have elevated him through Our Revelation, but he clung to the earth and followed his own lustful desires '(7:176)

Every day you should begin with a strong belief in your infinite potential and Allah will always be there to help you.

My daily wish is that we may
See good in those who pass our way; Find in each a worthy trait
That we shall gladly cultivate. A softly spoken word of cheer A kindly face, a smile sincere.
I pray each day that we may view
The things that warm one's heart anew
The kindly deed that can't be bought
That only from good are sought.

A burden lightened here and there, A brother lifted from despair,
The aged ones freed from distress;
The lame, the sick brought to happiness. A soothing hand given to one in pain A sacrifice for love–not gain;
A word to ease the troubled mind of one whom life has been unkind.
So my friend my wish is that we may
See good in all who pass our way.

'O our Sustainer! Grant us good in this world and good in the life to come, and keep us safe from sufferings and agony of the fire' (2:201)

2 SELF-CONTROL

'Allah grants firmness to those who have attained to faith through the work that is unshakably true in the life of this world as well as in the life to come; but the wrongdoers. He lets go astray: For Allah does whatever He wills' (14:27)

When we see ourselves in a situation which must be endured and gone through, it is best to meet it with firmness and accommodate everything to it in the best way practicable. This lessens the evil, while fretting and fuming only increase your torments (Thomas Jefferson)

Self-control is the ability to manage your actions, desires and feelings. It is the quality of your mind with which you resist and control temptations and urges to which you should not submit as they will bring disastrous results and may destroy the peace and happiness of those who are around you. It also means to keep your thoughts and emotions to yourself. It involves your willpower, which should be strong enough to regulate your actions, attitude and behaviour. It is the action itself that is right or wrong. It is not made right or wrong by its consequences. Actions are understood in term of intentions.

'Allah will not call you to account for your unintentional and meaningless oaths; but for the intention in your hearts. He is often Forgiving and most Merciful' (2:225)

NEGATIVE REACTIONS

As a young man, you may become angry sometimes and may become violent and aggressive. These are negative reactions and ultimately harm you. You have to learn gradually to take control of your feelings. It is wrong to believe that anger, aggression and violence can help you fulfil your desires.

'As for those who do not believe in the hereafter, We make their wrong actions seem fair to them, so that they wander about blindly in confusion' (27:4)

Such persons are never accepted or liked in society as anger shows weakness of character.

'Allah loves those who spend their wealth generously in the way of Allah, whether in adversity or in prosperity; who hold in check their anger and forgive their fellow men' (3:134)

Contrary to the beliefs in other religions, Islam asserts that man is born innocent and as he grows up he absorbs vice and virtue that influence his character. The Quran pronounces:

'He is indeed successful who causes his self to grow; and he is indeed a failure who stunts it' (91:9,10)

HOLES IN THE FENCE

There was once a little boy who had a bad temper. His father gave him a bag of nails and told him that every time he lost his temper, he must hammer a nail into the back of the fence. The first day, the boy had driven 37 nails into the fence. Over the next few weeks, as he learned to control his temper, the number of nails hammered daily gradually dwindled down. The boy discovered that it was easier to hold his temper than to drive those nails into the fence. Finally the day came when the boy did not lose his temper at all. He told his father about it and the father suggested that the boy now pull out one nail for each day that he was able to hold his temper. The days passed and the boy was finally able to tell his father that all the nails were gone.

The father took his son by the hand and led him to the fence. He said, "You have done well, my son, but look at the holes in the fence. The fence will never be the same. When you say things in anger you leave a scar just like this one. You can throw a stone at a person and cause injury and pain."

Courtesy, respect and politeness breed love and affection and not only strengthen your character, but helps others to understand the virtues of life.

OUR ACTIONS

As you grow up you will be driving cars. This will need your skills and self-control not only in controlling the car but yourself as well. Young people who have obtained their driving licenses are considered to be in a phase of life in which they are beginning to develop a sense of what they are able to control. Your ability in this regard will show that your actions influence what happens in your life. We all have duties regarding our own actions.

'Whosoever acts righteously, whether that person be male or female, and is a believer, We shall give such a person a life that is pleasant and pure, and also reward such a person in the Hereafter in accordance with the best that they ever did' (16:97)

It makes us feel good to do something we feel like doing; but in reality, we cannot do all these things. Take for example, the desire to eat. Most children who allow their appetite to dictate what food to eat and how much to eat become overweight. That is why so many children are obese nowadays. Self- control helps in overcoming such eating disorders and other harmful habits.

It is said that the best day of your life is the one when you decide that your life is your own. No apologies or excuses; no one to lean on, rely on or to blame. In other words you are yourself responsible for your actions and deeds:

'Every soul is responsible for its own deeds and no person shall bear the burden of another person, and ultimately you shall all return to your Sustainer' (6:164)

DIFFERENTIATING BETWEEN RIGHT AND WRONG

Train yourself to be independent in differentiating right from wrong, and just from unjust.

'If you follow the right path shown by Allah, He will give you the faculty of moral evaluation to judge between right and wrong, and will cleanse you of your evil deeds' (8:29)

This will help you in finding solutions to problems rather than slamming doors or yelling. Remember that such behaviour may force your parents and teacher to take away some of your privileges. Your ability to control and discipline yourself will make you a trustworthy and responsible human being capable of overcoming laziness, shyness and fear, and will guide you on the road to success in life.

'For all those who believe in Allah and in the last Day of Judgment; and for those who are conscious of Allah in all their acts, Allah will surely find out a way (to relieve them of their problems) and would provide for them support from sources they could never imagine. If anyone trusts Allah, He is sufficient for them' (65:2,3).

SELF-DISCIPLINE

Self-discipline is the giving up of instant pleasure and satisfaction for a distant goal. It gives you the power to follow your decisions, stick to them and not to change your mind too often. These are steps needed for achieving the desired goals in life.

You do not have to be afraid or be apprehensive of disciplining yourself. It will not limit your initiative or restrict your lifestyle. It is a very useful inner-power that enables you to persevere and not give up in spite of failures and setbacks. Lack of self-discipline leads to failure of reaching even minor goals.

'Nor be among those who reject the Divine Revelation (Guidance) of Allah, or you too will be one of those who perish' (10:95).

'Evil is the example of those who denied Our Revelation and harmed their own souls' (7:177).

ANGER

Anger is perhaps the most destructive emotion. It never helps anyone. It wastes your energy and causes you to miss opportunities. Life can be happier without anger. So, avoid anger as much as possible. You should even be tolerant towards those you do not like and react calmly in all kinds of situations. Drinking water when you are angry will help you overcome negative emotions. Don't take everyone too seriously; It is not worth it. Your attitude determines your altitude. When you talk to someone who is aggressive, proud and agitated, your tone should be mild, gentle and tolerant (20:44)

Everyone knows the importance of self-control and self-discipline, but very few take real steps to develop these qualities. These can be developed like any other skill. This is what you have to realize. Remember that for every minute you are angry, you have lost sixty seconds of happiness.

'If you have to respond to their aggressive and militant arguments, then match them in the same manner; but if you exhibit patience that will indeed be the best for you' (16:126).

'Allah is with those who practice self-restraint, are pious and devout, and do that which is good' (16:128).

'Those who spend in Allah's way in time of plenty and in time of hardship and hold in check their anger, and pardon their fellow-men because Allah loves the doers of good' (3:134)

WILLPOWER

Willpower is the ability to overcome laziness and indecision. It is the ability to control or reject unnecessary or harmful impulses and desires. It is the ability to arrive at a decision and follow it with perseverance until it is successfully accomplished. It is the inner power that overcomes the desire to indulge in unnecessary and useless habits. In fact, it is the corner stone of success.

'Allah is always with those who persevere steadfastly' (2:249)

Everyone possesses some addiction or bad habits they wish they could overcome such as smoking, excessive eating, lack of assertiveness, etc. To overcome these habits or addiction, one needs to have willpower and self-discipline. These two qualities give inner strength and the power to decide.

'Indeed, if you remain patient and firm, and have trust in Allah, He will help you' (3:125).

Here are some examples from our daily lives:

1. You are sitting in a bus or train and an old person walks in. You should stand up and give up your seat even if you prefer to be seated. Do this not just because you

are doing something that you are reluctant to do. In this way you can overcome the resistance of your body, mind and feelings and develop a helping attitude.

2. You may feel that your body needs some physical exercise, but instead you keep on sitting doing nothing or watching a movie. You should get up and walk, run or do some other physical exercise.

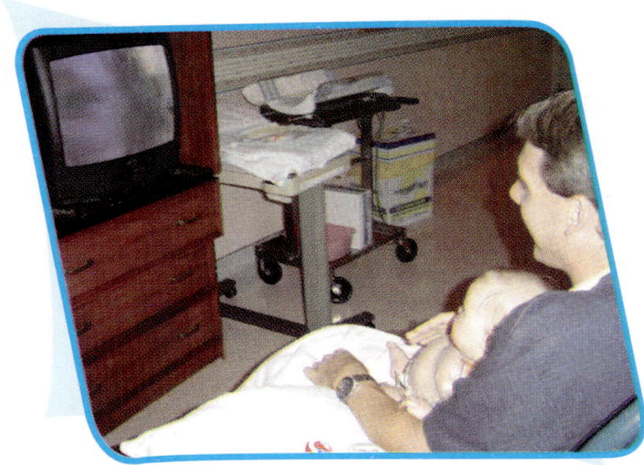

3 CONSIDERATE AND BENEVOLENT

'The true servants of the Most Gracious Allah are those who walk gently on earth, and who, whenever the foolish address them, reply with words of peace' (25:63)

Treat everyone with consideration and benevolence, even those who are rude to you- not because they are nice, but because you are (T. Maxwell)

You are considerate when you are polite and concerned about others. Also when you are thoughtful about those around you and show concern for their well-being and happiness. Benevolence is a positive gesture of kindness and generosity. When you donate to a charity or hospital service, you are both considerate and benevolent.

Consideration for others and benevolence are two very important ingredients of the Islamic way of life. In the absence of these two qualities, a Muslim can never be true to his faith. Consequently, he will never be able to tread the right path that would lead him to his ultimate goal of a peaceful and blissful life on this earth and manifold rewards in the hereafter.

The famous poet Emily Dickinson reminds us that acts of compassion add meaning to our lives:

IF I CAN STOP ONE HEART FROM BREAKING

If I can stop one heart from breaking,
I shall not live in vain;
If I can ease one life the aching,
Or cool one pain,
Or help one fainting robin
Unto his nest again,
I shall not live in vain.

Students are expected to conduct themselves in a considerate manner when going to and coming from school, in classrooms, on school grounds and in school buses. They should also be considerate of the thoughts and feelings of others.

The Quran stresses that we should be kind to our parents, kindred, poor and orphans; and that we should speak kindly and politely to people (2:82)

HEAVEN AND HELL

A Saint was having a conversation with the Lord one day and said," Lord, I would like to know what Heaven and Hell are like"

The Lord led the Saint to two doors. He opened one of the doors. In middle of the room was a large round table. On the table was a large pot of stew which smelled delicious. The people sitting around the table were thin and sickly. They appeared to be famished. They were holding spoons with very large handles that were strapped to their arms. They found it impossible to reach into the pot of stew and get the spoons into their mouths.. The Saint shuddered at the sight of their misery and suffering. The Lord said," You have seen Hell"

Then they went to the next room to Heaven. The door was opened. It was exactly the same as the first one. There was the large table with the large stew pot on it. The people were equipped with the same long-handle spoons, but they were well nourished, healthy, laughing and happy. The Saint said," I don't understand."

"It is simple", said the Lord, "it requires but one skill. You see, they have learned to feed each other, while the greedy think only of themselves.

This attitude should not end with people, but should also include animals and birds.

GREED

The opposite of benevolence is greed, and that of considerate is inconsiderate and mean. An inconsiderate person lacks regard for the rights and feelings of others and keeps his own interest above all.

The Quran points out, 'Allah bestows upon him abundant wealth and children to be besides him, and provides for him resources for smooth and easy progress and development, yet he is greedy to have much more from Him' (74:12,13,14,15).

'Misery to those who amass wealth and hoard it, thinking that this wealth will remain forever. No, certainly not! They will, in fact, be flung in the consuming flame of hell' (104-1,2,3,4).

GOOD MANNERS

In modern times, the use of cellular or mobile phones is very common. It has become necessary to develop a new set of manners that would show your consideration for the privacy of others. The use of this device is also disturbing for those around. In places like hospitals, schools, aeroplanes, places of worship like mosques, temples, churches, cinema houses and banks, the use of mobile phones is not allowed. You just need to be considerate of those around you and use a little common sense when deciding the appropriate times to use your mobile phone. The rest is up to you.

'Do not enter homes other than your own unless you have obtained permission and greeted their inmates. This is for your own good. If you do not find anyone within the house, do not enter it until you are given leave; and if you are told to turn back, then turn back' (24:27,28)

NEIGHBOURS

Living in a city means to have neighbours. Having neighbours sometimes means to put up with noise. This is the case both in apartments and houses. While indulging in unavoidable noisy work you should be considerate enough to inform your neighbours. Unnecessary noise and clatter should be avoided and all should behave like good neighbours.

'And do good unto your parents, and near of kin, and unto orphans, and the needy, and the neighbour from among your own people, and the neighbour who is a stranger,and the friend by your side, and the wayfarer (4:36)

When I was young there were regular announcements on the radio and television to keep the volume low in case someone is sick in your neighbourhood or a student is preparing for his examination.

The worst abuse of courtesy today is the tendency to make honesty an excuse for rudeness. Nothing justifies rudeness and unkindness.

BENEVOLENCE

Benevolence should also be mild and courteous in nature. It is not necessary to announce or propagate your benevolent acts:

'Those who spend their wealth in the way of Allah and do not follow their charity with reminders of their generosity; nor hurt the feelings of the recipients, shall get their reward from Allah and they shall have no fear or sorrow of any kind' (2:262).

So do not negate your good deeds of benevolence by propagating them.

In the Quran, Allah, while telling Prophets Moses and Aaron (Musa and Haroon RA) to go to Pharaoh, ordains them to be gentle to him, so that he might pay heed (20:44). This shows that we are not supposed to be rude or unkind to even those who do not subscribe to Allah's existence and His laws.

'And tell my servants that they should speak in the most kindly manner; verily Satan is always ready to stir up discord among them' (17:53).

THE CONSIDERATE BROTHERS

In the days of King Solomon there lived two brothers who were farmers and reaped wheat in the fields. One night, the elder brother gathered several sheaves of his harvest and left it in his brother's field, saying to himself: "My brother has seven children. With so many mouths to feed he could use some of my wheat. And he went home.

A short time later, the younger brother slipped out of his house, gathered several sheaves of his wheat and carried it into his brothers field, saying to himself. "My brother is all alone, with no one to help him harvest, so I'll share some of my wheat with him."

When the Sun rose, each brother was amazed to find that he had just as much wheat as before! The next night they paid each other the same courtesy and still woke to find their stores undiminished. But on the third night, they met each other as they carried their gifts into each other's fields. Each threw his arms around the other and shed tears of joy for each other's goodness, love and consideration.

The more considerate you are and help others, the more nature helps you and you are never short of the good things in life.

KINDNESS

There are many different ways we can show kindness to others, and it does not have to be in a big way. The simplest of things may make the difference. A smile, a door being held open, a friendly note, a kind word, the list can go on.

'You shall obey none but Allah, and you shall do good to your parents and relatives, and the orphans and the poor; and you shall speak unto all people in a kindly way' (2:83)

GREETING OTHERS

As we grapple with the complexities of the modern age, we must agree upon one principle; that a crucial measure of our success in life is the way we treat one another everyday of our lives. When we lessen the burden of living for those around us, we are doing well, when we add to the misery of the world, we are not. Life is what our relationships make it. Good relationships make our lives good and bad relationships make our lives bad. To learn how to be happy we must learn how to be considerate and live well with others. Consideration and benevolence is a key to this way of life. It allows us to connect successfully with others. Modern society is full of people who are uncaring and inconsiderate. Rude and inconsiderate manners show the insufficiency of a person's character. Speaking loudly on cell phones in public is one such example. You don't have to be a person who acts only according to his own wishes.

Those who are conscious of Allah, and stood before Him in submission, and had restrained their inner self from vain desires; paradise shall truly be their goal (79:40,41)

CONSIDERATE ABOUT NATURE

Human beings should not be the only object of your consideration. You should be considerate about nature as well. So, when you visit protected areas like gardens, zoos, parks, rivers and mountains, you should take care not to spoil the beauty of nature by throwing rubbish like empty food cartons and juice cans. Avoid playing music or operating machinery in a way that affects the enjoyment of other visitors and disturbs wildlife. Try to leave everything as you find it.

BENEVOLENCE AND MALEVOLENCE

Benevolence is a word often used in reference to God, to indicate the idea that He is All-Good and Merciful. Benevolence and its opposite malevolence also refer to ideas and actions that take place in everyday life.

'Whoever grows in virtue does so for the good of his self' (35:18)

We have a clear choice between the two opposite shades of a value. A benevolent person is kind, helpful and tolerant; while a malevolent person acts deliberately to cause harm. The Quran explicitly refers to these two types of people and says, 'Among those whom We have created, there are people who guide others to the Truth and act justly in its light. As for those who are bent on rejecting Our Revelation- We shall bring them low, step by step, without their perceiving how it came about' (7:181,182).

'If they cannot respond to your (Muhammad) demand, then you ought to know that they are only slaves of their own likes and dislikes and who could be more astray than he who follows but his own likes and dislikes without any guidance from Allah. Verily Allah does not Grace with His Guidance people who are given to evildoing' (28:50).

Maligning or hurting someone physically or mentally is malevolent. The basic goals of a good life compatible with human nature can be termed 'benevolent' while those that deny life and happiness are 'malevolent'.

BEAUTIFUL FACES

Beautiful faces are they that wear
The light of a pleasant spirit there;
Beautiful hands are they that do
Deeds that are noble, good and true;
Beautiful feet are they that go
Swiftly to lighten another's woe

4 ENCOURAGING AND CONSOLING

'Now surely the friends of Allah will have no fear nor shall they grieve' (10:61)

So I never quite despair' Nor let my courage fail;
And some day when skies are fair,
Up the bay my ships will sail (Robert Barry)

Those who give courage, hope and confidence to others are encouraging them. The main goal is to see them through troubles and cheer them to continue working for successful results. Encouragement is also a kind of help which is necessary, for at times it *seems that all is lost and there is no way to successfully move ahead.*

THE UNDERSTANDING TEACHER

As a class teacher, John was very popular among the students and his colleagues. He always took keen interest in the problems and progress of his students. He always had the time to help them out. Shawn, his colleague and Science teacher, asked him the secret of his popularity and interest in the problems of students. John replied that as a young student he had a very strict teacher who asked him questions in class to which he had no answer. He was not a bright student and had difficulty in understanding and learning the different subjects. He was always punished in class and his classmates laughed at him. He even thought about leaving school as he considered himself lazy and with a weak brain. Even his father scolded him for his shortcomings, but his mother understood his problem and encouraged him to continue his studies. The following year his class was blessed by the arrival of a very nice teacher, Ms Brown, who helped him in improving his learning. She advised him not to take his studies as a burden, but to enjoy whatever he studied.

"You must take control and become the master of your studies. Keep a diary so you can plan your studies," she said.

He was never scolded or punished in class. She never once called him lazy or stupid. In fact, she did the opposite and praised him loudly in class. This also changed the attitude of his classmates and he was so encouraged that he passed with an 'A' grade in the final examination. That was the reason of John's appointment into the school as a teacher. His teacher's attitude and encouragements made him realize that weak students, who have learning problems, need to be understood and encouraged.

That is why he always had time for his students and never scolded, punished or disheartened any of his students.

Understanding leads to encouragement and improvement in our lives. That is what we all must do.

POSITIVE ENCOURAGEMENT

Children need encouragement from their parents and teachers; soldiers need encouragement from their officers; doctors are encouraged when their patients regain lost health. You must have seen cricket, hockey and football team members encouraging each other to win matches. Thousands of spectators watching these matches also encourage players to give their best. We do better when we are encouraged. In schools, prizes are given to students excelling in their class. This is very encouraging to even those who do not get these prizes, as they try to improve so that they would also receive these honours. Even a simple nod of the head by the teacher is enough to encourage a student in his studies. This encouragement shall be for actions and deeds that yield positive results

'You ought to help each other in righteousness and piety; and also do not encourage or help in sin or evil acts' (5:2)

When you encourage someone, you support him in his work. We all need this support at one time or the other in our lives.

'Even the Exalted Messenger Muhammad ﷺ was asked to encourage and support those who contribute to the community at large as his support and encouragement would be a great source of peace in their hearts' (9:103)

TEAMWORK

A man was lost while driving through the countryside. As he tried to reach for the road map, he accidentally drove off the road into a ditch. Though he was not injured, his car was stuck deep in the mud. So the man walked to a nearby farm to ask for help. At the farm, he met a farmer who pointed to his old mule and said, "Warwick can you get the car out of that ditch?" The man looked at the weak old mule and also at the farmer who kept on saying, "Warwick can do the job." The man figured that he had nothing to lose and led the farmer and the mule to the ditch. The farmer hitched the mule to the car. With a snap of the reins, he shouted "Pull, Fred! Pull, Jack! Pull, Ted! Pull, Warwick! And the mule pulled the car out of the ditch.

The man was amazed. He thanked the farmer, patted the mule, and asked, "Why did you call out all those names before you called him by his real name, Warwick?"

The farmer smiled and said, "Old Warwick is just about blind. As long as he believes he's part of a team, he doesn't mind pulling."

Teamwork leads to encouragement in which each person subordinates his or her individual interests to the unity and efficiency of the group. The most effective teamwork is produced when all those involved harmonize their contributions and work towards a common goal.

Members of a family should be proud of each other by believing that each member makes valuable contribution to the family in his or her own way. This is positive encouragement that every family needs.

The opposite of 'encourage' is 'discourage' which disheartens people and they lose hope and confidence. Traffic controllers and planners use devices to discourage heavy use of a route. Speed bumps and breakers discourage high speed in residential areas. Another example is the posting of security guards at banks and shops to discourage robbers.

CONSOLING OTHERS

Console means to give hope to someone in times of grief or pain. It brings comfort and relieves many burdens. Its opposite is annoy, depress, disturb or hurt.

The young generation has an important role to play in bringing hope and happiness to people who are sad and gloomy. Just as despair can come from one human being, hope, encouragement and consolation can be given by other human beings. Encouragement is a great quality because it gives you hope and confidence. If you encourage a particular activity, you support it actively. Encouraging an attitude or a kind of behaviour makes it more likely to happen. Those who develop this quality bring about good and positive changes.

TAKING THE RIGHT PATH

Accepting your value as a human being may help you feel happier and more confident because the image you have of yourself is responsible for the way people see and treat you.

You should develop success from failures. Discouragement and failure are two of the surest stepping stones to success. Go ahead with whatever you are doing. Do not wait for success, as it would eventually come. Make sure that you are on the right path. The Quran has this to say about such people:

'They are the ones who are on the right path getting true guidance from Allah and it is they who shall attain success' (2:5)

'Indeed, he succeeds who purifies his soul' (91:9). *'Do not lose heart. You will definitely succeed if you are steadfast in your beliefs'* (3:139) *'If you follow the guidance given to you, nobody can hurt you'* (5:105) *'Muslims who do righteous deeds are the best of creatures'* (98:7).

ENCOURAGEMENT

Two frogs fell into deep pit and though they tried hard they couldn't hop out. Their comrades peered down from the top and croaked in sympathy.

We feel for you but there is no way you can get out from there."

On hearing this, one of the frogs lost heart and died of fear. The other frog was deaf. He thought his comrades were encouraging them. Emboldened by their faith in him, he gathered up all his reserves of strength in one great jump that landed him out of the pit.

PRINCIPLES OF RIGHT APPROACH

At times we feel that results could have been different if a matter was handled in a different way. Our minds are conditioned to find excuses. An intelligent persons knows that time does not wait for anyone and results that have taken shape cannot be changed. However, all situations should be used to evolve towards a better resolution of problems the next time they occur. It is no use crying over the spilt milk as it only creates more problems and is a source of constant discouragement.

Here are some principles of life that should be kept in mind at all times:

1. Whomsoever you encounter is the right one. No one comes in our life by chance. All those with whom we interact represent something whether to teach us something or to help us improve a current situation.
2. Whatever happened is the only way it could have happened. Nothing, absolutely nothing of that we experience could have been any other way.

3. Each moment in which something begins is the right moment; neither earlier nor later.
4. Whatever is over, is over. It is that simple. When something in our life ends, it helps our evolution. It is better to let go and move on.

Even your reading this book is not a coincidence. If you can learn something from this book, it is because you meet the requirement, and understand that not one single snowflake falls accidentally in the wrong place.

5 SENSE OF RESPONSIBILITY

'And certainly you will be questioned about what you did' (16:93)

Ability is what you are capable of doing. The truth of the matter is that you always know the right thing to do. The hard part is doing it (Lou Holtz)

Living in this world means that there are rights, duties and responsibilities. Fulfilment of responsibilities as an obligation shows how much one is dutiful. People around you expect you to do things because they are due or ought to be done. This willing obedience is dutifulness and shows how much your sense of responsibility makes you committed or devoted to this value. It also shows your humble, submissive, polite and obedient nature. The Divine Guidance is sound and clear. Following these directives will ultimately bring positive results. Those who draw away from these injunctions do so at the risk of great loss and harm:

'Clear proofs have come to you from your Sustainer. Whoever, therefore, chooses to make use of sight (to understand) he will do so for his own good; and whoever behaves like a blind person does so to his own hurt' (6:104)

DIVINE GUIDANCE

It is man's sense of responsibility that makes him aware of the various aspects of life. He also realizes that ethics, philosophy, poetry, art, sciences of mathematics, astronomy, chemistry, physics, medicine and industrial techniques encompass his mind and contribute a great deal in his progress and development. Islamic values tell us that Divine Guidance control and divert these sources of knowledge to virtue and piety. The choice of choosing the right path rests solely on man. That is why he is totally responsible for what he does and the best path for him to adopt is that which is given in the Quran:

'This is a Divine Scripture. In this there is no doubt guidance for all those who are conscious of Allah' (2:2)

END OF A DEDICATED CAREER

An elderly carpenter was ready to retire. He told his boss of his plans to leave and live a more leisurely life. The contractor was sorry to see such a good worker go, and he asked the Carpenter to build just one more house as a personal favour. The Carpenter agreed but in time it was easy to see that his heart was not in his work. He resorted to shoddy workmanship and used inferior material. It was an unfortunate way to end a dedicated career.

When the Carpenter finished the work, his contractor came to inspect the house. He handed the keys to Carpenter; "This is your house." The contractor said, "It is my gift to you" The Carpenter was shocked. If he had known he was building his own house, he would have done it differently.

This story tells us that we should do everything with a dedicated sense of responsibility.

This quality of realizing the sense of responsibility should become a part of education and upbringing. When the youth realize the importance of being dutiful, they affect the entire surroundings. A family becomes strong as a unit; a community benefits largely in its development and ultimately a whole nation progresses as this individual quality combines collectively to express solidarity and strength.

If a nation is left behind on the path of progress, development and well-being, it means that its people are not motivated by a sense of responsibility. No doubt you have rights in the society you live, but every right implies a responsibility; every opportunity you come across has an obligation. The more this society and nation gives us, the more dutiful we have to be.

In order to discharge our duties and responsibilities we have to strive ceaselessly. Our perseverance and steadfastness is bound to produce positive results:

'Those who patiently persevere and are steadfast will surely receive immeasurable rewards' (39:10)

GOALS AND OBJECTIVES

Visualize your goals clearly, add desire, faith and a sense of responsibility, and you will surely achieve them. In order to attain any kind of success, in any field, with minor everyday goals or major goals, you need to exercise this virtue. The opposite of dutiful is irresponsible, undutiful and faithless.

Instilling a sense of duty among children is not only the responsibility of teachers and parents; but the youth too have to realize that apart from a social obligation, it is a moral obligation as well. It means that being dutiful is an important part of goodness and its absence is truly bad and is a vice.

THE THORNY BUSH

A man once planted a bramble bush in the middle of the road. The passers by reproached him and repeatedly told him to dig up the thorny bush, but he did not do so. The bramble bush grew larger. Its thorns tore the people's clothes and wounded their feet.

The mayor told the man to dig the bush up, and he answered, "Yes, I will dig it up tomorrow". For a long time he promised to do 'it tomorrow and tomorrow.' Meanwhile the thorny bush grew firm and robust.

The mayor said to him one day, "O promise-breaker, come to do what you said you would do." But the man replied, "The bush is too large now, and I no longer have the strength to pull it out." The mayor said, "you who say tomorrow, should learn that in every day which time brings, that evil tree grows younger and stronger, and he who should dig it up grows older and weaker. The bramble bush every moment grows green and fresh, while you become more helpless and withered. Be quick, therefore and do not waste your time."

Your responsibility lies in getting rid of the thorns of life as soon as possible before it is too late.

Whenever parents, teachers and elders praise the children and students, the sense of responsibility is always mentioned. This quality makes one a good and popular student, a loving and devoted child, a loving friend and a cooperative and helping neighbour.

People have different responsibilities and contribute accordingly. They are like the various parts of a clock, each having a different function. Some parts may have diamond tips worth much more than a small iron screw. Separately the screw and the diamond have no similarity in value, but inside the watch the value of the screw and the diamond is such that should the screw become loose and stop performing its duties, the whole watch becomes useless and even the diamond is of no use:

'Those who desire for the good of the life hereafter and strive to achieve the same with all possible efforts, and maintain strong belief,they shall be the ones who would find favour with Allah' (17:19)

A BALANCED SOCIETY

The Islamic way of life aims at achieving the state of equilibrium in the society by exhorting its followers to meet the responsibilities and obligations. Since with every right there is a corresponding responsibility, if everyone in the society meets his obligations, the society as a whole shall prosper. Foregoing one's rights in favour of others is 'Eesar' or magnanimity and is regarded as an act of piety.

'Dispel evil with good' (23:96)

PREPARE FOR THE WORST IN ADVANCE

Years ago a farmer owned land along the Atlantic seacoast. He constantly advertised for hired hands. Most people were reluctant to work on farms along the Atlantic. They dreaded the awful storms that raged across the ocean, wreaking havoc on the buildings and crops. As the farmer interviewed applicants for the job, he received a steady stream of refusals. Finally, a short, thin man, well past middle age, approached the farmer. "Are you a good farmhand?" The farmer asked him. "Well, I can sleep when the wind blows," answered the man. Although puzzled by this answer, the farmer, desperate for help, hired him. The little man worked well around the farm, busy from dawn to dusk, and the farmer felt satisfied with the man's work.

Then one night the wind howled loudly in from offshore. Jumping out of bed, the farmer grabbed a lantern and rushed next door to the hired hand's sleeping quarters. He shook the little man and yelled, "Get up! A storm is coming! Tie things down before they blow away!"The little man rolled over in bed and said firmly, "No sir. I told you, I can sleep when the wind blows."Enraged by the response, the farmer was tempted to fire him on the spot. Instead, he hurried outside to prepare for the storm. To his amazement, he discovered that all of the haystacks had been covered with tarpaulins. The cows were in the barn, the chickens were safe, and the doors were barred. The shutters were tightly secured. Everything was tied down. Nothing could blow away. The farmer then understood what his hired hand meant, so he returned to his bed, also to sleep while the wind blew.

The Moral: When you're prepared for all eventualities you have nothing to fear. Can you sleep when the wind blows through your life? The hired hand in the story was able to sleep because he had secured the farm against the storm.

OUR RESPONSIBILITY TO PARENTS AND ELDERS:

One of the main duties upon us is to show kindness towards our parents. Respecting and obeying one's parents is a way of showing gratitude to them for bringing us into this world, and for rearing and taking care of us when we were young.

There are many ways in which one can show them kindness and respect; paying them a visit is one form of dutifulness to parents, in addition to treating them well, addressing them politely, trying to humble oneself before them, giving them gifts and showing our love and devotion.

We have our duties towards those who are close to us; especially those who looked after us and made our life comfortable and easy when we were very young and helpless. Thus true happiness is all about loving and caring for those who love you. Loving one's parents is also a moral duty.

The Quran points out:

"Your Sustainer has commanded that you worship none but Him, and that you be kind to your parents. If one or both of them reach old age with you, do not say to them a word of disrespect, or scold them, but say a generous word to them. And act humbly to them in mercy, and say, 'My Sustainer, have mercy on them, since they cared for me when I was small." (Quran-17: 23-24)

The duty of caring for one's parents and elderly in our society, in this most difficult time of their lives, is considered an honour and a blessing and an opportunity for great spiritual growth. In Islam, it is not enough that we only pray for our elders especially our parents, but we should act with limitless compassion, remembering that when we were helpless children, they preferred us to themselves.

When people reach old age, they should be treated mercifully, with kindness and selflessness. In Islam, serving elderly, in particular one's parents is a duty second to prayer, and it is their right to expect it. It is considered despicable to express any irritation when, through no fault of their own, the old become weak and vulnerable and need our special attention and care :

'Show kindness and affection to your parents' (4:36) *' Be kind to your parents'* (2:83) *'Be good to your parents and treat them kindly'* (6:151) *'We have enjoined man to show kindness towards his parents'* (29:8, 31:14, 46:15)

The reason for this is that it is the parents who bring a person into existence and it is they who nourish and look after him. The way this directive is mentioned in Quran shows that parents have rights on the children:

'And We have counselled man to show kindness to his parents. His mother bore him with much [hardships which resulted in] weakness upon weakness, and he is not weaned before he is two years of age. We said: "Show gratitude to Me and to your parents and towards Me is the return." (31:14)

'We have enjoined on man to be good to his parents' (46:15)

The Almighty has counselled man to be thankful to both his parents the foremost after Allah. This gratitude is not to be expressed merely through the tongue. There are some essential requisites of this gratitude which the Qur'ān has related in the above quoted verses of Sūrah Banī Isrā'īl.

The first thing mentioned is that a person should treat his parents in a manner that he shows respect to them not only outwardly but also from the depth of his heart. He should not show any aversion to them in his heart and also not say something before them which is against manners. In fact, he should treat them with love, affection and decency and in a manner that reflects his obedience to them. He should obey them and in the frailty of old age comfort them and be a means of re-assurance to them.

GRANDMOTHER'S TABLE

There was an old feeble woman whose husband died and left her all alone, so she went to live with her son and his wife and their little daughter. Every day the old woman's sight weakened and her hearing grew worse, and sometimes at dinner her hands trembled so badly that the peas rolled off her spoon or the soup fell from her cup. The son and his wife got annoyed at the way she spilled her meal all over the table. One day, when she knocked over a glass of milk, they decided that enough was enough.

They set up a small wooden table for her in the corner next to the closet and made the old woman eat her meals there. She sat all alone, at her table, with tear filled eyes looking sadly at the others. Sometimes they spoke to her while they ate, but usually, it was to scold her for dropping a bowl or a fork.

One evening just before dinner, the little girl was busy playing on the floor with her building blocks, and her father asked her what she was making. "I'm building a little wooden table for you and mother," she smiled, "so you can eat by yourselves in the corner somebody when I get big and you become old."

The parents sat staring at her and then suddenly both began to cry. That night they led the old woman back to her place at the big table. From then on she ate with the rest something every now and then, The son also realized how his mother cared for him when he was small and messed up things all the time.

FAILURE AND SUCCESS

There is no shortage of persons ready to claim credit for contributing to an enterprise that goes well; however few would accept responsibility for mistakes and failures. There is no end to the good you can do if you don't care who gets credit for it all the good work you do:

'Whoever follows the right path follows it for his own good, and whoever goes astray, does so for his own loss' (17:15)

CODE OF SOCIAL ETIQUETTE

Islam has exalted the level of obligations and responsibilities in prescribing its own code of social etiquette. By putting these rules into practice, we can have a society free from malice, hatred, tension, conceit, greed ill-will, ostentation, envy and numerous similar social evils.

Those who have a sense of responsibility always give preference to a positive attitude. This quality makes them solution-providers and problem-solvers.

Here is a comparison of the difference between those who have a positive attitude and those who treat every opportunity in a negative way;

POSITIVE PERSON	NEGATIVE PERSON
Considers accomplishment a commitment.	Treats accomplishment as a promise.
Discharges his responsibilities promptly.	Always has an excuse.
Sees a solution to every problem.	Sees a problem in every solution.
His slogan 'Treat people as would like them to treat you.'	His slogan 'Deceive people before they deceive you.'

Sees hope in work.	Sees pain in work.
Looks at the future and thinks of what is possible.	Looks at the past and thinks of what in impossible.
Chooses what he says.	Says what he chooses.
Adheres to values and gives up the trivial.	Adheres to the trivial and gives up values.
He makes events.	Events make him.

POND OF MILK

Once there was a king who told some of his workers to dig a pond. Once the pond was dug, the king made an announcement to his people saying that one person from each household has to bring a glass of milk during the night and pour it into the pond. So, the pond should be full of milk by the morning.

After receiving the order, everyone went home. One man prepared to take the milk during the night. He thought that since everyone will bring milk, he could just hide a glass of water and pour inside the pond. Because it will be dark at night, no one will notice. So he quickly went and poured the water in the pond and came back.

In the morning, the king came to visit the pond and to his surprise the pond was only filled with water! What has happened is that everyone was thinking like the other man that "I don't have to put the milk, someone else will do it."

The episode can have so many different conclusions. Here are a couple of them:

1. When it comes to helping poor people, do not think that others will take care of it. Rather, it starts from you, if you don't do it, no one else will do it. So, change yourself and act like a responsible person and that will make the difference.
2. Be honest in your actions regardless of thinking about others. Your honesty is related to your character.

'Do not oppress those who are orphans and helpless, and do not drive away those who are in need of help, and keep recounting the favours of Allah' (93:9,10)

6 THE MEANING OF LIFE AND DEATH

'There is no Allah but He. He gives life and causes death' (7:158, 44:8, 53:44)

Even death is not to be feared by one who has lived wisely (Buddha)

Nothing is more certain than death, but humans are forever haunted by the fear of death. Perhaps it is the mystery of the life beyond the grave that makes death an enigma. Human life is always punctuated and tinged by a brief encounter with death; the people in general and the young in particular tend to be oblivious of this stark reality. The reminder comes with someone close to the heart coming under its relentless grip. Mortality of man never before assumes such sure character as on such days. Humans, in sending off the deceased, are reminded of the similar fate that awaits them in the future. Surprisingly, after the funeral services, people rejoin the mainstream of life and life continues as before. Death at best is an episode, but it causes emotions of fear in man. Those who have lived their lives in accordance with the directives of the Quran have to fear nothing. The Quran points out:

'They shall enter the Gardens of Eden, underneath which flows the pleasant stream flows, and there they shall have their heart's desire. Thus Allah rewards all righteous people (16:31)
'Remember, the friends of Allah have no occasion for fear or for sorrow' (10:62)

LIFE

Life is sweet and beautiful. Things surrounding us grow within ourselves casting an imperishable imprint on our minds. It is an unconscious and imperceptible journey from childhood to youth, adulthood and to the old age.

We all describe life in different ways. The scientific definition says that life is the sum total of functions which resist death. Philosophers would say that all living creatures and processes have a final cause or purpose. Science does not address our inner needs. Human beings have perennially been in search of a knowledge that would help them to understand life and how to transcend their limitations and fulfil the mandate of their existence.

DEATH

Death, like life, is a reality everyone has to face. Humans have no authority or control over death:

'It is Allah Who takes their consciousness upon death, and of the living during their sleep. He withholds it from those whom He has passed the decree of death, and restores until an appointed time. Herein are signs for people who think' (39:42)

'Wherever you may be, death will overtake you even though you hide in lofty and fortified towers' (4:78)

'And tell also (Muhammad) the death from which you flee is sure to overtake you and then you will be sent back to Him Who is in the knowledge of all that unseen and seen, and He will narrate everything that you had been doing' (62:8)

' And then behold ! After all this you are destined to die' (23:15).

PURPOSE OF LIFE

What is the purpose of life? Is it to acquire success, to gain wealth, or to help others who are less fortunate than we are? Do we live for the satisfaction of our desires or just to fulfill the expectations of our parents and peers? A positive and humane answer would hold that life should be lived in such a way that in the end we have no regrets; that we are satisfied and feel that our presence in this world brought happiness to others or at least did not bring unhappiness to anyone.

Life and death are the two poles of existence. This existence is the space that we have in the form of time that provides ample opportunities to live a life worthy of respect and remembrance. The time that passes never returns no matter what we do. Nobody comes back from the valley of death; so we should reflect upon the purpose of our existence and strive to perform good deeds before our time runs out. The Quran points out:

'As for those who will not believe in the life to come, they go on lying to themselves] until, when death approaches any of them, he prays: "O my Sustainer! Let me return, let me return [to life] so that I might act righteously in whatever I have failed [afore time]!" Nay, it is indeed but a [meaningless] word that he utters: for behind those [who leave the world] there is a barrier [of death] until the Day when all will be raised from the dead!' (23:99,100).

Islam treats death as a part of the journey of life. The birth is the journey's first stage; while death is the stage from where the journey to the next world starts. Death only heralds an end to our physical existence.

The Quran emphatically says:

'Every self shall have the taste of death' (3:185) and 'Every living soul shall have a taste of death .And We test you with evil temptations and by the good things of life, by way of trial, and to Us you must finally return' (21:35) .

Death brings an end to all activities of life and, in a way, deprives us of whatever we are doing. The main difference between Islam and other beliefs about death is that according to Islam death is merely a turning point, a new phase and facet of life in the hereafter. This life may be termed as the spiritual life of eternity.

DEVELOPMENT OF PERSONALITY AND CHARACTER

At the time of birth every human being is in a natural state and is innocent. With the passage of time, he develops his self. This is known to us as personality and character. A true Muslim , in his transient life, abstains from sin; controls his unruly passions and lives his life in accordance with the directives of the Almighty. These directives are enshrined in the last and final Revelation , the Quran.

The Quran pronounces, 'He is indeed successful who causes his self to grow. And indeed he is a failure who stunts it (91:9,10). It also points out, 'He created death and life so that He may test which of you is best in deeds'(67:21)

DAY OF JUDGEMENT

With the concept of an after-life firmly embedded in Islam, a believer acts upon a prescribed code of right and wrong throughout his worldly life. His strivings in a proper direction (Sirat-e-Mustaqeem) results in a continued, sustained progress of his self and he becomes eligible for the coveted rewards promised by Allah

'Those who believe and keep away from evil, they shall have the good news of happiness in this present worldly life, as well as, in the life to come after death' (10:63,64).

Thus the rewards of living a righteous life cannot be confined to the life hereafter. These rewards make our lives blissful here, in this world too. The Divine system is therefore, a logical necessity, short of which the whole process of creation, death and re-birth becomes a place of purposelessness without any objective in sight.

'Every soul shall have a taste of death and in the end it shall return to us' (29:57)

'And in the end Allah causes him to die' (80:21)

SUCCESSFUL LIFE

Fear not that you may die, instead, fear that you will reach death and realize that you have never truly lived .Some people say that life should be successful, but the word 'success' holds different meanings for different people. To some people success means to acquire fame, for some to accumulate wealth and for a handful few, to have happiness and peace of mind. The famous scientist Albert Einstein said "I have never looked upon ease and happiness as ends in themselves. Such an ethical basis I call more proper for a herd of swine. The ideals which have lighted me on my way and time after time given me new courage to face life cheerfully have been Truth, Goodness and Beauty. Without the sense of fellowship with men of like mind of preoccupation with the objective, the eternally unattainable in the field of art and scientific research, life would have seemed to me empty. The ordinary objects of human endeavour–property, outward success, luxury-have always seemed to me contemptible."

There are no specified criteria for leading a successful life as different people have different aims and goals. Whatever aims you have or whatever field or profession you are in, you should do justice to your work. Thus sincerity should not only be to one's profession, but to all human beings as well. A wise man once said 'Live amongst people in such a way that if you die, they weep over you, and while you live, they crave for your company.'

In contemporary times the quality of trust is missing in our life and makes us feel insecure. We have moulded our lives in such a self–centred manner that we do not see beyond our noses. In this materialistic world, our values have also changed. Everyone wants to be a part of the rat race and lead it too. Morality and ethics have been relegated to an obscure and unimportant position. It is no doubt true that life has to move on. Every new day should bring progress and prosperity. At the same time our main principle of life should be that any intelligible conception of progress must be directional; that is to say, it must imply the simultaneous conception of a goal and the manner in which that goal is conceived and achieved. If a completed individual life does not amount to something that can be called attainment or achievement, that life has been lived in vain.

The best use of life is to spend it for something that will outlast it. Death gives value, and in a sense almost infinite value, to our lives and more urgent and attractive the task of using our lives in achieving something for others which apparently embodies more or less the meaning of life.

'And We test you with evil temptation, and by the good things of life, by way of trial and to Us you must return finally' (21:35)

ABSOLUTE STANDARDS

The Quran is Allah's book of guidance which deals with all aspects of life. It is meant for us,therefore, our lives should be modelled on its standards of right and wrong.

'We have sent down to you (O people) a Divine book which contains 'Reminders of matters concerning you. Will you still not understand? (21:10).

Despite this fact there are those who simply reject the guidance of Quran and prefer to follow their own standards of right and wrong.

'And indeed We have sent forth in the Quran every kind of similitude (example) for mankind, yet, if you recite to them a single verse , they are bound to say that you preach falsehood' (30:58)

According to the teachings of Islam, death is not a punishment despite its extremely tragic ramifications. It is not a punishment because it is not selective.

'Everything that exists on earth shall eventually perish, but forever will abide thy Sustainer's Self' (55:26,27).

TRUE IMMORTALITY

It is an irony of life that people are no longer judged by the qualities of piety, trust, justice and honesty, but by their status. Even human relationships are now based on profit and loss. Mankind has drifted away from the true purpose of life and the spirit of love, justice and sacrifice. Everyone knows in his heart, whether it be through the teachings of religion or of science or of both, that all the works and ambitions of man will sooner or later be overwhelmed and lost as all life forms have to end.

True immortality lies in doing some noble work that benefits humanity at large:

'That which is foam passes away off like froth on the banks and that which is useful and beneficial for mankind, remains on earth' (13:17)

Life tells us to take a closer look at life itself and try to understand why we have become so selfish and materialistic? What has happened to our conscience? Why can't we take a few minutes to help others? We have lost the qualities of patience, tolerance and perseverance. Our thoughts, our feelings are too narrow and have only hindered our mental and spiritual development.

There is more pleasure in being righteous, just and honest, in controlling and disciplining one's desires and in sacrificing one's self-interest for the greater good of all human beings.

MASTERING POSITIVE QUALITIES

You will always be in the company of those who have a positive attitude towards life.A negative approach is an obstacle which should be feared or else it will overwhelm you and lead you to failure. Quranic values guide you to master your positive qualities so that the mosquitoes of negativity get zapped before they can get too close. As they say in Martial

Arts 'Leverage your opponent's weight against him.' If someone is being positive, he or she is focusing on a problem or a perceived problem. Your approach should be towards the solutions of the problem. The general principle is that you always do what you have always done, you will always get what you have always got.

Work for a cause, not for applause. Live life to express and not to impress. Do not strive to make your presence noticed, just make your absence felt. Give your best in whatever you are doing. Make sure it conforms to the permanent values of the Quran.

The meaning of life has one important objective and that is the purpose and goal you have to set for yourself. It begins with your awareness of the fact that everything and anything matters. As a human being with different roles, responsibilities and rights, every action that is taken produces a result and makes the differences. Do not act impetuously There are generations yet unborn whose lives will be shaped by what we do today, and tomorrow and the next day. Renunciation of the world is repugnant to the teachings and principles of Islam. Islam encourages its followers to make materialistic progress with reasonable limits. Between the extremes of stark materialism on the one hand and complete asceticism on the other, Islam shows a balanced course. The Quran advises mankind to seek good in this world as well as in the hereafter world (2:201)

'Those who believe and keep away from evil, they shall have the good news of happiness in this present worldly life, as well as in the life to come after death. No change can there be in the words of Allah' (10:64)

UNIQUE CREATION

Every human being is unique and there has never been any one like you; and there will be no one like you. Your thoughts, feelings the ability to reason and act, all exist in no one else. You have to realize this and commit yourself to the concept that you have been created in order that you might make a difference. Your life and whatever you do with it matters forever.

It is pertinent to remember that if you were to live for a thousand years or ten thousand years you could not lose any other life than the one you have, and there will be no other life after it. So the longest and the shortest lives are the same. The present moment is shared by all living creatures, but the time that is past is past gone forever. No one can lose the past or the future, for if they do not belong to you, how can they be taken from you ?

Life may be full of conundrums. It may not be fair, but it is good in many respects. It is not a very long affair, so it should not be wasted in hating others. Human relationships play a crucial role in making life livable. So keep in touch with people, friends and relatives. A rose given during lifetime is better than orchids on the grave.

There are positive motivations in the human spirit that is not born of fear and guilt of hate and anger; but of life and love. The life instinct not only battles against the death instinct, it has a purpose of its own.

INAPPROPRIATE ATTITUDE

In our daily life we tend to dominate others. This is an incongruous attitude. Such an approach fends people away. We don't have to win every argument ; learn to agree to disagree. Sad moments are part of life. When the chips are down, it is better to cry with someone, it is more healing than crying alone. There is nothing wrong in getting angry at God. He can take it. Time is a big healer that heals everything. Give time to time. The only unchangeable thing is change itself. Value what is yours.

THE SONGS OF THE BIRDS

The owner of a small business, a friend of the poet Olavo Bilac, met him on the street and asked him, "Mr. Bilac, I need to sell my small farm. The one you know so well. Could you please write an announcement for me for the newspapers?"

Bilac wrote, "For sale, a beautiful property where birds sing at dawn in extensive woodland, bisected by the brilliant and sparkling waters of a large stream. The house is bathed by the rising Sun. It offers tranquil shade in the evenings on the veranda."

Sometime later, the poet met his friend and asked whether he had sold the property; to which he replied, "I have changed my mind. When I read what you had written, I realized the treasure that was mine."

Sometimes we underestimate the good things we have. As a result we start chasing the mirages of false treasures. We often see people letting go of their children, their families, their spouses, their friends, their possessions, their parents and their professions. They throw out of the window what life has given them so freely without realizing that these are truly their precious treasures.

'O mankind! Bear in mind the favours of Allah to you. Is there any other Creator besides Allah, Who provides you sustenance from heaven and earth ? Indeed there is no God save He. How can you then turn away from Him (35:3)

MAKING LIFE LIVABLE

Comparing your life with that of other should be avoided. You do not have the idea what their journey of life is all about. Some say that every moment of life is worth living and should be enjoyed. So burn the candles, wear nice clothes and enjoy nature; but do not hurt anymore. No one is in control of your happiness but you. What others think of you is none of your business. Envy is a waste of time. You already have so much. The best is yet to come. Running water does not flow back. So is life; make it happy and livable. Laugh and smile every day. Loving yourself, within limits, is a positive attitude because we cannot give what we do not have.

'Life is no brief candle to me. It is a sort of splendid torch which I have got hold of for the moment, and I want to make it burn as brightly as possible before handing it on to future generation' (Bernard Shaw)

A well directed goal or vision of life sets you free from beliefs that are not true. It frees you from self-doubt and insecurity, and from self-imposed perfectionism. It also gives you the courage to heed your intuition in all her guises finding your voice to speak the truth, to create fulfilling work and to build great relationships. You have to have strong belief in your strength, generosity and wisdom. So variegate you life and remember that we are all mutually bonded to support one another sharing our experiences, hopes and efforts so that all may enjoy and live a satisfactory life.

'Everyone has a goal towards which he aims. Try to surpass others in good deeds' (2:148)

THE CRACKED POT

An elderly Chinese woman had two large earthen pots, each hung on the ends of a pole which she carried across her neck. One of the pots had a crack in it while the other pot was perfect and always delivered a full portion of water. At the end of the long walk from the stream to the house, the cracked pot arrived only half full. For a full two years this went on daily with the woman bringing home only one and a half pots of water. Of course, the perfect pot was proud of its accomplishments. But the cracked pot was ashamed of its own imperfection, and felt miserable that it could only do half of what it had been made to do. After two years of what it perceived to be bitter failure, it spoke to the woman one day, by the stream "I am ashamed of myself because this crack in my side causes water to leak out all the way back to you house."

The old woman smiled and said "Did you notice that there are flowers on your side of the path, but not on the other side? That is because I have always known about your flaw, so I planted flower seeds on your side of the path, and every day while we walk back, you water them. For two years I have been able to pick these beautiful flowers to decorate the table. Without you being just the way you are, there would not be this beauty to grace the house."

We all have our cracks and flaws; but they make our lives interesting and rewarding.

DEATH- AN INTEGRAL PART OF LIFE

Death is the opposite of life and yet it is an integral part of life. The meaning of life can never be complete without realizing life's inevitable termination in death. It is a natural phenomenon, a physical change that overtakes the human body. The life cycle of birth, growth, death and decay is a reality and we cannot negotiate our way out of it. Unlike all the creatures on this planet, we are the only ones who are aware that our time is limited.

'And in the end Allah causes him to die and brings him to the grave' (80:21)

This knowledge shapes us as human beings. This feeling for the poignancy and transience of our lives has been at the root of so much that we value in human culture. Throughout history this knowledge of life's impermanence has driven human beings to search for a way out. This acme has been provided by many religions of the world that promise eternal life, time without end. Those who believe in the material concept of life consider death to be the end of all activities.

The basic fact remains that death is universal, inevitable and irreversible. It can be gradual as well as abrupt. It can truly be understood only when it happens as no one returns after dying to relate the experience.

We should not be like those who are so afraid to die that they never begin to live. One must be willing to die in order to live. The beauty of life lies in its uncertainty.

FREEDOM OF CHOICE

The path of life given by nature is simple - survive until you die. What you do in between is up to you. Human beings are the only creatures who have freedom of choice and can shape their lives as they deem fit, Instead of fearing death, the life span should be properly planned with a purpose and objective. Life can only be propitiated by good deeds.

Perhaps the best cure for the fear of death is to respect that life has a beginning as well as an end. There was a time when we did not exist. So why should it trouble us that a time will come when we shall cease to exist ?

The Quranic values can be adopted practically to benefit humanity at large. Such a life is not a dream or utopia, but can be actualized as a living reality.

The meaning of life should not exclude death as it is a vital ingredient of the life process and as a wise man once said that the strongest protection to life is given by death.

One has to live till the very end of life. The tragedy of life is not that it ends so soon, but that we wait so long to begin it. So live better by understanding life and not just standing under it and letting time pass by.

'Consider the flight of time !Verily man is at a loss unless he is one of those who has firm faith, and does deeds of righteousness and urges one another towards the path of truth, constancy and patience in adversity' (103:1,2,3,)

Death comes only once, but life is a day to day affair. In order to be in the front line of the race of humanity, the following principles will help you:

1. **Follow Your Curiosity**

   The great scientist Einstein once said," I have no special talent. I am only passionately curious."

   The success of one person and the failure of others should cause you to think and study the rules of success. The pursuit of your curiosity is the secret to your success.

2. **Perseverance is Priceless**

   Through perseverance the turtle reached the finishing line. Are you willing to persevere until you get to your intended destination? They say the entire value of the postage stamp consists of in its ability to stick to something until it gets there. Be like the postage stamp; finish the race that you've started! Be resilient when misfortune strikes.

3. **Focus on the Present**

   You cannot ride two horses at the same time.. Learn to be present where you are; give your all to whatever you're currently doing. Focused energy is power, and it is the difference between success and failure.

4. **Imagination is Powerful**

   Imagination is more important than knowledge. Are you using your imagination daily? Your imagination pre-plays your future. The true sign of intelligence is not knowledge, but imagination. Are you exercising your "imagination muscles" daily? Don't let something as powerful as your imagination lie dormant.

5. **Make Mistakes**

   Never be afraid of making a mistake. A mistake is not a failure. Mistakes can make you better, smarter and faster, if you utilize them properly. Discover the power of making mistakes. A person, who never made a mistake, never tried anything new.

6. **Live in the Moment**

   The only way to properly address your future is to be as present as possible "in the present."

   You cannot "presently" change yesterday or tomorrow, so it's of supreme importance that you dedicate all of your efforts to "right now." It's the only time that matters, it's the only time there is. Remember that it makes no difference whether you think about the future or not, it comes soon enough

7. **Create Value**

   "Strive not to be a success, but rather to be of value."

   Don't waste your time trying to be successful, spend your time creating value. If you're valuable, then you will attract success.

   Discover the talents and gifts that you possess. Learn how to offer those talents and gifts in a way that most benefits others. Values always remain extant.

8. **Don't Expect Different Results**

   You can't keep doing the same thing every day and expect different results. In other words,

   you can't keep doing the same workout routine and expect to look differently. In order for your life to change, you must change, to the degree that you change your actions and your thinking is to the degree that your life will change.

9. **Knowledge Comes From Experience**

   Knowledge comes from experience. You can discuss a task, but discussion will only give you a philosophical understanding of it; you must experience the task first hand to "know it." What's the lesson? Get experience! Don't spend your time hiding behind speculative information; go out there and do it, and you will have gained priceless knowledge.

10. **Learn the Rules and Then Play Better**

To put it all in simple terms, there are two things that you must do. The first thing you must do is to learn the rules of the game that you're playing. It doesn't sound exciting, but it's vital. Secondly, try to play better than all others.

In our daily lives let us re-evaluate and assess ourselves regularly. Here are some questions that will help you to judge yourself:

- Are we selfish?
- Do we speak the truth?
- Do we lie as much as others do?
- Do we make false excuses?
- Do we deceive people with words?
- Do we deceive them with actions?
- Do we respond to phone calls, emails and letters that the other person considers important?
- Do we keep our promises?
- Do others see us as trustworthy?
- Are we more generous or more stingy and greedy?
- Do we convey messages to others?
- Do we practically believe that we are accountable for our actions in this life?
- Do we have a good moral character?

PRICKS OF TIME

It was the coldest winter ever. Many animals died because of the cold. The Porcupines, realizing the gravity of the situation, decided to group together to keep warm. This way they covered and protected each other; but the quills of each one wounded their closest companion. After sometime, they decided to distance themselves one from the other and they began to die alone and frozen. So they had to make a choice, either accept the quills and pains of their companion or die. Wisely , they decided to go back being together. They learned to live with their wounds caused by being close to each other. This way they were able to survive.

Life and death are the two sides of a picture.All living beings try their hardest to survive. As human beings we should also learn to live with the pricks of time. There will be moments in life that would not be comfortable. We all depend upon each other in many ways. This makes us thankful to our brethren and we also learn to respect them.

FAREWELL LETTER FROM A NOBEL PRIZE WINNER

Gabriel Garcia Marquez, the famous writer from Colombia and Nobel Prize winner for Literature in 1982, retired from public life for reasons of health. Realizing that he had not much time left in life, Marquez wrote a farewell letter to his friends. The brilliant letter expresses his views about the different facets of life. It is thought provoking and makes us aware of how a life should be lived:

If God, for a second, forgot what I have become and granted me a little bit more of life, I would use it to the best of my ability. I would give merit to things not for what they are, but for what they mean to express. I would sleep less and dream more because I know that for every moment that we close our eyes we waste sixty seconds of light. I would walk while others stop; I would dress in a simple manner; I would place myself in front of the Sun, leaving not only my body but my soul naked at its mercy.

To all, I would say how mistaken they are when they grow old without knowing that they grow old when they stop loving. I would give wings to children, but I will leave them to learn to fly by themselves. I have learned that everyone wants to live on top of the mountain without knowing that true happiness is obtained in the journey taken and the form used to reach the top of the hill.

I have learned that when a new born baby holds with its little hand his father's finger, it has trapped him for the rest of his life. I have learned that a man has the right to look down at another man only when that man needs help to get up from the ground.

Say always what you feel and not what you think. There is always tomorrow and life gives us another opportunity to do things right. Keep the loved ones near you, love them and treat them well; take your time to tell them, "I am sorry", "forgive me",

"Please", "thank you", and all those loving words you know. Nobody will know you for your secret thoughts. Show your friends and loved ones how important they are to you.

LIVE A LIFE THAT MATTERS

Whether you are ready or not, someday life will come to an end. There will be no more sunrises, no minutes or hours or days. All the things you collected whether treasured or forgotten will pass on to someone else. Your wealth, fame and temporal power will shrivel to irrelevance. It will not matter what you owned or what you were owed. Your grudges, resentments, frustrations and jealousies will finally disappear; so too your hopes, ambitions, plans, and the to-do lists will expire. The win, the losses that once seemed important will fade away. It will not matter whether you were beautiful or brilliant.

So what will matter? How will the values of days be measured?

What will matter is not what you bought, but what you built; not what you got, but you gave. What will matter is not your success, but your significance. What will matter is not what you learned, but what you taught. What will matter is your act of integrity, compassion and sacrifice that enriched, empowered or encouraged others to emulate your example. What will matter is not how many people you knew, but how many will feel the loss when you are gone. What will matter is how long you will be remembered, by whom and for what.

We are here, on this planet, for a specific period of time we call life. During this period our goal must be to try to do something good, something useful with our lives. If we contribute to other people's happiness, we will find that goal. Help others in their march of life. You will always stand taller with someone else on your shoulders.

Living a life that matters does not happen by accident. It is a matter of choice. 'Cultivate tolerance, enjoin justice, and avoid the fools' (7:199)

PARABLE OF THE PENCIL

The Pencil Maker took the pencil aside, just before putting it into the box. "There are 5 things you need to know," he told the pencil, "Before I send you out into the world. Always remember them and never forget, and you will become the best pencil you can be.

"One: You will be able to do many great things, but only if you allow yourself to be held in someone's hand."

"Two: You will experience a painful sharpening from time to time, but you'll need it to become a better pencil."

"Three: You will be able to correct any mistakes you might make."

"Four: The most important part of you will always be what's inside."

"And Five: On every surface you are used on, you must leave your mark. No matter what the condition, you must continue to write."

The pencil understood and promised to remember, and went into the box with a purpose in its heart.

Now replace the pencil with yourself

(Always remember and never forget, and you will become the best person you can be.)

One: You will be able to do many great things, but only if you allow yourself to be held in the hand of moral values. And allow other human beings to access you for the many gifts you possess.

Two: You will experience a painful sharpening from time to time, by going through various problems in life, but you'll need it to become a stronger person.

Three: You will be able to correct any mistakes you might make.

Four: The most important part of you will always be what's on the inside.

And Five: On every surface you walk through, you must leave your mark. No matter what the situation, you must continue to do your duties.

Allow this parable of the pencil to encourage you to know that you are a special person and only you can fulfil the purpose to which you were born to accomplish

Never allow yourself to get discouraged and think that your life is insignificant and cannot make a change.

CONSOLATION

The Quran provides plenty of solace to the mourners of those who have departed. The solace is hidden in the promise of resurrection in the next world where immortality will replace transience of the present world. The Quran points out:

'No soul shall be wronged but will be requited justly and those who merit paradise shall on that day have joy in whatever they do' (36:54,55)

This promise spurs all survivors of their departed near and dear ones to do good deeds to earn a place in paradise and then enjoy their everlasting companionship.

There is a definite purpose behind creation and that is what we have to remember:

'We have not created the heavens and the earth, and all that lies between them in vain as is the opinion of those who disbelieve. And sorrow and misery is for those nonbelievers' (38:27)

7 JUSTICE-FAIRNESS

'O you who believe, be maintainers of justice and bearers of witness for Allah, even though it be against your own selves or your parents or near relatives whether he be rich or poor' (4:135)

If we do not maintain justice, justice will not maintain us. (Bacon)

Justice is the concept of moral righteousness which is based on ethics, rationality, natural law, religion, fairness, truth and equity. Justice demands punishment of those who break these values. Justice is also the quality of being fair and just; the conformity to the principles of truth and rectitude in all matters. Happiness, prosperity and success can be your achieved if the positive values of justice and fairness are practised in a society.

'Allah commands justice, the doing of good and the giving of gifts to your relatives and forbids indecency, impropriety' and oppression. He warns you so that you may remember' (16:90)

In the Quranic context justice is not confined to the courts of law. In fact, it covers justice in all spheres of life. It also signifies the condition where every individual gets what is due to him. And 'due' means not only what is due to him economically, but all the fundamental rights that belong to him by virtue of his position as a human being. The Quran has laid great stress on the establishment of justice as the ultimate end of the social order.

'We sent Our Messengers with clear evidence of truth and through them We sent the Book (Quran) and the Balance (of right and wrong) so that men may stand forth in justice' (57:25).

HUMAN RIGHTS

All rights of human beings are derived from the Divine Laws of Allah and are given in the Quran. We have before us the example of the rightly guided Caliphs who followed these laws in letter and spirit. These laws were binding on them like any other believer who was a member of the Muslim community. The Caliphs themselves were answerable to Allah and to their people. In their own right they had no special privileges or position. They were accountable to the courts of justice and could be summoned there as ordinary citizens.

The most evident wrong is done in the name of right. This is something which our inner 'Satan' had promised at our birth:

'O my Lord ! Grant me then respite till the Day when all the dead shall be raised. (To which) Allah said 'All right! You are granted respite till the appointed Day'. Iblis (Satan) said,' swear

by your might that I will lead them all astray' (38:79-82)

'I shall certainly bring his (Adam's) descendents completely under my subjugation, except a few (who will not succumb to my influences due to their sincere devotion to You).(17:62).

SATAN'S ROLE

Thus we should be aware that Satan is always there to misguide us and show the wrong way. We are reluctant to accept our wrong actions as wrong and unjust because they appear right to us. Here Satan plays his dubious role of presenting vice as virtue, wrong as right and falsehood as truth:

'There are those whose efforts go astray n the pursuit of the pleasures of this world, and yet they are in the impression that they are doing good work' (18:104).

This is further confounded when the misguided ones twist and change the true spirit of Islam to serve their purpose. The tussle between right and wrong and just and unjust goes on. Whosoever takes guidance from the Quran locks up his Satan as the Messenger of Allah ﷺ had said.

Let us stand up to what is just and fair and prove Allah's trust in us when He said to Satan:

'But, you will have no authority ever over any of My sincere and devoted servants, excepting those who would voluntarily follow you' (15:42).

RULE OF JUSTICE

To establish the rule of justice is the basic responsibility of all states.

As a fundamental value, justice has been ordained on all (16:90), even if we deal with nations that are our declared enemies (5:8). The same principle applies to individuals. We should not be unjust simply because we do not like anyone. Another important factor to realize is that it is not only enough to be just to others, you should also not allow others to be unjust to you' (2:279)

According to the common concept of justice, the duty of a law-court is to decide the disputed affairs according to the code of law that is prevalent, so that a decision taken by the law courts shall be considered as based on justice. But if the law itself is not based on justice, then the decision based on it can never be considered just. Justice itself should be based on truth. If the law is devoid of truth, then any judgment according to this law, cannot be considered as meeting the requirements of justice. All members of a society, especially the youngsters, would have to cooperate in ensuring a system based on merit, honesty and impartiality. If a society practises these values, then it is a just society.

'Those who break the law should be brought to justice' (2:179)

Justice has a different meaning to everyone. It is interpreted in many ways. Many believe that standards of justice are not applied to everyone, only the rich benefit from it and the poor suffer. The Quran points out that during the course of justice, no distinction should be made between relatives and non-relatives, both the status of rich and poor, not even personal benefits should affect one's judgment. The judgment in all matter must be based on justice even if it goes against you. This is a tall order but not impossible. In this respect the Quran points out :

'O you who believe ! Be ever steadfast in your devotion to Allah bearing witness to fair dealings, and not let the hatred of anyone lead you into the sin of deviating from justice; this is the closest to being Allah-conscious and remain conscious of Allah. Verily Allah is aware of all that you do' (5:8).

We should be fair even to our enemies. The Quran does not permit us to deviate from the path of justice in any circumstance. If an oppressor has deprived any one of his basic right, then justice demands that those rights should be restored to him:

'Be conscious of the Day when no human being shall in the least be benefited by another, nor shall intercession be accepted from any of them; nor any ransom taken from any of them; nor will anyone be helped from any source' (2:48).

Consequently:

'Those whose scales are heavy, they are the successful. And those whose scales are light are those who lose their self' (23:102,103).

This is what the Divine system of Justice does. Every deed is assessed on merit without any bias or prejudice.

'And on every man We have fastened his/her record around his neck; and We shall bring forth to him at the time of judgment with a scroll that would be made open to him' (17:31)

INTEGRITY, TOLERANCE AND JUSTICE

The second caliph of Islam Omar Ibn Khattab bought a horse from a Bedouin, paid its price and rode off. After a while the Caliph noticed some defect in the horse, so he returned to the seller asking him to take it back.

The Bedouin refused telling the Caliph that the horse was perfectly healthy when it was sold. The Caliph asked him to choose a judge and the Bedouin suggested the name of Shuraih Bin Haris, whom the Caliph accepted. After listening to the testimony of the Bedouin, the judge asked the Caliph "Was the horse healthy. When you bought it?" The Caliph answered in the affirmative. Shuraih decided the case and said, "Then keep what you bought or return it as you took."

The Caliph looked at Shuraih with admiration and complimented the judge for his fair decision.

The story reflects the integrity and moral uprightness of both the judge and the Caliph. It also shows that a just social order ensures and enables a common man to seek justice even against the most powerful man in the land, refusing to take back what he had sold minutes before and deciding which judge to go to and the Caliph accepting the judge's decision.

In the prevailing circumstances this story may seem like a myth, something impossible; but such instances are common in societies that honour and respect justice.

JUSTICE IN THE PRESENT DAY WORLD

Justice today is mush more complicated than it used to be, but it revolves round the principle that every action has a consequence. Youngsters of today may be judicial officers, law enforcers, law makers and judges of tomorrow. They should know that legal justice mandates procedural fairness in treating those who are alleged to have broken the law and in arbitrating between aggrieved parties; while social justice, by contrast, refers to the fairness or rightness of the overall distribution of benefits and burdens in society like food, clothing, housing etc. All aspects of justice cannot be taken up in this book, but the general purpose is to convey the concept of justice.

As regards the courts of justice, we are clearly guided by the Quran:

'Confound not the truth with falsehood' (2:42).

'Not knowingly conceal the truth' (2:42)

'Hide not testimony' (2:283)

Evidence must be given truthfully (4:135)

'Never be supporter of the guilty' (28:17)

'Not be an advocate for the fraudulent' (4:105)

SINS AND CRIMES

Crimes and sins, according to the Quran, are not only those that are actually and physically committed, but even the mere thought of a breach of the Moral values is an a offence. No doubt such offences do not fall within the jurisdiction of a court of law; nevertheless they are offences in the eye of the Divine Laws of Retribution, and adversely affect the character and personality of the perpetrators. Our innermost wishes, desires and intentions are all known to Allah:

'For Allah is aware of the stealthy glance of the eyes and that which hearts conceal' (40:19).

FIRST PRIORITY OF JUSTICE

For young people the first priority of justice should be to perform their assigned duties and responsibility efficiently and with dedication. Their other job is to assess their relationship with their family, relatives, neighbours, friends and all those who come in contact with them. The next step would be to honestly prioritize what they are required to do for them. In this respect this book will help you to determine your relationship values.

HARMONY IN NATURE

Justice and fairness in nature can be seen working at the macro and micro levels both and any injustice or violation leads to natural disasters like earthquakes, floods, shortage of natural resources and the affliction of humans by deadly bacteria and virus.

The perfect working and harmony that is seen in the universe is due to the balance that Allah has ordained through His standards of justice. The message for us is loud and clear; if we want a similar smooth system in our lives, we have to apply justice in all walks of life and also refrain from creating chaos by being unjust.

'The plants and trees bow in adoration to Allah. He has raised the skies high and has set a balance for all things so that you may not transgress and upset the set scales. Therefore, strictly weigh all things with justice and cheat not in the measures' (55:6-9).

INJUSTICE

In many religions, injustice is punishable in accordance with the Divine Laws of retribution and requital. Fairness demands that we honestly hand over the rightful possessions to whom they belong.

'Do not defraud people of what rightfully belongs to them and do not spread mischief in the land by corruption and dishonesty' (11:85)

Justice turns to injustice when a wrong is committed and the culprit tries to justify and pass it as a right. He usually bribes his way out and a long chain of socially disastrous events take shape. A just and fair individual has the qualities of gratefulness and humility. There is a direct relationship between humility and justice because humility is inextricably bound up with truth. The humble person makes an accurate assessment of himself and willingly accepts the truth of his status. An unjust person considers himself everything and others as nothing.

Justice demands relationship on the basis of equality with all human beings. Anyone who believes in justice will not do to others what he will not like to be done to himself. He recognizes that he is the beneficiary of the labour of countless others.

So much of what we take for granted, has come about through the establishment of social conditions that preceded us, such as the existence of schools, universities, hospitals, neighbourhoods, a just legal system etc. Most of those who laboured for us are not alive but this should not stop us form being generous, and fair to those around us.

THE BELL OF JUSTICE

This is a legendary story of the Mughal emperor Jehangir and his queen Nur Jehan. While on a hunting trip in the jungle, Nur Jehan accidentally killed a man when her arrow missed its mark. The Emperor was famous for his justice and fairness. He had a bell of justice in his palace and citizens, who had a complaint, were free to toll the bell. The widow of the slain subject shook the bell of justice and the Emperor responded promptly. The widow related the whole tragedy of how the Queen had killed her husband and pleaded for justice. The Emperor thought for a moment and pronounced his judgment. He asked the widow to retaliate in the same manner as the Queen and kill Nur Jehan's husband with an arrow, which in this case was the emperor himself.

The Emperor's fair judgment made the aggrieved widow forgive and pardon the Queen for the sake of the just and kind Emperor.

Emperor Jehangir did not hesitate to do justice even though it would have resulted in his own death.

DISTRIBUTORY JUSTICE

Distributory justice is a form of justice that exists in those having charge of the common weal. It is the virtue that inclines the will of those who hold political office to apportion to citizens what is their due through the process of proportional equality. A man who holds a position of authority should by prudent and of eminent integrity.

PRODIGALITY

Prodigality is a vice by which a person is inclined to use his excess wealth to gratify his passions. The result is that he takes no delight in virtue and is more inclined towards covetousness. This leads to a number of other vices against justice such as fraud, treachery, perjury, violence and insensibility to mercy.

Justice also means getting what one deserves, which is scary if you have done something wrong. But it also means having one's rights being respected and not being subjected to oppression. Any form of injustice should be reported to the proper authorities.

PUNISHMENT

The Divine Laws also takes into consideration the concept of punishment for injustice. Liars, deceivers, crooks and bullies do not usually reform their behaviour unless there are serious consequences. But these consequences should be meted out with compassion and not anger or revenge to have a just and beneficial effect. Harsh punishments yield retaliatory cycles of crime. One injustice cannot be redressed by another injustice.

'Allah commands you that when you judge between the people, judge with justice. Noble are the counsels of Allah and Allah hears all and sees everything' (4:58)

'Yet amongst those whom We have created, are people who guide others to the Truth, and establish justice in its light' (7:181)

SOME QURANIC RULES OF PRACTISING JUSTICE

1. Be fair in all your dealing and relationships
2. Avoid favouritism
3. Encourage impartiality and merit
4. Set clear boundaries and rules
5. Thank those who stick to these boundaries.

6. Do not be influenced by rumours, Find out the facts yourself and judge accordingly
7. Do not hurt others and do not let others hurt you
8. Avoid taking revenge
9. If you are in a position of authority, ensure equity and fairness
10. Speak with wisdom to preserve everybody's dignity
11. Respect your elders
12. Do not force your beliefs
13. Respect rights of others without prejudice
14. Accept the responsibilities that go with your rights.

All human beings are bound to face tests and trials in their lives. Their character and personality has the ability to choose and act. There are those who let their weaknesses rule them and are unable to be fair and act unjustly. Frailties or weaknesses are common to all of us.

Weaknesses that the Quran refers to are:

* *Inability to resist lust (4:27)*
* *Leaning towards injustice, in gratitude and unfairness (14:34)*
* *Hastiness and impatience (17:11)*
* *Ingratitude (17:67)*
* *Contentiousness and belligerence i.e. not prone to easily accepting one's faults (18:54)*
* *Niggardliness i.e reluctance to part with what one has (17:100)*
* *Impatience and anxiety (17:19,20)*
* *Transgressors and mischievous (7:162)*
* *Proud (7:166)*

Human beings have been endowed with faculties like wisdom, reasoning, creativity, vision and mercy. Through these faculties they have the ability to make distinction between right and wrong with regard to their own actions and conduct. And above all they have been provided necessary guidance (76:3). There is no logical excuse for being unfair and unjust. The Islamic way of life stands firmly on the pillars of justice and fairness.

8 SINCERITY-HYPOCRISY

'Say (Muhammad) Do you dispute with us about Allah. Allah is our Sustainer and your Sustainer and for you your deeds and for us are our deeds, and we are sincere to Allah' (2:139)
'The hypocrites waver between belief and disbelief, belonging neither to these nor to those' (4:143)

No man can, for any considerable time, wear one face to himself, and another to the multitude, without finally getting bewildered as to which is the true one. (Hawthorne)

Sincerity means to be earnest, true, open, simple, honest, straight forward and natural. These are qualities of character that have become rare. In order to be sincere you have to speak your heart with your words fully in accord with your actions. Thus sincerity is pure thought and action; being who you are, not who you think you are. Sincerity also demands a person to be free of all fears and inhibitions with no ego problems of being hurt.

The Quran clearly declares that those who follow its directives and guidance, in letter and spirit, have nothing to fear or be apprehensive of:

'Allah has promised those of you who sincerely believe in Him and do acts of righteousness that He will surely make them masters in the land, as He had made their ancestors before them, and He will certainly establish for them their religion which He has chosen for them; and He will grant them security and peace in place of fear' (24:55).

'Those who remain steadfast there shall be nothing to fear nor anything to grieve about' (46:13).

'In fact, whoever submits his whole self entirely to Allah, and does good in life, he will get his reward from Allah. All such persons will have no fear, nor shall they grieve' (2:112).

The golden rule of Sincerity is immediacy, spontaneity; spur of the moment responses that are genuine and not polished. The overlays of caution, attempted perfectionism and even sugar-coating, destroys the genuineness of sincerity and drags you in the domain of hypocrisy.

GOLDEN RULE

Do not praise those you do not like. Can there be greater insincerity than the respect you pay to people whom you deeply despise in your heart?

Those who wish to lead their lives sincerely and in accordance with the Divinely ordained values, should ensure that their belief is reflected in their deeds. The Quran condemns those hypocrites who do otherwise:

'O you who believe! Why do you profess what you do not practice ? It is most loathsome in the sight of Allah that you do not practise what you profess' (61:2,3,)

OBJECTIVE ASSESSMENT OF SINCERITY

The intensity of our desire increases our desperation and fogs our sincere and honest approach to life. The world does not encourage sincerity. It is a quality that has to be deliberately developed and cultivated. Even our small actions that seem insignificant make great difference. It is we, ourselves, who have to decide whether we are sincere or not.

Although we all believe that we are sincere, yet the truth becomes evident when we assess ourselves objectively.

Once again the criterion of this judgment has to be the Quran. If we fulfil the standards of sincerity set by it, we can rest assured that we have achieved our goals:

'Those men and women who submit to Allah's guidance and are true believers, devout, truthful, patient, humble, charitable, chaste and who observe fast, and who remember Allah unceasingly; for such people Allah has prepared forgiveness and a mighty reward' (33:35).

SINCERE LOVE

It was a busy morning when an elderly gentleman in his eighties arrived at a hospital to have stitches removed from his thumb. He said he was in a hurry and had an appointment. The doctor examined the wound and found that it was well healed. He asked the old patient if he had another appointment as he was in such a hurry. The old gentleman said that he needed to go to a nursing home to have breakfast with his wife. The doctor inquired about her health and found out that the old patient's wife had been at the nursing home for a while and was suffering from Alzheimer's disease. As they talked the doctor asked the patient if his wife would be upset in case he was late. He replied that she had not recognized him for five years. The doctor was surprised and asked, "And you still go there every morning even though she does not know who you are?" The old gentleman smiled as he patted the doctor's hands and said, "She doesn't know me, but I still know who she is."

The doctor had to hold back his tears as the old patient left and said to himself, "That is the kind of sincere love I want in my life."

True and sincere love is an acceptance of all that is, has been, will be and will not be. The happiest people are not hypocrites and do not necessarily have the best of everything, they just make the best of everything they have.

HYPOCRISY

The opposite of sincerity, truthfulness, forthrightness and honesty is hypocrisy. It is a show or expression of feelings and beliefs one does not actually hold or possess. It is a kind of lie and is inconsistent with one's actions. A person who acts in such a way is called a hypocrite. Such a deceitful person always pretends and is never sincere and true in his work, attitude and relationship. The Divine Guidance advises you to keep away form such attitudes and traits of character.

'When they come to you they say,"We believe", but unbelieving they came and unbelieving they go; and Allah is aware of what they conceal in their hearts' (5:61)

In religious terminology 'Kufr' is an antonym or negation of 'Eeman' (belief). One who denies the truth in fact seeks to conceal it. It does not mean hypocrisy because a hypocrite professes to believe in a thing that he does not accept with conviction in his heart.'The Hypocrites encourage what is bad and discourage what is good' (9:66)

'They waver between belief and disbelief, belonging neither to these nor to those' (4:143)

'They may hide their evil deeds from the people, but they cannot conceal them from Allah. He is amidst them even when they hold secret discussions by night, of matters that are displeasing to Him; for Allah surrounds all that they do' (4:108) .That is why the Quran condemns the hypocrites to the lowest depths of hell:

'The hypocrites will be in the lowest depths of hell, and you will find no help for them' (4:145).

'And one day the hypocrites, men and women, will say to those who believe 'wait for us a while to enable us to borrow a light from your light'. They will be told to go back and seek their lights elsewhere. Then a wall to separate them shall be raised between them with a gate therein, on the inside of which there will be grace and mercy and on the outside there will be retribution of Hell' (57:13).

HYPOCRITE'S SORROW

A hypocrite's sorrow will also be pretentious like the proverbial crocodile who moans and cries to lure passersby into its clutches, and then, still weeping, devours them. A hypocritical approach in any matter is devoid of conviction and is bound to falter and fail.

The Quran has this to say about such people:

'There is a certain type of man whose views on the life this world impresses you, and he calls Allah to witness about the good intentions he cherishes in his heart; whereas in truth, he is the deadliest opponent of Truth' (2:204).

EVIL NEVER SUCCEEDS

The golden principle of life is that evil, in any form, never succeeds. It may appear to be successful but this success is temporary and not everlasting. No decent human being can justify dissimulation or a concealment of one's real character and motives. The assuming of false appearance of virtue or religion should be identified, discouraged and condemned. This form of hypocrisy has always existed and attracts people with the delusion of immediate success and self-serving gain. It is better to speak the truth that hurts and then heals, than assume falsehood that comforts, but finally destroys.

'When you see them, their outward personality may please you. When they speak, you are attracted to listen to their speech as to what they have to say. They are like worthless timber leaning against a wall. They presume that every cry is directed towards them. They are your enemies, so be on guard against them! The curse of Allah be on them ! How are they deluded away from the Truth' (63:4)

'Allah will punish the hypocrites, both men and women' (33:75)

It is not easy to observe a strict code of conduct. The inner struggle between our base impulses and the rigorous demands of our moral system is quintessentially human. It is how we conduct ourselves in that struggle which determines how we may be judged by others.

SHINING LIGHT

Dr Paul Brand was speaking to his medical college students on the impermanence of deceit and hypocrisy. In front of the lectern was an oil lamp with its cotton wick burning from the shallow dish of oil. During the lecture the lamp ran out of oil, the wick burned dry and the smoke made him cough. He immediately used the opportunity to make his point about hypocrisy and deceit so common in everyday life.

"Some of us are like this wick" he said, "We try to appear forthright, righteous and just; but we stink. That is when we use ourselves as fuel of our desires and ambitions. Wicks can last indefinitely, burning brightly and without irritating smoke, if the fuel of our true selves is in constant supply."

'Allah has reserved for hypocrites, whether men or women,and for unbelievers, the fire of Hell where they will live forever. This is sufficient for them: They have Allah's condemnation and lasting torment' (9:68)

In 'Little Red Riding Hood' the wolf pretends to be her grandmother in order to lure her into the house so he can eat her. In 'Cinderella' you have the ugly sisters pretending that the glass shipper is theirs. In 'Hansel and Gretel' the children's parents twice abandon them in the woods, promising to return, but do not do so.

All these are examples of insincerity; deceit and hypocrisy that fail to succeed in the end are a lesson for us all to adopt moral values in our lives.

INTEGRITY

Integrity is the intelligible human good of harmony or integration between various elements of the self. For a hypocrite there is no correspondence between what is in him and his words. There is a separation between the content of his words and his own mind. Although the truth is in his mind, it is not evident in his words and actions. So our words should be an extension and expression of ourselves.

No circumstances can change the status and nature of insincerity. If we are required to withhold information from others, at the very least we have a duty not to lie to them. For a hypocrite affability is a means of deception, an opportunity to mislead and trap others.

The hypocrites forget that ultimately they will be answerable for their deeds and the insincerity that they so prized in this earthly life will be of no use.

'On the Day of Judgment, Allah will raise them all together and inform them of what they did. Allah has maintained a full account of their deeds although they may have forgotten. Know that Allah is Witness over everything' (58:6).

'How would they fare when We will gather them together on the Day of Judgment which is certainly to come, when each will receive the reward without any favour or injustice' (3:25)

BASIC DUTY

Our basic duty is to be sincere and honest in our deeds. The rest should be left to Allah Who has absolute authority over our lives and Who is never unjust.

'Nothing shall befall us except what Allah decrees for us. He is our Supreme Protector and in Him should all believers place their trust' (9:51)

'Those who keep their utmost trust in Allah should know that if Allah bestows upon them good fortune, there is none who can impair that good fortune' (6:17)

9 GOOD EDUCATION AND UPBRINGING

'Those who possess knowledge, maintain justice and acknowledge Allah as Supreme' (3:18)

Education commences at the mother's knee, and every word spoken within the hearsay of little children tends towards the formation of character. (N. Ballou)

TOP PRIORITY

Islam gives top priority to education, knowledge and wisdom. The exalted last Messenger also prayed to Allah to enhance his knowledge:

'O my Sustainer ! Cause me to grow in my knowledge' (20:114)

EDUCATION

In the broader sense education is an act or experience that has a formative effect on the mind, character and ability of a person. It is also considered a progressive discovery of a person's ignorance, helping to replace an empty mind with an open and enlightened one.

The foremost objective of good education is to understand and subdue the forces of nature through knowledge. This can only be achieved if the system of education is well-balanced, adequate and all embracing. This ultimately helps to harness the human potential and its utilization in subservience to the Quranic values for the benefit of mankind. The outer world is the true image of man's inner-self.

'The truth is that Allah never changes the condition of the people, unless they themselves exert to change their own characteristics and inner-selves' (13:11).

If work in accordance with the teachings of the Quran and adequately educate the potential users, then the flow of this information and knowledge, like water, will ultimately find its own level. The expected result will definitely discourage and eliminate the negative forces:

'The negative forces as a result of the clash between truth and falsehood pass away like scum and that which is beneficial for mankind remains on the earth' (13:17).

The Quranic teachings give birth to the most precious, delicate, fragile and dear of all institutions – an entity where students are encouraged to develop a deep insight for formulating the right solutions to problems and difficulties confronting them.

ORIGINAL IDEAS

A really good education is meant for those who insist on knowing, the rest is mere sheep-herding and rote-learning. Some look upon education as a medium of acquiring skills. This points to an activity which teaches to think objectively so that a person becomes capable of conceiving original ideas and contributes positively to the society he lives in.

At ebb tide I wrote
A line upon the sand,
And gave it all my heart
And all my soul..
At high tide I returned
To read what I had inscribed
And found my ignorance upon the shore.

Good education is not to teach facts, theories or laws or make children good earners. It is to unsettle their minds, widen their horizons, inflame their intellect and teach them to think straight if possible, but to think nevertheless. Every piece of marble has a statue in it waiting to be released by a man of skill to chip away the unnecessary parts. Just as the sculptor is to the marble, so is education to the mind. Minds are like parachutes. They only functions when they are open. It is the ability to listen to almost anything without losing your temper or your self-confidence.

USAGE OF SENSES

Education also involves the maximum usage of the senses that Allah has given. They are sources of educating us in all matters. Those who ignore and do not use their senses and their minds are not living their lives on a human level.

'Many among human beings have adopted a lifestyle that will lead them to hell. They have minds but they do not use them, they have eyes but do not see; they have ears, but cannot hear. They are not human beings and are even worse than animals. They are neglectful' (7:179).

OBJECTIVES OF GOOD EDUCATION

Providing good education to the youth should be the goal of every teacher, of every educational institution and of every government of every country in the world. When we think of a well educated person, the image of someone who is knowledgeable on a wide range of subjects and topics comes to mind. Such a person is well-mannered, able to communicate well, verbally and in writing and is up-to-date on current events. He is also capable of solving problems and is cultured with a good command and taste for the arts, music, literature, politics and possibly other languages.

Parents consider it their duty to provide the best possible education to their children that would guide and help them to become useful human beings. Parents also desire that their children should have a balanced personality capable of assessing how things in the world fit together in the 'big picture' of life. Good education creates life- long learners.

The Quran emphasizes that education is a life-long process and at no stage should one consider that he does not need any more knowledge.

'They say our hearts are full of knowledge and we need no more! No, but Allah has rejected them because of their refusal to acknowledge the truth' (2:88).

KNOWLEDGE AND LEARNING

The first revelation of the Quran 'Al-Alaq' revealed to the Messenger Muhammad ﷺ pertained to knowledge and learning.

'Read (Iqra) in the name of your Sustainer (Allah) Who created man from a clot. Read and your Sustainer is the most Bountiful who teaches the use of the pen; teaches man that which he knew not '(96:1-5).

'Iqra' in the above verse implies reading, writing, study, research, knowledge including science, technology and observation of nature and promulgation of the Divine Book. It also enlightens the righteous in adoration of Allah and imbues him to draw closer to the Creator and Cherisher.

Young people love tackling problems and real problems should be given to them for practical and down to earth solutions. Elders should never underestimate the potential abilities of young people.

Facts can be memorized, but problem solving skills, reason and critical analysis provide the learner with tools to question, inquire and conclude. These tools train the sensibility of pupils in such a manner that in their attitude to life, their actions, decisions and approach to knowledge, they are governed and guided by moral and ethical values.

Good education trains and mentally disciplines children in such a manner that they want to acquire knowledge and expertise not merely to satisfy intellectual curiosity or just for material worldly benefit, but to grow up as rational righteous human beings. Not only that, it also ensures the overall welfare and prosperity of their families, their community and country.

'And tell my servants that they should speak in the most kindly manner to those who do not share their beliefs; surely Satan is always ready to stir up discord between men – for surely, Satan is man's open enemy' (17:53)

BASIC EDUCATION

Basic education begins at home long before formal education takes place in the school and college. Parents are naturally the child's first teacher. They can be most effective for their children's academic growth. Teaching by example and encouraging the young ones natural interest in learning is the key to incorporating good education in their daily lives.

The entire purpose of creation rests on the Quranic system of values. All social, economic and political activities have to base their principles on this nucleus if they wish to succeed.

In the education system, the Quranic guidance provides the best possible opportunities for self-development because the individual is the focus of these values. The society exists to enable the individuals to develop and express themselves to the full extent of their capacity.

EDUCATION SYSTEM

In present times the youth seems to be wandering in a rudderless ship with no clear objectives.. Even our curriculum and education system has nothing concrete to offer.

Good education need not be purely theoretical, Development of the right perspective to living a fuller life is equally important. Learning important life skills like doing chores in the house, gardening and cleaning are all an integral part of education. Youngsters should also be encouraged to participate in debates, sports, exhibitions, presentations, essay writing and other competitions. Character building can be reinforced at home where basic human values like honesty, kindness and empathy are taught and instilled right from the early stages of a child's development. These could and should be effectively reinforced and incorporated in schools, colleges and universities by teachers.

The society is full of those people who can neither read nor write. The Quran directs the literate and the educated to help those who have not been fortunate enough to acquire these skills:

'No scribe should refuse to write, as Allah has given him the gift of literacy' (2:282)

A FATHER'S LETTER TO HIS SON'S TEACHER

Teach him that all men are just, all men are not true. But teach him also that for every scoundrel there is a hero; that for every selfish politician, there is a dedicated leader.

Teach him that for every enemy there is a friend.

Steer him away from envy if you can, instil in him the wonder of books but also give him quiet time to ponder the eternal mystery of birds in the sky, bees in the Sun, and the flowers on a green hillside .

In the school teach him to fail than to cheat. Teach him to have faith in his own ideas, even if everyone tells him that he is wrong. Teach him to be gentle with gentle people and tough with tough people.

Teach him if you can how to laugh when he is sad. Teach him that there is no shame in tears. Teach him to scoff at cynics and to beware of too much sweetness. Teach him to sell his brawn and brain to the highest bidders but never to put a price-tag on his heart and soul.

Teach him to close his ears to a howling mob and to stand and fight if he thinks he is right. Treat him gently but do not cuddle him, because only the test of fire makes fine steel.

Let him have the courage to be impatient; let him have the patience to be brave. Teach him always to have sublime faith in himself, because then he will have sublime faith in mankind.

This is a big order, but see what you can do he is such a fine little fellow my son!

QUALITIES OF A GOOD STUDENT:

Positive:

- Thinks positively and enthusiastically about people and what they are capable of becoming.
- Sees the good in any situation and can move forward to make the most of difficult situations when confronted with obstacles.
- Encourages others to be positive.

Communicative:

- Shares with others in a manner that encourages effective two-way communication.

- Communicates personal thoughts and feelings on a wide spectrum of issues and can listen to other students in an empathetic manner.
- This brings him closer to those around him.

Dependable:

- Honest and sincere in working with others.
- Consistently lives up to commitments to teachers, fellow students and others.

Social:

- Establishes and maintains positive mutual working relationships.
- Likes to be social.
- Has many ways of getting to know his friends, fellow students and well wishers as persons while building trust and appreciation through personal interaction and involvement.

Organized:

- Makes efficient use of time and moves in a planned and systematic direction.
- Knows where he or she is heading and is able to co-ordinate and help others

Committed:

- Demonstrates commitment to his studies and is self-confident, poised and personally in control of situations.
- Has a healthy self-image; is neat and clean.

Motivational:

- Enthusiastic with standards and expectations of his institution and teachers.
- Understands the intrinsic motivations of individuals, and knows what the true value of motivation.
- Does not treat assignments as work to get done just for the sake of good grades, rather treats them as an important part of the learning process.

Compassionate:

- Caring, empathetic and able to respond to people when they need him.
- Knows and understands the feelings of other students; is always willing to help his class-mates in their studies.

Flexible:

- Willing to alter plans and directions in a manner which assists people in moving toward their goals.
- Seeks to reason out situations with teachers and parents in an amiable manner.

Value Based:

- Focuses upon the worth and dignity of human beings.
- Is sensitive to community values.
- Strives to work in an environment consistent with the prevailing social and moral values.
- Recognizes the importance and power of modelling constructive behaviour.

Knowledgeable:

- Is in constant quest for knowledge.
- Keeps up in his or her speciality areas, and has the insight to integrate new knowledge.

Creative:

- Versatile, innovative, and open to new ideas.
- Strives to incorporate techniques and activities that enable students to have unique and meaningful new growth experiences.

Patient:

- Strives to look at all aspects of the situation and remains fair and objective under most difficult circumstances.
- Believes that problems can be resolved if enough input and attention is given in a forthright manner.

Sense of Humour:

- Knows how to take the tension out of tight situations. Uses humour, spontaneously, in a tasteful manner

Disciplined and hard working:

- Knows that a good result is not possible without effort and devotion to hard work

Well prepared:

- Knows the importance of preparing for the future.
- Has high dreams and knows their limits.
- Is practical and goal oriented; always keeps in mind that failure is one thing that should be faced and overcome to achieve goals

Punctual and attentive:

- Is attentive in class and does not disturb the class or stare out of the window.
- Asks questions that the teacher knows many other students may also have.

Diligent and enthusiastic:

- Keeps in touch with his teachers and benefits from their knowledge and experience.
- Is not afraid to ask questions and express his opinions within bounds of decency.

Extra-curricular activities:

- Takes active part in extra-curricular activities like sports, drama, debates and literary discussions.

UPBRINGING

The parents bring their children into this world. The protracted infancy of the human child necessitates close association of parents with the children over a number of years. In this close companionship, tender emotions germinate and develop strong ties of love and affection. This binds the parents and children closely and permanently. In the upbringing of children, home symbolizes peace, security, happiness and mutual sympathy. It is the basis for satisfying social relationships and fruitful cooperation under parental care. Children not only attain physical maturity, but they also become humanized and socialized beings. The family is the matrix in which the personality is shaped and moulded.

FORMATIVE YEARS

It is the care and training of young children during their formative years and paves the way for their future life All aspects of a man's life—his character, sense of responsibly, good and bad habits, ability to cope with difficulties, and his piety—are shaped, during his childhood. If children and young people are brought up in an atmosphere where their enthusiasm is stimulated with higher feelings and moral values, they will have vigorous minds and display good morals and virtues. Importance should also be given to the teaching of cultural values.

Improvement in a community is possible by elevating the young generations to the rank of humanity and not by ignoring or obliterating bad ones. A child's mischief and impudence arises from the environment in which he or she has been raised. A dysfunctional family life is reflected upon the spirit of the child and influences the whole society. Good manner, in school and at home, should be considered as important as other subjects. Those with good manners are liked, even if they are uneducated.

ROLE OF PARENTS

Almost everyone can train their bodies, but few can educate their minds and feelings.

In the process of upbringing the first educators are mothers. Thus it is imperative for a nation's progress, existence and stability that girls be brought up and educated to be good mothers and educators for their children. Those who wish to predict a nation's future can do so accurately by analysing the education and upbringing being given to its young people. If parents are educating and bringing-up their children properly, if a school is awakening hope, faith and moral values in its pupils, then we can say that they are serving their purpose, otherwise they are like fatal traps that divert us from the truth.

IMPORTANCE OF MORAL VALUES

Any upbringing, either within the family or the school, can only pursue temporary aims related to the needs of the family and society when divorced from moral values. For instance, the aim of education in socialist totalitarian countries is to make a person an obedient instrument of the government. In the Western capitalist countries the object of education is not a person's highest welfare or integrity, but the material needs of the government and community. Good education and upbringing shapes people as good, considerate, kind and helpful human beings. This enables them to differentiate between right and wrong, vice and virtue and true and false. If the parents strive to give their children a good education and upbringing, there would be very little need for laws, courts and punishments. At an early age children become lazy, are prone to slyness and deceit and manifest greed and cruelty toward other children. If parents do not teach them to overcome their bad inclinations, these may grow into passions and vices. A child should always know what is permissible and what is not. Sometimes sensible prohibitions and light punishments are necessary.

While children have been directed to be kind to their parents (2:83, 4:36) and not to show any kind of anger or disgust, nor snub them, but speak to them gently with kind words when they attain old age (17:23); the parents too should do justice while bringing them up. Parents have been specifically warned to desist from unduly favouring their children when their acts negate the Quranic principles.

'And know that your worldly possessions and your children are merely a trial and temptation; and that it is with Allah with Whom greater rewards await you' (8:28)

EFFECT OF ENVIRONMENT AND GENES

Children are products of both their environment and their genetics. The manner in which children are raised has a great deal of effect on their eventual adulthood. Those raised with sufficient love, respect and guidance are more successful than their peers who are not. Parents influence the lives of their children in every aspect and leave an impression which remains throughout their lives. For example, it is natural for a boy to imitate his father in driving a car or a girl desiring to acquire the culinary expertise from her mother. The seeds of thought which parents sow in the minds of their wards will go a long way in defining their courses of lives. Thus it is the duty of parents to see that they set fine standards for their children to grow up, emulate and groom into dignified human beings.

Each person's knowledge of how to bring up a child usually comes from his or her own upbringing. This may result in patterns from the parent's own social experiences being repeated and passed on to their children. Raising a child is the most difficult and responsible task a human being can face. It is a responsibility for which the least formal training is received.

THE JUNGLE BOOK

This famous collection of stories by Rudyard Kipling was published in 1893. There is a story of an abandoned infant Mowgli, who is brought up by wolves in an Indian jungle. Mowgli is also helped by Balloo the bear and Bagheera the black panther. Balloo and Bagheera undertake the task of educating Mowgli. He grows up in the jungle more like an animal. He is taught all tricks of survival and combating predators. Ultimately Mowgli, being a human and not afraid of fire, helps the wolves in eliminating their old enemy Shere Khan the lion.

The story beautifully illustrates the process of learning from the environment in which a child grows. Mowgli is brought up as an animal, but he finally returns to his fellow beings who refuse to accept him. His intelligence as a human being helps him to overcome problems faced both by humans and animals.

Parents who compliment and show respect, kindness, love, honesty friendliness, hospitality and generosity to their children will encourage them to behave in the same way. Parents' love should be unconditional and they should provide continuous support to the children. This will make the children self-assured, confident and happy.

PARENTS' EXPECTATIONS

It is also important that parents set reasonable expectations from their children. The children should be plainly told what is expected from them. Young people do not reject reasonable boundaries. Setting boundaries within limits helps them to cultivate better behavioural habits. Inconsistency and lack of discipline among the parents and family leaves a very bad influence on the children's minds.

Children should realize the importance of the Divine Guidance as part of the process of being raised in a Muslim family. They are expected to understand, believe and act in accordance with the principles laid down in the Quran. The basic principle of this Guidance is the belief in the Divine Law of Retribution which states that every action of man has consequences and the doer will have to bear the consequences whether he likes them or not.

'Whoever follows the right path, follows it for his own good; and whoever goes astray does so for his own loss. No bearer of burdens shall be made to bear the burdens of another' (17:15)

FAMILY LIFE

Youngsters also need the quality time of their parents and elders. Being together all the time is not possible. At breakfast in the morning and at dinner in the evening, the whole family can get together. Everyone can join in the conversation and parents should give attention to what the children say. It is also good for a family to do a variety of things together such as playing games, going to the movies or the sea-side or watching television.

The children should be encouraged to ask questions. If the family has a problem that concerns the children, involve them in the discussion to find possible solutions. This creates confidence among the children and a healthy bond between the children and the parents. Young people are quite capable of helping their parents in all matters.

A good family life is an epitome of love, understanding , cooperation and righteousness. The older generation guides the young in matters of right and wrong. The younger generation, with more energy, adopts the right path and earns Allah's blessings.

'Surely those who have attained to faith and have forsaken the domain of evil and are striving hard in Allah's cause – these are the ones who may look forward to Allah's Grace for Allah is much-Forgiving, a Dispenser of Grace' (2:218)

10 CONSERVATION AND WASTEFULNESS

'He it is Who produces gardens, the cultivated ones and the wild, and the date-palms and land sown with corn and any other seeds and olives and pomegranates, alike and yet unalike. So eat of their fruit when it comes to fruition and give unto the poor their due on harvest day. And do not waste Allah's bounties. Surely He does not love the wasteful'(6:141)

To him who in the love of nature
Holds communion with her visible forms
She speaks a different language. (S. Bryant)

NATURE AND MAN

The Quran puts man on a meaningful relationship with nature. To grasp the significance of the Quranic view let us compare it with two popular views. According to one of them, nature is hostile to man. The other view considers nature to be completely indifferent to man and his ideals. This view does not care whether man succeeds or fails. Opposing both these views, the Quran presents nature as friendly to man, responsive to his intellect and sympathetic to his moral endeavours. According to the Quran both man and nature have been created by a wise and benevolent Allah and fundamentally there is no conflict between them. Man can progress with the help of nature. This help he can obtain provided he acquires knowledge of nature and utilizes it positively for the moral ends in the light of the Divine Guidance.:

It is Allah Who has created the heavens and earth and sent down rain from the sky, producing fruits for your sustenance' (14:32).

'He has made subservient to you by His Grace all that is in the heavens and on the earth. Verily, in this are signs for those who reflect' (45:13).

While harnessing the forces of nature we have to maintain a balance so as not to exceed the limits of our genuine necessities. Allah does not like those who are transgressors and waste by excess' (7:31)

CONSERVATION

In the present day world, conservation means the efforts that are made to reduce energy consumption in order to preserve for the future and reduce environmental pollution. An important factor essential for conservation is the efficient supervision of rivers, forests and all other natural resources. Another titan the world is facing today is global warming due to the indiscriminate burning and consumption of fossil fuel. Conservation can slow down this harmful activity and prevent the depletion of natural resources.

The old concept was that the total amount of energy in the universe was fixed and unchangeable. Modern day scientists are tapping new sources of energy, like nuclear energy, to cater to the everyday demands of unlimited energy.

HUMAN BEHAVIOUR

All living beings affect the environment they live in. For example the fan, air-conditioner or light we leave on while away from home create a chain of harmful events involving the electrical company supplying electricity, our homes and neighbourhood. Apart from the wastage it causes, the environment is also affected. Smoke emitting vehicles cause breathing problems. Even the excessive amount of fresh water wasted in the bathrooms and watering of lawns and plants is depleting the water resources. A large percentage of the population has no access to clean drinking water and consume polluted unhygienic water and become victims of numerous fatal diseases. We have to realize that water is a valuable asset and should be judiciously and economically used. A shower can wash and clean our body as much as a bathtub of over flowing water or even a tumbler of water. The amount of clean water that is flushed down the drain can also be economized by using sub-soil or recycled water. This practice is already in vogue in many countries.

All the gifts of nature are the blessings of Allah and we should use them judiciously. The Quran specifically says:

' Allah does not like those who are given to excess' (5:88)

More and more people are using public transport to avoid unnecessary consumption of petrol and gas. Many prefer to walk or cycle to their jobs resulting in a better environment and healthy.

OIL LEAK

On April 20, 2010 an oil rig in the Gulf of Mexico owned by British Petroleum Company exploded, killing eleven workers. Following the explosion, millions of barrels of crude oil leaked into the ocean, shutting down fisheries across the region and leaving tar balls and oily smudge on faraway shorelines. Marine life was adversely affected and entire region suffered untold hardships and miseries.

An oil tanker that ran aground near the Karachi port a few years ago, spilling huge quantities of oil and the entire Karachi coastline and adjoining areas suffered the environmental disaster and its ill effects for a very long time.

POLLUTION

Every year toxic chemicals, some capable of travelling thousands of miles from their source and lasting decades in the environment, are released into the earth's atmosphere. Many environmental problems have no boundaries or borders and threaten the health, prosperity and even the national security of nations. Pesticide contamination of food and water, polluted air, invasive plant and animal species (The flora and fauna that are non-native and dominate, disrupt and adversely affect the areas they invade or move in) can take their toll on our bodies and our national economy. A quarter of the life-saving drugs come from rapidly disappearing tropical forests. Ultimately our sources of energy, food and livable environment are bound to vanish and life will be very difficult on this planet.

THE GREENHOUSE EFFECT AND THE OZONE LAYER

People usually mention the 'Greenhouse Effect' without realizing its true meaning. The Greenhouse is a large room made of glass through which the Sun's rays pass and warm up the inside. This helps a number of plants, kept in the Greenhouse, to grow well in the warm and moist atmosphere. The warmth inside the Greenhouse does not escape and this allows the plants to have a regular supply of warmth that is needed for their proper growth.

The Earth is like a Greenhouse. The Sun's rays radiate through the atmosphere which comprises various gases surrounding the globe. The atmospheric umbrella lets the Sun's radiation in but does not allow it be reflected back into the atmosphere. The gradual warming of the Earth is known as the "Greenhouse Effect". The indiscriminate burning of fossil fuels (petrol, diesel, kerosene, furnace oil, natural gas, coal etc.) is on the rise and consequently the level of Carbon Dioxide in the atmosphere is also rising.

There is a trace gas called Ozone at about sixty kilometres above the Earth's surface which is a protective layer that filters ninety percent of the harmful Ultraviolet radiation from reaching the Earth. It also helps in regulating planetary temperature. As a result of too much burning of fossil fuel and gases, this Ozone protective layer has broken around the South Pole resulting in the extraordinary warming of the planet.

The abrupt changes in temperature have resulted in Tsunamis, heavy rains, cyclones, hurricanes and major floods.

We have to be extremely careful in consuming the different sources of energy to avoid these disasters. It is high time that we reduce the emission of those materials that can harm the Ozone layer.

PROTECTION FROM HARMFUL ACTIVITIES

The world needs protection from the various harmful activities of the human race. Knowingly or unknowingly we are involved in wastefulness, pollution and the introduction of invasive species and the release of genetically modified organisms and toxic material in the environment. We all have to realize this imminent danger and resolve to avoid wastefulness and the indiscriminate consumption of natural resources.

The satisfaction in the fulfilment of our needs is a favour and blessing of Allah. The Quran addresses us and says:

'He (Allah) fulfils all your requirements and needs, and if you try to count the favours, you shall not be able to calculate them (for they are innumerable and immeasurable). The truth is that man is unjust and ungrateful' (14:34)

RECYCLING

Recycling means the process of turning used material or waste into new products and reduces the use of fresh raw material. This process of reconditioning unwanted material or waste into new products prevents wastage of potentially useful materials. Recycling also means to reduce the consumption of fresh new materials and energy.

Recycling is of many types. For example paper recycling is the process of recovering waste paper and remaking it into new paper products. Ninety percent of the paper is made of wood. Recycling paper saves thousands of trees that we need for our survival. Recycling of clothes, old computers and mobile phones, plastic, textile products, tyres and many other materials is helping in saving the earth's environment from further deterioration.

Recycling is now an accepted form of combating wastefulness and pollution.

Not everybody realizes how environmentally important it is to shop consciously. We should support products and packaging that make recycling easier and reduce the amount of garbage that is thrown away. Plastic bags are absolutely out; use paper bags for shopping purposes. All batteries leak poison into the air. Whatever type of batteries and cells that are used in toys, cameras, laptops, musical instruments and other devices, have chemicals inside them that can cause health problems if not properly disposed off. Rechargeable batteries are a cost-effective way to power your proper recycling. The recycling slogan is "Reduce-Reuse-Recycle".

BALANCE IN UTILIZING NATURE

Life is a movement that appears to be running against the directions of main currents of nature. Nature demands humans to distribute its harvest equally among all living beings, yet the fear of starvation and greed for more forbids letting go of material gains. Nature wants human beings to live in peace. Yet, distrust, doubt and hunger for power makes us go to war regularly. Nature is silent in horror after observing the icy deceptions in human relationships. This silence is perhaps a humble request to human life to stay within truthful confines. We have no other place to go except this planet. We must cooperate with nature and accommodate each other in a comfortable manner.

Islam, while advocating care and respect for all animate and inanimate creations in nature, prohibits wanton killing of animals, expect for food, and cutting of plants and trees except for utility purposes. It, therefore, distinguishes between the rights of man and those of other things in nature. According to the Quran :

'Everything on earth has been created for man's benefit' (2:29).

This unqualified affirmation from the Almighty grants full authority to human beings to put to use the flora and fauna, rivers and rivulets, mountains and minerals etc., but this permission is only to utilize and avail and not to pollute and destroy. The natural resources are meant for all living beings:

'The earth He has spread for all of His creatures. With fruits of all kinds and palm trees containing clusters of dates; and a variety of corn with husk and sweet smelling plants' (55:10,11,12).

Light pollution is caused by our over expanding cities and outdoor street lighting. Safety at night and well lit streets are necessary, but too much electrical energy is wasted on advertisements, billboards, and decorations. We cannot even enjoy the beauty of stars at night.

We can all contribute in conserving nature and saying no to pollution by following these simple rules:

1. Plant trees. They will clean the air we breathe and produce oxygen.
2. Participate and encourage cleanup days at a beach, park or neighbourhood.
3. Discourage littering. Ensure the use of outdoor garbage containers.
4. Ask the local authorities to clean the drains. Trash tossed carelessly outside often washes into the storm drains and blocks them.
5. Report the burning of garbage to the authorities.
6. Ensure that your cars and other vehicles do not emit poisonous fumes.
7. Live a clean, simple and healthy life.

'So keep yourself exclusively on the true faith, turning away from all that is false, in accordance with the creational law of Allah according to which He created man with the quality of choosing right and wrong, not to allow any change to corrupt what Allah has created – this is the purpose of the one true faith, but most people know not' (30:30)

11 COURAGE AND BRAVERY

'Man never gets tired asking for the good things of life; but if evil fortune befalls him, he abandons all hope, giving himself up to despair' (41:49)

"It is curious that physical courage should be so common in the world and moral courage so rare."
— Mark Twain

COURAGE

Courage is the quality of mind or spirit that enables a person to face difficulties, dangers and pains without fear or anxiety. The youth usually shows more courage while standing up to injustice and cruelty. Great things are often done through courage than through wisdom. The act of courage is called bravery. Both these values/qualities insist to do the right thing even in the face of certain defeat or loss without promise of reward or return.

Think of the time when you should have done something or acted in a particular way, but did not do so perhaps due to some hidden fears and apprehensions. Had you acted courageously and with bravery, you might have succeeded. This shows that lack of courage and bravery leads to inaction and ultimate failure. All problems become smaller if you do not dodge them or look the other way, but face them head on. It is not about being fearless, but overcoming fear. You cannot be brave if you only have good and wonderful things happening to you.

In true courage there is always an element of choice . There is always a flame of spirit in it, a vision of some necessity higher than oneself.

Firefighters are honoured the world over for being courageous and brave facing great dangers while saving others. Such people are always respected, honoured and loved. They are the kind of heroes most people would like to be. You too can be a hero by stepping forward in times of need; to stand up for justice. This is what makes life worth living.

'You will surely be victorious if you believe and place your trust in Allah' (5:23)

HAZARDOUS JOURNEY

British Antartic explorer Sir Ernest Shackleton placed this advertisement in London newspapers in 1900 in preparation for the National Antartic Expedition.

MAN WANTED FOR HAZARDOUS JOURNEY: Small wages, bitter cold, long months of complete darkness, constant danger, safe return doubtful, Honour and recognition in ease of success. Ernest Shackleton

The expedition subsequently failed to reach the South Pole. Shackleton later said of the call for volunteers that "it seemed as though all the men in Great Britain were determined to accompany me, the response was over whelming."

FEAR AND COWARDICE

The opposite of bravery and courage is cowardice, timidness and weakness. The values of courage and bravery are needed at every moment in life. Remember that even a lion has to defend itself from flies. While your courage and bravery can help you or those around you; it will also leave a positive and lasting effect which never stops.

Whatever you do, you need courage. Whatever course you take, there is someone to tell you that you are wrong. There are always differences arising that tempt you to believe your critics are right. To map out a course of action and follow it to the end requires some courage similar to that of a soldier. Peace too has its victories, but it takes courage to win them.

Being afraid is a perfectly appropriate emotion when confronted with fearful things. The brave person is not one who is never afraid. This is rather the description of a rash and reckless person. On the other hand, a coward is a person who lacks confidence and is overly fearful in challenging situations. For example the fear of the dark is almost universal among younger children, and it provides relatively safe opportunities for first lessons in courage.

The message of the Quran is loud and clear. Those who believe in the Divine Values have nothing to fear:

'In fact, whoever submits his whole self entirely to Allah and does good in life, he will get his reward from Allah. All such persons need have no fear, nor shall they grieve' (2:112).

COURAGE AND WISDOM

There is nothing courageous about taking stupid, unnecessary risks just for thrills or to show off. Again, true courage requires wisdom of being able to distinguish between those circumstances you fear but need to face and those circumstances you fear and rightly need to avoid. False courage is dangerous and risky and serves no purpose.

Courage is not something that comes in a package. It is a way of life and is as much a habit as anything else like brushing your teeth. Courage is usually spoken in terms of deeds. For instance, soldiers showing their courage in a battle or rescue workers' act of courage in the face of natural disasters like floods, fires and earth quakes. But courage is also a lot more. The real test of courage is in our daily lives like the courage to speak the truth and stand up for what you believe in. The sign of a courageous person is in someone who feels fear, recognizes it and still goes on to do what is right.

'Those who listen and refrain from evil and make amends in their lives, will have no cause for fear, nor any cause for grief' (7:35)

VALUE OF LIFE

A man risked his life by swimming through the treacherous tides of the sea to save a youngster who was swept away by powerful waves. After the youngster recovered from the harrowing experience, he said to the man "Thank you for saving my life". The man looked into the boy's eyes and said, "That's okay young man. Just make sure your life was worth saving".

STANDARDS OF COURAGE AND BRAVERY

A life worth living should be based on the values and principles given in the Quran by Allah. Such a life is far superior to the life that ignores these values and principles:

'What do those who do evil expect that We will them and the righteous people on the same pedestal so that their lives and deaths are alike ? How erroneously they judge' (45:21).

The standards of courage and bravery should also be in line with the Divinely prescribed values that prohibit excess and intolerance, and encourage the use of wisdom and intelligence.

If you are afraid of smoking and you decide to smoke. That is not being courageous, in fact that is just acting foolish. You have to differentiate between foolish acts and bravery. Lowering your moral standard to go along with the crowd should never pass for courage or bravery.

A true believer follows the right path and avoids those who are ignorant:

'We have set you on the right path and not the whims of ignorant persons who do not know' (45:18)

Follow your conscience instead of 'following the crowd'. It will make you heroic and worthy of respect and admiration.

12 AESTHETIC SENSE AND TASTE

'Say."Who is there to forbid the beauty which Allah has provided for Hs creatures, and the good things from among the means of sustenance ?' (7:32)

Nature holds the key to our aesthetic, intellectual, cognitive and even spiritual satisfaction. E. O. Wilson

Aesthetic sense or taste is the ability to appreciate, praise and enjoy the different facets of life. The one who has this quality is called an 'aesthete'. If you have an aesthetic taste, you love beautiful things and appreciate works of art like paintings and sculptures, poetry, music, and theatre and admire all sights of nature's beauty like colourful flowers, clear blue skies and vast green fields and mountains, etc. All this is a reminder of Allah's creative powers. The Almighty has not forbidden the joys and beauty of life. In fact the Quran discourages those who insist on denying the beautiful gifts that Allah has bestowed on them.

'O children of Adam! Beautify yourselves – for every act of worship, and eat and drink, but do not be wasteful for Allah does not love the wasteful' (7:31)

AESTHETIC SENSE AND YOUTH

Young people think that it is very difficult to have an aesthetic sense and that only grown up and highly educated people have it. This is not correct. Even young people are quite capable of appreciating good music and art. In our everyday life, there are new situations at every moment of the day. The stress and pressure of modern age has made life rather mechanical. It is our aesthetic taste that focuses on the beautiful, colourful and soothing aspects of the world around us. This sense is already there in all of us and develops as we grow old. So look around at the beauty of nature and the creative genius of young and old and appreciate and enjoy the moments of joy they bring. Whenever you get a chance, make sure to visit art and historical museums, art galleries, theatres and cultural shows. They satisfy your aesthetic taste and also improve it.

'Behold We have adorned the skies nearest to the earth with beauty of stars' (37:6)

AESTHETIC TASTE

The word 'taste' does not only involve one sense, but all of your senses. A balanced structure of all the five senses plus your education, intelligence and knowledge is responsible for your aesthetic taste. That is why it is said that beauty lies in the eyes of the beholder. In a world where there are so many problems and sorrows, this sense enables one to appreciate the brighter sides of life and makes life worth living. It also reveals to us the beauty of creation in countless forms, and above all, it improves our personality. It also enables us to value and come close to those we call artists, painters, musicians, architects, dramatists, and poets, etc.

Youngsters usually show this sense in reading good books, stories, poems and plays by famous writers. This creates a love for reading which is important for acquiring knowledge and wisdom. For this purpose schools and colleges have libraries. Even community libraries are common in many cities. Taste is also a result of your education and awareness of cultural values and it can be learned and developed. It varies according to your surroundings and upbringing. It shows your manners and good habits and your appreciation of beauty. A good life is not devoid of leisure and recreation. The tensions of everyday life are released by games, contests and involvement in cultural activities. By creating games and contests man has devised a healthy way to compete and let loose his accumulating emotions and energies.

BEAUTIFUL CITIES AND MONUMENTS

On a larger scale this sense is seen in well-planned cities and monuments. For example, Mughals constructed symmetrical cities and monuments that are admired even today for

their aesthetic and artistic beauty. The Al-Hamra gardens in Spain constructed by the Muslims and modern cities like Beijing, Paris, New York, etc. reflect aesthetic qualities. Those who love travelling have first hand experience of the variety of life and creation.

The Quran also encourages us to traverse the world and experience Allah's supreme authority:

'Travel through the land, the wide span of the earth and see for yourself how Allah has brought the creation into being' (29:20).

Those who do not possess this sense, treat all objects of beauty, art and culture without truly appreciating their value. Art galleries, flower shows and literary seminars are meaningless and of no value to them. Art itself is an anti-dote for violence. An aesthetic sense which can appreciate a work of art in any form gives ecstasy, the self transcendence that could otherwise take the form of drug addiction, terrorism, suicide and intolerance. Even the picture of Paradise that Quran presents, reflects beauty in different forms. They are enough to satisfy our aesthetic taste and sense:

'Behold! Allah will admit those who attain to faith and righteous deeds, into gardens through which running waters flow, wherein they will be adorned with bracelets of gold and pearls, and where silk will be their garments' (22:23)

13 FORGIVING AND FORGETTING

And seek the forgiveness of Allah, certainly, Allah is Ever Oft-Forgiving, Most Merciful. (4:106)

"Throughout life people will make you mad, disrespect you and treat you bad. Let God deal with the things they do, cause hate in your heart will consume you too." — Will Smith

FORGIVENESS

Forgiveness is a Godly quality and brings people close to each other. As human beings, we are bound to make mistakes and do wrong things. If there is no forgiveness, there will be anger, bitterness, revengeful behaviour and constant quarrels. This is harmful for everyone and no one benefits from it.

'And whoever does evil or wrongs himself but afterwards seeks Allah's forgiveness, he will find Allah Oft-Forgiving,Most Merciful. (4:110)

'Those who endure with patience and also forgive, exhibit great courage and resolution in the conduct of affairs' (42:43)

You have to trust people, overlook slight lapses and even bigger ones, and believe that people can change. So make it a point to find out the shortcomings in your belief and thinking that block your ability to forgive and forget.

'Whether you do some good openly or in secret, or forgive an ill done to you, know that Allah is Forgiving and All-Powerful' (4:149)

Forgiveness may not solve all the problems, but it is capable of solving issues more than punishment and revenge. You cannot win all the time so learn to forgive and forget as all situations are bound to change.

If you have a forgiving nature, you will not get angry at the faults, mistakes and wrong doings of others. It also means that you have no hard feelings or grudges against people. It is the highest form of human behaviour that also includes forgetting or letting go.

'Whoever pardons his enemy and seeks reconciliation, his reward rests with Allah for He does not like those who do wrong' (42:40)

AVOID AND IGNORE REVENGE

It shows your good nature and intentions not to think about taking revenge. By such a behaviour you support, reinforce and encourage others to rebuild and re-establish a loving, caring, healthy relationship with you, and others in this world. The opposite of these qualities is to blame, condemn, punish, and be inexcusable and vindictive. When someone hurts you intentionally or otherwise, you may begin experiencing negative feelings of anger, sadness and revenge. These feelings may start at a small level, but if you do not deal with them quickly, they can grow bigger and more powerful. They may even start overcoming your positive feelings. Soon you will be full of anger and hatred. It will become difficult for you to get out of this trap. It is better to understand and recognize the value of forgiveness in order to avoid this trap.

'Allah loves those who spend their wealth in the way of Allah, whether in prosperity or in adversity; who restrain their rage and forgive their fellowmen' (3:134).

THE UNDERSTANDING TEACHER

Once there was a prince of dark complexion and he was not very particular about his appearance. Someone mistook him for a slave and employed him for digging trenches. Thus he continued working for a month. No one suspected who he was. When the truth was known, the employer shivered with fear. He fell on the prince's feet begging for mercy. The prince smiled and said, "I forgive you for you have taught me a great lesson. I, too have a slave and frequently from whom, I take difficult labour. Nevermore, when I remember the hardships of my work with you, will I trouble him."

If you suffer hardship at the hands of others, make sure you will not treat others similarly. The prince could have punished the employer, but he forgave him as he realized what hard labour meant.

BENEFITS OF FORGIVENESS

Sometimes forgiveness can be very challenging; it may be hard to forgive someone who does not admit wrong or shows remorse for his actions. You should keep in mind that the benefits of forgiveness are for you. You should also reflect on times when you have hurt others and on those who have forgiven you. This will help you to understand the position of the person who hurt you. Forgiveness may not be easy, but it can change your life. Instead of sticking to revenge, unforgiveness, bitterness and anger, you can move ahead towards mercy, peace, joy and kindness.

It is said that the weak cannot forgive. In other words forgiveness is the attribute of the strong because when you forgive you gain strength and come out a winner.You break free of the control of the actions of others. We should also remember that we too are prone to mistakes and yet Allah's mercy is always there to help us:

'Whatever misfortune befalls you, it is the result of your own doings, yet Allah forgives most of your faults' (42:30)

SAND, STONE & FRIENDSHIP

There were two friends walking through a desert. During some point of the journey they had an argument, and one friend slapped the other one on the face. The one who was slapped got hurt but without saying anything, wrote on the sand 'Today my best friend slapped me on the face.'

They kept on walking until they found an oasis, where they decided to take a bath. The one who had been slapped, got stuck in the mire and started drowning but his friend saved him. After the friend recovered from nearly drowning, he wrote on a stone, 'Today my best friend saved my life.' The best friend asked, "After I hurt you, you wrote on the sand, and now you have written on a stone, why?"

The other friend replied "When someone hurts us we should write it down on sand where winds of forgiveness can erase it away. But, when someone does something good for us, we must engrave it on a stone where no wind can erase it."

Learn to write your hurts in the sand, and carve your benefits in stone.

FORGIVE AND FORGET

Sincere forgiveness is not coloured with expectations that the other person apologize or change. In human relationships one should remember the good things. Ultimately, life is bound to feed back truth in its own way. Forgiveness may not change the past, but it will definitely enlarge the future. To forgive and not to forget is like burying the hatchet with the handle sticking out.

Forgiveness is not about forgetting. It is about letting go of another person's throat. When you forgive someone you certainly release them from judgment. It allows you to reach out and begin to build a bridge of reconciliation.

Allah has promised those who believe (in the Oneness of Allah - Islamic Monotheism) and do deeds of righteousness, that for them there is forgiveness and a great reward (i.e. Paradise). (5:9).

The Quran points out that Allah's forgiveness demands that the person committing a wrong act should realize his mistake, retract and amend his deeds and resolve never to commit that mistake again:

"Say: (My slaves) who have transgressed against themselves (by committing evil deeds and sins)! Despair not of the Mercy of Allah, verily, Allah forgives all sins. Truly, He is Oft Forgiving, Most Merciful"(39:53]

Conditions to receive forgiveness from Allah.:

1. You should give up the sin
2. You should regret having done it
3. You should resolve never to go back to it.

'Allah is indeed an absolver of sins, much-Forgiving' (4:99, 22:60, 58:2)

14 SENSE OF HYGIENE

'Most truly Allah loves those who refrain from evil and keep themselves pure and clean (2:222)

In every aspect of life, purity and holiness, cleanliness and refinement, exalt the human condition . . . Even in the physical realm, cleanliness will conduce to spirituality. Take care of your body. It's the only place you have to live. (Jim Rohn)

HYGIENE

Hygiene is the practice of keeping yourself and your surroundings clean, especially to avoid the spread of diseases. Personal hygiene means keeping yourself and your body clean. It also helps in improving your appearance.

Muslims throughout the world have extremely high standards of personal hygiene, because Islam places great emphasis on both physical and spiritual cleanliness and purification. While humankind in general usually considers cleanliness to be a pleasing attribute, Islam insists on it. Muslims are required to take care of their personal hygiene by assuring that they are well groomed, and that their bodies, clothing, and surroundings are clean. Messenger Muhammad ﷺ, may the mercy and blessings of Allah be upon him, informed his companions and thus all of us, about the importance of cleanliness when he said, "cleanliness is half of faith."

CLEANLINESS

Taking a bath regularly is a very old practice of cleanliness. This is not only hygienic but healthy as well. This has to be learned from childhood. If children are brought up in a clean and hygienic environment, it becomes a part of their daily life. Keeping their rooms and homes clean makes them aware of the benefits of cleanliness. This positive trait is then carried by them into the community and neighbourhood and the result is a healthy nation capable of speedy progress. That is why it is said that a healthy body has a healthy mind.

It is a pleasant sight to see school-going children on their way to school in clean and smartly dressed uniforms. In school they are regularly checked for clean body parts, trimmed nails and brushed teeth. Having clean teeth and healthy gums will really give you something to smile about. All this is meant to create awareness about the importance of hygienic living. Personal hygiene means to wash your hands regularly, especially before meals and after using toilets. The opposite of hygienic and clean is unhygienic, dirty and untidy. Nose-picking and biting fingernails are unhygienic habits and should be avoided. The nose and mouth should be covered when coughing or sneezing. Disposable tissue papers are a great help in cleanliness.

STANDING BEFORE ALLAH

When a person stands before Allah in the special connection that is prayer, he must ensure that his heart is free from sin, arrogance, and hypocrisy. Once this is accomplished, or at least greatly desired, he is able to cleanse himself from physical impurities. This is usually achieved by using water:

"O you who believe! When you intend to offer the prayer, wash your faces and your hands (forearms) up to the elbows, and pass your (wet) hands over your head and your feet up to the ankles. " (5:6)

DECENT LIVING

Decent living also means that houses, neighbourhoods, streets and shopping areas are not littered with dirt and trash. In all civilized countries it is a crime to throw dirt or even paper anywhere. Garbage bins, trash cans and waste-paper baskets, also called waste containers and wheelie bins, are placed in shopping areas, streets, homes, schools, parks, offices and other places in which all waste, trash and garbage is placed. This makes the environment clean and healthier and the city also looks neat and beautiful. We live in a world where serious health conditions and illnesses are on the rise. At the same time, the level of toxins (poisonous contents) in the food we eat, the air we breathe and water we drink, is also at its peak.

Islam is a holistic religion that takes into account humankind's need for a balance between physical, emotional, and spiritual health and well-being. Personal hygiene and cleanliness, both physical and spiritual, keeps both the body and mind free from disease. Cleanliness is an important part of the high standards and values that are inherent in Islam.

EATING HABITS

We are also careless about our eating habits. Food and cooking hygiene is meant to prevent food contamination and spread of diseases like cholera, jaundice, typhoid and food poisoning. Only clean, fresh and properly covered food should be consumed. Most of the food available in big cities, especially in schools, is not only prepared unhygienically but also sold in dirty and unclean conditions.

The Quran is very particular about the food that Muslims consume. The body becomes what the foods are, as the spirit becomes what the thoughts are:

'O Mankind ! Eat what is lawful and clean and good on earth and follow not Satan's footsteps' (2:168).

Allah is aware what is pure, clean and wholesome for us and that is why He has forbidden unhealthy and unhygienic food.:

'He has forbidden for you only animals that die by themselves, and blood, and the flesh of swine, and that on which any other name is invoked other than that of Allah; but if one is forced by necessity- neither coveting it nor exceeding his immediate need- no sin shall be upon him, for behold, Allah is much forgiving, a dispenser of Grace' (2:173)

Hygiene standards are different around the world, but the purpose remains the same–to promote healthy living and prevent diseases. Remember that he who has health has hope and he who has hope has everything. So make it a point to live a clean, hygienic and healthy life.

The Quran points out:

'The unclean and the pure are not equal even though the abundant volume of the unclean may be more alluring for you. So be mindful of your duty to Allah, O you who understand so that you may be successful and prosper in life' (5:100).

COMMUNITY HEALTH & CLEANLINESS

Shamina Shetu is a young Bangladeshi lady who goes door to door in her home community of Comilla. She is armed with a set of simple instructions and a watercolour painting. The painting has two sides depicting two versions of the world–one where water is dirty and sanitation practices are unhealthy; the other where water is clean and community sanitation is very good. Shamina and her friend Dolly Ahater are playing an important role in cleaning up their slum neighbourhood through United Nations Hygiene and Water Supply Project. They visit 20 homes in a day, checking whether neighbours are drinking clean water, using hygienic toilets, washing their hands before eating and after going to the toilet and disposing garbage properly.

GOOD HEALTH

Health remains the single most important factor in getting maximum enjoyment out of life. One may have the riches of the world but without good health, there will not be any joy in life.

PERSONAL HYGIENE

Apart from other things, hand washing is the basis of staying healthy. As you go through the day touching objects, dirty surfaces, food, even people and animals, germs tend to accumulate on your hands. If you do not wash your hands frequently, you can infect yourself with these germs by touching your eyes, mouth, nose and other parts of the body. At the same time you end up being responsible for the spreading of bacteria and germs by touching doorknobs, pens, doors, clothes and shaking hands with your friends. Make it a habit to wash your hands before and after eating, after blowing your nose, after coughing or sneezing, after using the toilet, after touching animals, after playing and coming back from school or college, before and after touching a sick person and whenever you see or feel that your hands are dirty.

Poor personal hygiene can result in a risk of infection and illness and also cause many social problems as a result of odours and appearance.

Oral hygiene is frequently over-looked. Simple actions such as cleaning of the teeth can significantly raise a person's morale and help in feeling better.

Poor education and lack of knowledge are some other reasons why people have different ideas on hygiene. It is important for children to understand and be taught how to maintain their own hygiene at as early an age as possible.

'Allah created me and showed me the way. He gives me food and drink. And heals me when I am sick' (26:78,79,80)

PETS

Caring for any animal requires a disciplined attitude, if you want to ensure your pet stays healthy and clean, besides showering your pet with love, you will also have to ensure that your pet–whether it is a cat, a dog, a rabbit or a bird-stays healthy and germ-free.

HEALTHY LIFE

Allah has given us five senses and a conscious mind to help us survive threats from the external world, and a sixth sense, our healing system, to help survive internal threats. We should be thankful to Allah for the abundance of gifts that He has bestowed for our sustenance. Therefore, it is our duty to discern the healthy from the unhealthy and the pure from the impure.

Looking after the different parts of your body and maintaining a good standard of personal hygiene helps in leading a healthy life.

15 GOD (ALLAH)-CONSCIOUS

'Proclaim; He is Allah, the One and Only Allah the Eternal and Absolute. He begets not, nor is He begotten. And there is none comparable to Him' (112:1,2,3,4,)

'TAQWA'

'Taqwa' is a term that occurs frequently in the Quran.It is a verbal noun which means to shield oneself and/or to protect oneself. Many Islamic scholars like Allama Asad have translated 'Taqwa' as God-consciousness.

Omar ibn Al-Khattab once asked Ubay ibn Ka'ab: How would you describe Taqwa? In reply Ubay asked, "Have you ever had to traverse a thorny path?" Omar replied in the affirmative and Ubay then continued, "How do you do so?" Omar said that he would carefully walk through after first having collected all loose and flowing clothing in his hands so nothing gets caught in the thorn. Ubay said: "This is the definition of Taqwa.". It means to implement the commandments given in the Quran and avoid those which are prohibited."Taqwa is to fear the most Exalted One, work upon His revelation, become content and ascetic and always prepare for the departure from this life. This consciousness and fear of Allah is understood as a protection and a shield against wrongdoing. The abstention of evil through this fear, consciousness and establishing a cautious awareness of Allah, ultimately develops one's love of Him.

The universal principle of submission to the Divine Will is beautifully expressed in the character of one who is a servant of Allah, known as an "Abd-Allah" which is an ideal state of Taqwa.

THE MESSENGERS OF ALLAH

We are all aware of the fact that everything in the universe has been created by Allah, Who is not only the Most Powerful, but Kind and Merciful. He is everywhere and knows everything we think and do. He sent His messengers with guidance for the people of the world.

The Quran clearly points out that all the Messengers of Allah were sent to guide us onto the right path:

'All Messengers were sent as bearers of good news and as warners to humanity, so that after their coming, people should have no excuse or argument against Allah; and indeed Allah is All-Powerful and All-Wise' (4:165).

Since man came into this world, these messengers have been coming with the Divine Message. These messages have come down to us in the form of books. Almost all religions have sacred and holy books which they follow.

'Say:'We believe in Allah, and in that which has been revealed to us from above, and that which has been revealed upon Abraham (Ibrahim) and Ishmael (Ismail) and Isaac and Jacob (Yaqoob) and their descendents, and that which was revealed to Moses (Musa) and Jesus (Isa) and that which has been revealed to all other Messengers by their Sustainer.We make no distinction between any of them, and it is to Him that we submit ourselves' (2:36) .

'We revealed upon Isaac (Ishaq) and Jacob (Yaqoob) and We guided Noah (Noh) before them, and also rightly guided David (Daud), Solomon (Suleman), Job (Ayub), Joseph (Yusuf), Moses (Musa) and Aaron (Haroon),from among his offspring, for thus we reward the doers of good .And among his other descendents Zachiarah (Zakaria), John (Yahya), Jesus (Isa) and Elijah (Alijah); each of them was a righteous person' (6:83,84).

SIMPLE RULES

Allah's guidance is very simple and straightforward. We have to respect everyone and lead a life in a positive way that includes being honest, kind, helpful, understanding, truthful, thankful, law abiding, generous and tolerant. The simple rule is that if you do good, you will be rewarded and if you do bad things, you will be punished. When you know and believe that Allah is watching all your actions, you will avoid doing wrong things. This is Allah-consciousness and is an important part of Islam and other religions. For example, a man had diabetes and the doctor advised him to avoid sweets, otherwise his condition would become serious. The doctor took great care in his treatment, but instead of improving his condition got worse. The patient had been eating sweets secretly when he thought no one was looking and in doing so he was harming his own body. Similarly a driver who does not follow traffic rules, may get involved in a serious accident. In both cases, the offenders suffer as they think no one is watching.

'Whosoever commits a wrong, commits it only against himself'(4:111)

This is not the case with Allah's system. He is always watching all our actions and hence we have to be conscious about the things we do. His laws never change and we cannot bribe our way out of punishment as we do in this world.

'To Allah belong the East and the West. Wherever you turn, there is the presence of Allah, for Allah is All-Pervading, All-Knowing' (2:115)

'You shall never find any change in the Law of Allah' (33:62)

'Nor will you find any alteration in the manner of His dealings. Each man shall be judged by his own deeds' (35:43)

The consciousness of Allah's presence contributes to the form and the content of ideals that guide the aspirations we harbour for our own lives, and it affects the way we regard and behave with respect to others. The moral values of love, joy, peace, patience, kindness, generosity, gentleness and self control has its parallels in all major faiths and religions almost universally.

THE MOST HONOURED

The most honoured in the sight of Allah is the believer with the most Taqwa, i.e. the most conscious and most aware of Him. The Glorious Quran illustrates this in Surah Al Hujurat :

"O mankind! We created you from a single (pair) of a male and a female, and made you into nations and tribes, that ye may know each other (not that ye may despise (each other). Verily the most honoured of you in the sight of Allah is (he who is) the most righteous of you (Muttaqi). And Allah has full knowledge and is well acquainted (with all things)."(49:13)

The ideal Islamic society is a Taqwa conscious society, conferring its highest respect on those considered to be high in Allah-consciousness.

INTERVIEW WITH RICK WARREN

You will enjoy the new insights that Rick Warren has, with his wife now having cancer and him having 'wealth' from the book sales. This is an absolutely incredible short interview with Rick Warren.

In the interview by Paul Bradshaw with Rick Warren, Rick said: People ask me, What is the purpose of life?

And I respond: In a nutshell, life is preparation for eternity. We were not made to last forever, and God wants us to be with Him in Heaven.

One day my heart is going to stop, and that will be the end of my body-- but not the end of me.

I may live 60 to 100 years on earth, but I am going to spend trillions of years in eternity. This is the warm-up act - the dress rehearsal. God wants us to practice on earth what we will do forever in eternity..

We were made by God and for God, and until you figure that out, life isn't going to make sense.

Life is a series of problems: Either you are in one now, you're just coming out of one, or you're getting ready to go into another one.

The reason for this is that God is more interested in your character than your comfort; God is more interested in making your life holy than He is in making your life happy.

We can be reasonably happy here on earth, but that's not the goal of life. The goal is to grow in character.

This past year has been the greatest year of my life but also the toughest, with my wife, Kay, getting cancer.

I used to think that life was hills and valleys - you go through a dark time, then you go to the mountaintop, back and forth. I don't believe that anymore.

Rather than life being hills and valleys, I believe that it's kind of like two rails on a railroad track, and at all times you have something good and something bad in your life.

No matter how good things are in your life, there is always something bad that needs to be worked on.

And no matter how bad things are in your life, there is always something good you can thank God for.

You can focus on your purposes, or you can focus on your problems:

If you focus on your problems, you're going into self-centredness, which is my problem, my issues, my pain. But one of the easiest ways to get rid of pain is to get your focus off yourself and onto God and others.

We discovered quickly that in spite of the prayers of hundreds of thousands of people, God was not going to heal Kay or make it easy for her- It has been very difficult for her, and yet God has strengthened her character, given her a ministry of helping other people, given her a testimony, drawn her closer to Him and to people.

You have to learn to deal with both the good and the bad of life.

Actually, sometimes learning to deal with the good is harder. For instance, this past year, all of a sudden, when the book sold 15 million copies, it made me instantly very wealthy.

It also brought a lot of notoriety that I had never had to deal with before. I don't think God gives you money or notoriety for your own ego or for you to live a life of ease.

So I began to ask God what He wanted me to do with this money, notoriety and influence. First, in spite of all the money coming in, we never changed our lifestyle one bit.. We made no major purchases.

Second, about midway through last year, I stopped taking a salary.

Third, we set up foundations to fund an initiative we call The Peace Plan to assist the poor, care for the sick, and educate the next generation.

Fourth, I added up all that my work had paid me in the 24 years since I started work, and I gave it all back. It was liberating to be able to serve God for free.

We need to ask ourselves: Am I going to live for possessions? Popularity?

Am I going to be driven by pressures? Guilt? Bitterness? Materialism? Or am I going to be driven by God's purposes ?

When I get up in the morning, I sit on the side of my bed and say, God, if I don't get anything else done today, I want to know You more and love You better. God didn't put me on earth just to fulfil a list. He's more interested in what I am than what I do! That's why we're called human beings, not human doings.

Happy moments, PRAISE GOD!! Difficult moments, SEEK GOD!!

Quiet moments, WORSHIP GOD!! Painful moments, TRUST GOD!!

Every moment, THANK GOD!!!

The word Taqwa (Allah-consciousness) has been mentioned 151 times in the Noble Quran. Allah has taken us through the various aspects of His Guidance and Blessings in the Glorious Quran. The Quranic descriptions of Taqwa are so precise and distinct that it is an indication of the importance of the involvement of this concept in the life of Muslims. These numerous verses elaborate the different dynamics and dimensions of inner meanings of Taqwa that enable Muslims to be an ideal and a living example as a vicegerent of Allah.

The following verses summarize the guiding principle for those who are Allah-conscious:

' This is the Book; in it is guidance sure, without doubt, to those who fear (or are conscious) of Allah (Taqwa). Who believe in the Unseen, are steadfast in prayer, and spend out of what We have provided for them; And who believe in the Revelation sent to you, and sent before your time, and (in their hearts) have the assurance of the Hereafter.. They are on (true) guidance, from their Sustainer, and it is these who will prosper' (2:2,3,4,5),.

OUR DUTIES AND RESPONSIBILITIES

On a smaller scale when we abide by the laws of the society and country we live in, the result is peace, progress and happiness. This is also a kind of consciousness about our responsibilities as citizens. On a larger scale when we are Allah-conscious and obey his laws, there will be peace, happiness and prosperity on a much larger scale. Someone who acts according to the guidance of Allah is also religious. Thus Allah-consciousness does not only mean saving yourself from the forces of bad deeds, but also improving your life and character and purity of conduct following the laws of Allah. It also includes performing your duties that your religion has asked you for, in the system of Allah, we are judged according to what our deeds are and not our position, wealth, power or family.

'And those who perform good deeds, be they men or women, and are also believers will surely enter paradise and not the least injustice will be done to them' (4:124).

OBEDIENCE BY CONVICTION

Allah-consciousness is also obedience of the Divine laws, not by compulsion but obedience from the core of the heart. It is the accomplishment of these laws in such a way that one does not ever touch a thing unlawful. This value determines how our lives, individually and collectively, will unfold, from day to day. It teaches that the purpose of life is better served when you strive for the good of all humanity. The Quran outlines this principle and says:

'Only that survives which is for the benefit of all mankind' (13:17). This is one law of Allah that we can all submit to.

WORDS WITHOUT DEEDS

Tukla, king of Persia, once visited a devotee and said, "My life has been fruitless. I have spent all my life in fighting wars, palace intrigues and getting rid of my enemies. I have very few days of life left and I want to devote this time to praying."

The devoted old man listened to the king and was angered at his attitude. "Enough!" he cried, "Religion consists in the service of humanity; it finds no place in prayer rugs or tattered dresses. Be a king in your pure morals and help your people in their need. Action, not words, is demanded by God, for words without deed have no substance."

Tukla listened to what the devoted wise man said and returned to his palace with a new vigour and objective to serve his people. If you want to please God, serve His creation.

TOLERANCE

In today's multicultural world, the reliable path is that of coexistence, creative cooperation and loving tolerance. All religions should be respected and whenever there is a religious discussion, it should be logical, rational and tolerant. You cannot force others to change by laws, material might and scientific advances. The clear message for our guidance is that we should be mindful of God and see every day what we have invested for ourselves for tomorrow.

EAGLES IN A STORM

Do you know that an eagle knows when a storm is approaching long before the storm breaks. The eagle will fly to some high spot and wait for the winds to come. When the storm hits, it sets its wings so that the wind will pick it up and lift it above the storm. While the storm rages below, the eagle is soaring above it.

The eagle does not escape the storm. It simply uses the storm to lift it higher. It rises on the winds that bring the storm.

So, when the storm of life comes upon you, you can rise above by setting your mind and belief towards God. The storms do not have to overcome you. God enables us to ride the winds of the storm that bring sickness, tragedy, loss, failure and disappointment in our lives. We have the capability to rise above this storm.

Learn from the eagle. It is not the burden of life that weighs us down, it is how we handle it.

OUR ACCOUNTABILITY

Allah-consciousness makes us aware that we are accountable for whatever we do.Among the earlier people of the Book there were those people who falsely believed that Allah had exempted them from all moral responsibility towards followers of a different religion. The Quran explicitly rejects this belief and says:

'Among the people of the Book are some who, if you entrust them with a treasure, would faithfully return it to you intact. But among them are also people who will not return even a single, tiny gold coin unless you keep pestering them for the same. They justify this immoral behaviour towards the illiterate pagans. They obviously lie knowingly about Allah' (3:75).

The Quran also extols those who are Allah-conscious and put the interest others above their own even though their resources are limited (59:9).

We should also not forget how we have lived our lives.Human beings have the tendency of forgetting their bad habits and deeds; but Allah's system is fully aware of all that we do and on the Day of Judgment we shall have to account for all our deeds:

'On the day Allah will raise them all together and inform them of what they did. Allah has maintained a full account of their deeds, although they have forgotten. Know that Allah is Witness over everything' (58:6).

FREEDOM OF CHOICE

Allah does not force people to accept His guidance. He has endowed man with the power of understanding, judgment and free-choice. If man makes use of this ability, he can understand the Divine Revelation and can also profit by the guidance offered therein. He has to bear the consequences of his choice, whether they are pleasant or unpleasant. Thus the best path for Muslims is the straight path (Sirat-e-Mustaqeem). To take that path we have to be Allah-conscious every moment of our lives.

The following values are repeatedly stressed in the Quran:

- To be truthful (9:120)
- To shun lies (22:31)
- Not to commit adultery (17:33)
- Not to commit theft (5:39)
- Not to commit breach of trust (8:28)
- Not to commit murder (6:152)
- Not to be dishonest (8:59)

- To keep away from all that is vain (23:3)
- To fulfil our covenants (5:2)
- To strive for increased knowledge (20:115)
- To do justice (4:59)
- To be benevolent (16:91)
- To be steadfast (3:200)
- To be thankful (39:67)
- To ask others to do good (16:126)
- Not to preach that we do not practice (61:3)
- Not to be haughty and vainglorious (4:37)
- To be neither miserly nor spendthrift (17:30)
- To be humble (39:67)
- To speak kindly (2:84)
- To suppress our rage and forgive people (3:135)
- To repay evil with good (13:23)
- To be united (3:103)
- To avoid backbiting (103:2)
- To spend wealth for the cause of Allah (2:262)
- To spend wealth for the poor and needy (2:272)
- Not to ridicule one another or call names (49:12)
- To fear none but Allah (2:41)
- Top eat pure and clean things (2:169)
- To remain clean (2:223 and 74:6)

16 GRATEFUL AND THANKFUL

'Remember, your Sustainer proclaimed: ',"I will give more if you are grateful; but if you are thanklesss, then surely My punishment is very great (14:7)

Silent gratitude is not of much use to anyone. If thankfulness is not expressed, it is plain, old-fashioned ingratitude. (M. Eckhart)

THANKFUL

Thankful means to be appreciative for the acts of kindness and benefits received. Gratefulness is an expression of gratitude and thankfulness. Its opposite is ungratefulness and thanklessness which lead to rudeness and meanness.

Both the negative and positive aspects of these values are inherent in the nature of man. The Quran points out that majority of the human race is inclined towards ingratitude and thanklessness:

'The truth is that your Sustainer is full of Grace to mankind, and still most of them are ungrateful' (27:73)

'It is Allah Who has undowed you with the faculties of hearing, sight, feelings and intelligence, but seldom you are grateful and thankful' (23:78).

We should be thankful to Allah for the abundance of blessings that He has bestowed upon us. To those skeptics who refuse to do so, the Quran's reminder is enough:

'Say, 'Tell me if your water were to disappear in the earth, who then will bring you clean flowing water ? (67:31) 'Who is he that will provide for you, if He would withhold His provision' (67:22).

BLESSINGS IN LIFE

We should also be thankful for the blessings we have in our lives. We have families we love and enjoy, school and college life and jobs that help us provide the necessities of life, good health, friends to laugh and enjoy with, and freedom to move about. How many times do we stop, think and express our thanks for these blessings? Probably not as often as we should.

'It is We who have established you on the earth entrusting you with power and provided you with means of livelihood, but little are the thanks you give, and seldom you are grateful' (7:10).

PARENTS, RELATIVES AND FRIENDS

When you give gifts to your friends on birthdays, it makes them very happy and they spontaneously show their gratitude by saying 'Thank you, I just love it!'. This appreciation makes you happy and you like doing such acts more often. Gratitude is an attitude of thankfulness and joy. So tell your near and dear ones, especially your parents, what they mean to you. Embrace them and be thankful for their presence in your life.

'And We have enjoined on man to be good to his parents, with difficulty and pain his mother bore him..And in two and a half years was his weaning. Therefore, show gratitude to Me and to your parents. And ultimately it is to Me your final goal ! (31:14)

GIVING GIFTS

Being grateful or thankful should also be reflected on how we react and behave. Gratefulness and thankfulness should not only be confined to words; rather they should be translated into our positive attitude and an even better form of returning the favours. Giving and accepting gifts is encouraged in Islam. The Messenger of Allah ﷺ said,'Give presents and gifts to another as this act removes hatred and creates bonds of love and kinship. Whoever is given a present and has means, let him give in return and whoever has no means, let him thank (him).

'If you are grateful, then remember Allah is independent of you, and He does not favour ingratitude on the part of His creatures. If you are grateful He will be pleased with you' (39:7)

FATHER

All I knew was when I needed
Shoes and clothes I got 'em on the spot;
Every thing for which I pleaded
Somehow, father always got
Wondered season after seasons
Why he never took a rest.
And that I might be the reason
Then I never ever guessed.

Used to wonder just why father,
Never had much time for play,
Used to wonder why he never
Loafed around the road and shirked
Can't recall a time whenever
Father played while others worked

If he'd lived to have his way
He'd have sent me off to college
Had the bills been glad to pay
That, I knew, was his ambition:
Now and then he used to say
He'd done his earthly mission
On my graduation day.

Saw his cheeks were getting paler
Didn't understand just why;
Saw his body growing frailer
Then at last! I saw him die.
Rest had come! His tasks were ended
Calm was written on his brow;
Father's life was big and splendid,
And I understand it now.

APPRECIATING OTHERS

Instead of insulting or complaining about the people around you, try praising and appreciating them for all they have done for you. This act of gratitude will gain their respect and trust and they are more likely to continually assist and help you to achieve better. A simple thank you or gift card will show how much you appreciate them.

COUNTLESS GIFTS OF ALLAH

Every night you go to bed, think about the countless gifts Allah has given you. The absence of light makes us aware of what a gift electricity is, a sprained ankle lets us appreciate walking as a gift. Loneliness makes us aware of the value of friends. When you see the efforts of your family members and friends make you happy and satisfied; you are also motivated to serve them.

In many countries of the world 'Thanksgiving Day' is celebrated to express thanks to Allah for the many blessings given by nature and natural resources.

'If one is grateful, he is grateful for himself, and if one is thankless, surely Allah is unconcerned and magnanimous' (27:40)

Life is a curious mixture of highs and lows, pleasures and pains. When you go through times of life that are harsh and hard, express gratitude for other blessings that you continue to enjoy. Being thankful does not cost anything, but it can bring many rewards. This fact becomes clear as we grow older. Be thankful for what you have, and you will end up having more. Develop an attitude of gratitude, which, if not expressed, is like wrapping a present and not giving it.

'Allah rewards those who are thankful and are grateful' (3:144)

While referring to Messenger Abraham (Ibrahim), the Quran says that he was always grateful to Allah for His favours and consequently Allah rewarded him with His guidance (16:161, 14:37)

GRATEFULNESS

'Allah produced you from your mothers' wombs knowing nothing, but He gave you ears and eyes so that you may be grateful (16:78)

When you are grateful for the good you already have, you attract more good into your life. On the other hand, when you are ungrateful, you tend to shut yourself from the good you might otherwise experience. Gratitude is the key to the fullness of life. It turns denial into acceptance, a meal into a feast, a house into a home, a stranger into a friend. It makes sense of our past and creates a vision for tomorrow—something that is very important for the youth. You do not realize how much Allah has given you as gifts and benefits unless you are suddenly deprived of them. Be grateful to Allah and those who make your life liveable and see how your life changes for the better.

Young people with so much of energy and ideas need to move on in life, but they should not leave behind a trail of ingratitude and thanklessness. Design the life of your dreams, but do not forget to thank those who made it possible. Those who receive a good turn in life should never forget it and he who does one such good should not remember it:

'Remember Me and I shall remember you and give thanks to Me and do not be ungrateful of the bounties that I have bestowed upon you ' (2:152).

A day that begins with gratitude is a day you will be able to fill with positive progress. Begin with a positive thought and link yourself with the abundance that is all around you.

'It is He Who made the night and day an alternation for him who cares to reflect and be grateful' (25:62, 28:73)

There is always something for which you can be sincerely thankful. Be grateful, and you will create even more things in your life for which you can be grateful. The blessings you enjoy are blessings precisely because you see them as such.

'Allah presents the example of a town which enjoyed peace and security, the provisions coming

from everywhere in abundance, but it denied the favours of Allah, so Allah acquainted it with ultimate hunger and fear (as punishment) for what they had done' (16:112)

COUNT YOUR BLESSINGS

A poor and destitute man became rich. He was so successful that whatever business he ventured into yielded great profits. He started believing that all this was due to his intelligence and the right use of mind. He would give examples of this by relating to the time when he bought cotton and the World War began which made the cotton very costly giving him immense profits. Similarly he bought a useless piece of agricultural land and transformed it into a gold mine. He never thanked anyone for his richness and good fortune.

After a few days, things started changing and everything he tried did not work out. He suffered heavy losses and also lost his house. An epidemic in the village killed all his goats, buffaloes and sheep. Whatever cash he had was stolen by thieves. He became very poor and started blaming fate, luck and fortune for his poverty.

A wise neighbour pointed out to him that when he was a successful businessman and landlord, he attributed it to his intelligence and now when bad times had fallen on him, he was blaming his luck and fortune.

The story relates the fact that you should have a realistic mind capable of accepting the facts of life. Blaming others for your misfortune is unfair and unjust. You should always be thankful for the things you have.

WARNING TO THE UNGRATEFUL

There is clear warning from Allah to those who are ungrateful and betray the trust reposed in them:

'Certainly Allah will protect those who believe and have faith in Him; but He does not like such traitors who betray His trust and exhibit ingratitude' (22:38)

17 HAPPINESS AND CONTENTMENT

'O our Sustainer give us good in this world and good in the hereafter (2:201)

Happiness does not come from doing easy work, but from the afterglow of satisfaction that comes after the achievement of a difficult task that demanded our best. (Rubin)

HAPPINESS

Happiness is a condition of good spirit and well-being. It is found in satisfaction and delight. It is found in every kind of enjoyment. Contentment is satisfaction that brings joy and happiness. Its opposite is discontentment, dissatisfaction and unhappiness. If you are satisfied with things around you, then you are contented and at ease.

If you look at people around, you will realize that they all want to be happy. Thus, all your acts are in search of happiness. The secret of happiness is knowing that there are some things that we can control and some things we cannot.

The concept of happiness in Islam is expressed in the Qurân in different ways. First, we find the Qurân discussing the "good life". Allah says: "Whosoever does right, whether male or female, and is a believer, We shall make them live a good life, and We shall pay them a recompense in proportion to the best of what they used to do." [16:97]

This "good life" is happiness itself. It is realized through faith and good deeds. This does not mean that we will not face difficulties in our good life. Our worldly lives, even when they are bolstered by faith and good works, are never free from distress and vexations. This world is the abode of toil, as Allah says: "Certainly We have created man to be in toil." [90:4]

Allah also says: " We test you by evil and by good by way of trial, and to Us is your return." [21': 35]

WISHES, DESIRES AND TRUE HAPPINESS

Real happiness does not come from the fulfilment of every wish. You can chase an endless chain of wishes and desires, and still manage to be unhappy. A thief may steal because he desires to make quick money to spend. He is actually looking for happiness, but in a criminal and wrong way. Happiness should not be sought in a selfish way or by hurting others through stealing or taking away by force.

'Those who seek gain through evil means and are surrounded by their sinfulness; they are destined for the fire of punishment, wherein they shall abide' (2:82).

True happiness can only be achieved if the Divine Guidance is followed in letter and spirit. When one door of happiness closes, another opens, but often we keep looking at the closed door and do not see the one which has been opened for us. Sometimes the return of good deeds is not immediate. This should not discourage those who follow the right path because the Quran says:

'And be patient in adversity for Allah will not leave to waste the reward of the righteous' (11:115).

Happiness does not demand too much of the things you like. Abundance sometimes leads to problems of greed and impairs the satisfying nature of true happiness.

THE BOY & THE NUTS

A little boy once found a jar of nuts on the table. "I would like some of these nuts," he thought. "I'm sure Mother would give them to me if she were here. I'll take a big handful." So he reached into the jar and grabbed as many as he could hold. But when he tried to pull his hand out, he found the neck of the jar was too small. His hand was stuck, but he did not want to drop any of the nuts. He tried again and again, but he couldn't get the whole handful out. At last he began to cry.

Just than his mother come into the room, "What's the matter?" she asked,

"I can't take this handful of nuts out of the jar." Sobbed the boy. "Well, don't be greedy, "his mother replied. "Just take two or three, and you will have no trouble getting your hand out."

"How easy that was, "said the boy as he left the table. "I might have thought of that myself:-

So, how and when does happiness come? It comes quite simply when you allow it. Your life may have difficulties and challenges, still you can be happy and satisfied whether you are close to achieving your goals or far away or even beyond them. Real happiness is never too far away. Your friends and relatives may tell you that you need this or that to be happy. In truth, you need nothing else than to let it be. Instead of waiting and searching for a reason

to be happy, create for yourself a way to be happy. Something as simple as a smile can get you started on the road to happiness and that is something you can do right now.

GOALS AND OBJECTIVES

Goals, aims and targets are no doubt important in life. Without them you are shooting blanks in the air. Set well-defined goals and targets. As you do, you will discover a road to contented life. It does not matter if those goals are small. They are still goals and when you achieve them, you can move on to the next one with a sense of confidence and satisfaction. For example, you can set yourself the target of revising all that is taught in school. The next goal should be to master the topics that you have finished studying. Gradually you will prepare exercises and topics well before your teachers take them up in the class.

PEACE OF MIND

There are some principles that can be adopted for peace of mind :

1. Do not interfere in the business of others unless asked. We have a tendency to interfere because we are convinced that our way is the best way. For peace of mind, mind your own business.

2. Forgive and forget .It is the most powerful aid to your peace of mind. When we are insulted or ignored, we nurture grievances resulting in our own loss of sleep, development of stomach ulcers and other harmful diseases of the body and mind. This is something we have to get rid of. Forgive, forget and move on. What others think of us is none of our business.

3. Do not crave for recognition. The world is full of selfish people. They seldom praise anybody without selfish motives. They may praise you for your power and pelf and will forget your achievements when you are powerless Recognition by such people is not worthwhile and of no consequence. Do whatever you are doing sincerely, honestly, efficiently and responsibly.

4. Do not be jealous of others' success. Shape your own life and destiny. Jealousy will not get you anywhere. It will only take away your peace of mind.

5. Change yourself in accordance with the environment because it is difficult to change the entire prevailing environment and conditions totally and single handedly. Instead, a positive change in your approach will make the environment congenial and harmonious. This does not mean that you should compromise on principles and values.

6. Some inconveniences and irritations are beyond our control. We must learn to put up with them and endure them cheerfully. Ultimately your will power, inner strength and patience will make things bearable and peaceful.
7. Do not bite off more than you can chew. Only opt for those responsibilities that you can fulfil efficiently. Be aware of your limitations and leave your ego aside.
8. Give some time to yourself everyday and enjoy the company of those who love you.
9. Do not leave your mind vacant for the devil to step in. Actively follow a hobby that may not necessarily earn you more money. It will give you a sense of fulfilment.
10. Do not procrastinate and never regret. Days, months and years are wasted in this futile exercise. All future happenings can never be anticipated. Value your time and do things that need to be done. It does not matter if you fail the first time. Sitting back and worrying will get you nowhere. Lamenting and brooding over the past is a negative and worthless activity. Why cry over spilt milk when there is so much in the future to be done.
11. Do not isolate yourself because of any shortcoming. Seek opportunities to invest in constructive activities. We are not perfect. Do our best and let nature take its course.
12. Work at something you enjoy.
13. Give others more than they expect.
14. Become the most positive and enthusiastic person you know.
15. Be generous and have a graceful heart.
16. Commit yourself to constant improvement and to quality.
17. Understand that happiness is not based on possessions, power or prestige; but on relationship with people you love and respect.
18. Be bold, loyal , courageous, compassionate and decisive.
19. Take care of those you love and who love and respect you.

HAPPINESS BOOSTERS

It feels good to be happy. Laughing is fun. If you do not feel happy today, that does not mean there is something wrong with you. If you want to be happy there are a lot of things you can do to improve your mood. It is a well-known fact that those who frequently do kind things for both friends and strangers are the happiest. Each day do at least one act to make others happy. This can be a kind word, helping your friends, giving your seat in a bus to someone needy or helping someone cross the road. The possibilities are many. Do not be jealous of people who are happy. Instead, be happy at their happiness. Smile more often, it does not cost anything. Happiness boosters also include your future dreams, setting and pursuing goals, making friends family members a big part of your life, and playing games regularly.

INNER PEACE

If your mind is free from worry and concern, it is at peace. To achieve inner peace, happiness, satisfaction and joy, all you have do is to remove the layers of thought that have kept these hidden. You have to stop worrying about whether or not you are ever going to find these in the future, and realize that they are always here and now.

Happiness can be achieved by giving. You too can be happy by providing shade like the tree to those around you. This will bring happiness all around you.

The reward from Allah for those good deeds that one does for others is manifold:

'Those who spend their wealth in the way of Allah may be compared to a grain of corn which produces seven ears and each ear contains a hundred grains. Similarly, Allah multiplies manifold the charity for whomsoever He pleases for Allah is All- Embracing and All-Wise' (2:261).

'Who is there among you who will lend to Allah a beautiful loan, which He will return after multiplying it manifold ? Only Allah can increase and decrease your wealth and it is to Him that you have to return ultimately' (2:245).

OUR ATTITUDE

In the above verse it seems strange that Allah is asking for a loan when everything that we possess has been given by Him. This obviously relates to the way we help our brethren who are in need. Allah does not need anything. We are the ones who need His help all the time to remain happy and contended.

'O Mankind ! It is you who stand in need of Allah (Allah does not stand in need of you) for He is Self-Sufficient and above all need' (35:15).

If you can smile and be happy while watching a movie in which the people and incidents are not real, why can't you create similar situations in real life to have real happiness? Negative feelings like anger, fear, depression, sorrow and sadness can be driven out of life and replaced by hope and satisfaction. It is your attitude that makes you feel happy

THE CLUB 99

Some time ago, there lived a King. This King should have been contented with his life, given all the riches and luxuries he had. However, this was not the case! The King always found himself wondering why he just never seemed content with his life. Sure, he had the attention of everyone wherever he went, attended fancy dinners and parties, but somehow, he still felt something was lacking and he couldn't put his finger on it. One day, the King had woken up earlier than usual to stroll around his palace. He entered his huge living room and came to a stop when he heard someone happily singing away... following this singing... he saw that one of the servants was singing and had a very contented look on his face. This fascinated the King and he summoned this man to his chambers. The man entered the King's chambers as ordered. The King asked, "Why are you so happy?" To this the man replied: "Your Majesty, I am nothing but a servant, but I make enough of a living to keep my wife and children happy. We don't need too much, a roof over our heads and warm food to fill our tummy. My wife and children are my inspiration; they are content with whatever we have. I am happy because my family is happy."Hearing this, the King dismissed the servant and summoned his personal assistant to his chambers. The King related his personal anguish about his feelings and then related the story of the servant to his personal assistant, hoping that somehow, he will be able to come up with some reasoning that here was a King who could have anything he wished for at a snap of his fingers and yet was not contented, whereas, his servant, having so little was extremely contented. The personal assistant listened attentively and came to a conclusion. He said, "Your Majesty, I believe that the servant has not been made part of The Club 99."

"The Club 99? And what exactly is that?" the King inquired. To which then he replied, "Your Majesty, to truly know what The Club 99 is, you will have to do the following... place 99 Gold Coins in a bag and leave it at this servant's doorstep, you will then understand what The Club 99 is." That very same evening, the King arranged for 99 Gold Coins to be placed in a bag at the servant's doorstep. Although he was slightly hesitant and he thought he should have put 100 Gold Coins into the bag, but since his assistant had advised him to put only 99 Gold Coins that is what he did. The servant was just stepping out of his house when he saw a bag at his doorstep. Wondering about its contents, he took it into his house and opened the bag. When he opened the bag, he let out a great big shout of joy. "Gold Coins!! So many gold coins!!" He could hardly believe it. He called his wife to show her the coins. He then took the bag to a table and emptied it out and began to count the coins. Doing so, he realized that there were only 99 coins and he thought it was an odd number so he counted again, and again and again only to come to the same conclusion... 99 Gold Coins. He began to wonder, what could have happened to that last 1 coin? For no one would leave

99 Gold Coins. He began to search his entire house, looked around his backyard for hours, not wanting to lose out on that one Gold Coin. Finally, exhausted, he decided that he was going to have to work harder than ever to make up for that 1 Gold coin to make his entire collection an even 100 Gold Coins. He got up the next morning, in an extremely horrible mood, shouting at the children and his wife for his delay, not realizing that he had spent most of the night conjuring ways of working hard so that he had enough money to buy himself that gold coin. He went to work as usual—but not in his usual best mood, singing happily—as he grumpily did his daily errands.

Seeing the man's attitude change so drastically, the King was puzzled. He promptly summoned his assistant to his chambers. The King related his thoughts about the servant and once again, his assistant listened. The King could not believe that the servant who until yesterday had been singing away and was happy and content with his life had taken a sudden change of attitude, even though he should have been happier after receiving the 99 Gold Coins. To this the assistant replied "Ah! But your Majesty, the servant has now officially joined The Club 99." He explained: "The 99 Club is just a name given to those people who have everything but yet are never contented, therefore they are always working hard and striving for that extra one to round it out to 100." We have so much to be thankful for and we can live with very little in our lives, but the minute we are given something bigger and better, we want even more. We are not the same happy contented person we used to be, we want more and more and by wanting more and more we don't realize the price we pay for it. We lose our sleep, our happiness; we hurt the people around us just as a price to pay for our growing needs and desires. That is what joining The Club 99 is all about." Hearing this, the King decided that from that day onwards, he was going to start appreciating all the little things in life.

The Moral: Striving for more is always good, but let's not strive so hard and for so much that we lose all those near and dear to our hearts, we shouldn't compromise our happiness for greed. Let us be happy and content with whatever we have. This does not mean that we should give up our efforts for improvement in life. There are limits to our needs and wants.

or sad. It is also true that you come across all kinds of situations every day and some of them lead to gloom and dissatisfaction. You should not let such situations control your behaviour and attitude. Always look at the positive side of things. Think of solutions and not problems. Allah has placed ease and happiness in certainty of faith and contentment. He has placed worry and misery in discontent and doubt.

The contentment is to be reconciled to Allah's decree and with the portion that Allah has allotted to us. This is the way to attain peace of mind and happiness. By contrast, being discontented and resentful about one's circumstances, unsatisfied with one's portion that Allah has allotted, and having doubts about one's faith, this is the way to anxiety, misery, and distress.'Allah will reward those who are thankful and grateful' (3:143)

DAILY ROUTINE AND HAPPINESS

Each day read a few pages from a good book. Whenever you catch yourself having negative thoughts, start thinking about the good things in life. Always look at the things you have done and not at what you have not.

Every day do something good for yourself like buying a good book or magazine, eating something you like, watching your favourite programme on television or just having a stroll on the beach.

Do not place demands on your happiness like 'I'll be happy when I get the 1st position in class' or 'I'll be happy when I get a new disc player or a pair of jeans'. Why put off your happiness for some other day?

You also come across those who are never satisfied. Their faith hinges on the amount of happiness they have. This means that the faith of such persons in Allah is not based on sincerity and total submission. The Quran condemns such people and says:

' And among mankind is he who worships Allah as it were, upon the very edge (i.e. in doubt); if good befalls him, he is content therewith; but if a trial befalls him, he turns back on his face (i.e. reverts back to disbelief after embracing Islam). He loses both this world and the Hereafter. That is the evident loss' (22:11).

In a corruption ridden society the stock argument is,'While in Rome do as the Romans do'. This is a selfish and illogical attitude. It comes from the feeling of insecurity and helplessness in a society that is devoid of positive values. In such a society the evil forces dominate. The Quran relates to such situations and says:

Satan threatens you with poverty and enjoins upon you what is foul, whereas Allah promises you forgiveness and bounty' (2:269) 'And if you fear poverty, Allah will enrich you out of His bounty (9:28).

PRINCIPLES OF HAPPINESS

Life , as we know it, is surely complex; but there are certain principles that make it easy to understand and live a happy life. At times it all also depends upon the situation that one has to face. It is also a fact that life cannot always be lived according to set rules, but there are some generally accepted rules that can be followed. While reflecting on our daily lives, these tested principles will definitely help:

1. If you do not go after what you want, you will never have it.
2. If you do not ask, the answer will always be 'no'.
3. If you do not step forward, you will always be in the same place.
4. Remind yourself that it is alright not to be perfect.
5. Apologizing does not always mean you are wrong. It just means you value your relationship more than your ego.
6. Go as far as you can. When you get there you will be able to see further and farther.
7. Do not find faults. Find remedies.

Why not make life a little happier than it is. Rest assured that it can be done. The real fun in life is enjoying the present moment. You will be amazed by the joys of daily life.

The real fun in life is enjoying the present moment. You will be amazed by the joys of daily life.

'We settled you on the earth, and provided means of livelihood for you in it; but little are the thanks you give' (7:10)

18 HONESTY

'There are some amomg the people of the book who return a whole treasure entrusted to them; yet there are some who do not give back a Dinar you demand and insist because they say, "It is not a sin for us to usurp the rights of the Arabs", yet they lie against Allah and they know not'(3:75)

Honesty is the first chapter of the book of Wisdom. (Thomas Jefferson)

You are honest if you communicate and act truthfully keeping in mind the truth as a value. Your belief in honesty and truthfulness is shown in your overall behaviour. Only good intentions are not enough, your actions and attitude should also reflect that you are honest.

JAPANESE RETURN $78 MILLION

In March, 2011 a devastating earthquake struck, Japanese police say they've received $78 million in missing cash and valuables that citizens have found in the rubble and promptly turned in.

Thousands of missing wallets contained $48 million in cash, and nearly 6,000 more safes turned in by volunteers contained an extra $30 million, the Japanese Police reported that most of the found money has been returned to its owners, after police used identifying documents in the safes to track them down.

"The fact that these safes were washed away meant the homes were washed away too," Koetsu Saiki of the Miyagi Prefectural police force told ABC News. "We had to first determine if the owners were alive, then find where they had evacuated to." Some wallets and safes were most likely pocketed, but the scale of honesty in the wake of disaster is still striking.

The fact that a hefty 2.3 billion yen in cash has been returned to its owners shows the high level of ethical awareness in the Japanese people.

Children learn traits such as hard work, honesty, self-control in parts by imitating parents, other family members and friends. Parents and elders should exercise caution in their behaviour as they are being constantly observed by children.

THE HONEST FATHER

There was a man in England who needed a baby sitter and he contacted a woman who gave him two rates. One, if he reported it on his income tax return and a lower rate if he did not. This meant that if he did not report it, neither would the child minder on her income tax return. This is being dishonest and harmful for the people at large. The father chose to report it on his income tax return. Sometimes it is easy and tempting to be dishonest so we have to be on guard to be honest.

HONEST PERSON

An honest person has no confusions in his mind. He is honest to himself and to the purpose of a task assigned to him. This earns him the trust and respect of others and his position is also elevated in his own eyes. All great men and women in history had these qualities which made them role models. Honesty means never to misuse that which is given in trust.

Everything that is given as a trust has to be returned to its rightful owner. The command of the Quran in this respect is:

'Allah commands you to deliver all that you have been entrusted with unto those who are entitled thereto, and whenever you judge between people, do with justice. Verily, most excellent is what Allah exhorts you to do; He is All-Hearing and All-Seeing' (4:58).

"Woe unto those who give short measure, those who, when they are to receive their due from people, demand that it be given in full but when they have to measure or weigh whatever they owe to others, give less than what is due. Do they not know that they are bound to be raised from the dead (and called to account) on an awesome Day, the Day when all men shall stand before the Sustainer of all the worlds?" (83:1-6)

An honest person does not lie. He realizes that if he does not tell the truth honestly, others may be misled into believing facts that do not exist. The ultimate result would be disastrous for everyone. Knowingly one should not hide the truth (2:43), nor should they confuse truth with falsehood (2:42), and hide evidence (2:283)

Those who believe in the eternal message and guidance of the Quran have been asked not to violate knowingly the trust that has been reposed in them (8:27) Those who are honest and abide by their trust have been called the inheritors of paradise (23:8-11).

Honesty is not possessed by someone who tells the truth occasionally or whenever it is to his advantage. The honest person is truthful as a matter of course and habit. His actions spring from a firm and unchangeable character.

DECEPTIVE HONESTY

There are many ways of misleading people than by lying alone. There is the story of a traitor named James who was rowing on a river to escape from the state authorities who were looking for him. His persecutors came rowing from the opposite direction. As James had disguised himself, he was not recognized by the soldiers. "Where is the traitor James?" asked the soldiers.

"Not far away," replied James and rowed past his persecutors unsuspected. Although

James had told the truth, yet it was a deceptive truth.

The story stresses the point that intent and motive are very important in being honest.

Honesty is a virtuous value of respect in itself. An honest person keeps his word and people depend on him. Thus, relationships are built on trust. At times, it takes courage to be honest. When you have to accept your fault. It also takes courage to apologize for doing something wrong. You can surely think of a time when you were loved for your honesty. It is a very nice feeling and only an honest person knows its true worth.

HONESTY PAYS

Seemi was a young girl who worked in a house along with her mother. She was fascinated by the beautiful toys that the owner's daughter had and wanted similar ones for herself. Her mother pointed out that only rich people could afford such toys. Seemi looked at the toys lovingly one more time and went upstairs to clean the bedroom. "I wish I could be rich and have as many toys and clothes as I want," she thought to herself. Lost in her thoughts, she accidentally knocked a glass vase down. It broke into pieces, but the surprising thing was that the gold jewellery and diamonds contained in it were splattered all over the place.

Nobody was watching her. She could have all her toys and clothes and other valuable things she longed for, but her mind kept telling her to return everything. She decided to give everything to her mother to return to her employer. The mother was needy too and thought of keeping the valuables. She was sure that her employer would not miss the valuables as she was very rich. Seemi reminded her mother that it was dishonesty to keep something that did not belong to them. "We cannot buy a better life with money that does not belong to us," Seemi told her mother, so she returned the jewellery and diamonds to the lady of the house who was overjoyed as the jewellery was a gift from her mother.

Seemi and her mother's honesty was rewarded by a big raise in their wages, and the expenses of Seemi's education were also ensured by the employer.

The reward for honesty is always long lasting and satisfying.

You must accept the truth from whatever source it comes.

CLEAR CONSCIENCE AND HONESTY

Honesty is to speak with a clear conscience because it leads to a life of integrity. It is as distinct as a flawless diamond that can never remain hidden. The worth is visible in one's actions. An honest person never gives evidence that is not true even if it goes against himself or his parents or those close to him (4:135)

The world is full of people who are not honest. They are even dishonest to themselves. Such people have their own standards of honesty and consider all their actions as honest. The fact of the matter is that their inner self or conscience is aware of their dishonest deeds, but they themselves deliberately try to hide these deeds without realizing that Allah is aware of what they do and what their intentions are.

The Quran tells us that:

'Do not plead for those who are dishonest to themselves, for Allah does not love the treacherous and sinful people. They may hide their evil deeds from the people, but they cannot conceal them from Allah' (4:107,108).

When honesty is lost, then wait for the Hour (the Day of Judgment). These are the words of Messenger Muhammad ﷺ. They paint a picture of the time leading up to the Day of Judgement. We expect people to be honest in their dealings with us yet we ourselves are not honest in our dealings.

Without thinking, we teach our children that dishonesty is acceptable. When we expect our children to tell the caller on the telephone we are not home, this is a lesson in deceit. When we refuse invitations and pretend we are busy, this is lying. We admonish our children for lying, yet the reality is we have been their teachers. Whether we tell lies, or whether we allow our children to live in a world surrounded by deceit, the ultimate result is not encouraging as honesty begins to disappear from the hearts of the next generation.

Honesty incorporates the concepts of truthfulness and reliability and it resides in all human thought, words, actions and relationships. It denotes integrity and moral soundness. Islam commands truthfulness and forbids lying. Allah commands that a Muslim be honest.

"O you who believe! Fear Allah, and be with those who are true (in words and deeds)." (9:119)

HONEST BUSINESS AND MONETARY DEALINGS

Islam has stressed and asserted the importance of honesty in monetary dealings and highlighted its vital role in social stability and peacefulness.

The Holy Quran and Prophet Mohammad ﷺ have made it clear to us that the true Muslim is he who is honest and upright in his business and monetary dealing with others, even if they weren't Muslims. Also the true Muslim should keep his word and fulfil his promises, shun fraud and avoid deceit and perfidy, encroach not upon the rights of others, nor take part in wrongful litigation. A good Muslim does not give false testimony, and abstains from making unlawful money as from usury and graft. According to Islam whoever is not free from these vices is not a true believer but a renegade and a worthless transgressor. The Qur'an is rich with verses that confirms all this. Allah says in the Quran:

"Oh ye who believe! Eat not up each other's property by unfair and dishonest means." (4:29)

Allah forbids all unclean and corrupt means of making money, such as, dishonest trading, gambling, and bribery. And the Holy Quran has explained and described such practices in many of its verses. In this verse, for instance, Allah warns those traders who cheat in weighing, he says:

"Woe to those that deal in fraud, - those who, when they have to receive by measure from men, exact full measure, but when they have to give by measure or weight to men, give less than due. Do they not think that they will be called to account- on a Mighty Day when (all) mankind will stand before the Sustainer of the Worlds." (133: 1-6)

Another example is given in the coming verse, where Allah urges Muslims to be very particular about their trusts and about other people's rights.

"Allah does command you to render back your trust, to those to whom they are due." Quran(4:58)

At two places in the Quran a chief distinguishing feature of Muslims is said to be that they are:

"Those who faithfully observe their trusts and their covenants." Quran (24:8)

THE DISHONEST MAYOR

One day a neighbour knocked on the town mayor's door and asked, "Will you lend me your donkey for a while?"

"My good friend, "the mayor replied, "you know there is nothing in the world I wouldn't do for you. I'd love to lend you my donkey. But I am afraid he is away today".

Just then the donkey gave a bray loud enough to wake the dead.

"Well, this is my lucky day, "said the neighbour. "It seems that your donkey is here after all."

"How dare you!" protested the mayor, puffing up with shocked indignation. "Are you going to believe my donkey and doubt me, a man of honour status and distinction?"

So build a reputation as someone who is honest and always tells the truth. It will serve you well. Facts should not be hidden. Hiding them gives a wrong impression and the listener is misled into believing something that is not the truth. The final outcome is always bad.

THE TRUTHFUL SON

Shahid stared at the broken window. His football had crashed through the window. He realized that he should not have kicked the football towards the window. He knew that his Mom and Dad would be angry when they got home; and he would probably have to pay from his pocket money. He thought of keeping quiet. Then may be it won't be like lying. Then he remembered what his grandmother had told him. She had said, "Telling the truth is very important. Hiding a truth is another way of lying." So, when his parents returned, he told them the truth. His father said that accidents do happen and did not punish him. He told Shahid, "It is easy to lie without opening your mouth."

Value Achievement

Children should know that you appreciate their honesty.

- If they have done something wrong, parents should listen rather than being annoyed. If parents beat up children when they make mistakes, they will not depend on their parents if there is a bigger problem later on. Listening allows trust to bloom.
- Children should always be told the truth. They should know what is happening when there are changes about which they need to know.
- Honesty should be inculcated as a virtue and value for which the parents and teachers would have to be honest themselves.

EPITOME OF QURANIC VALUES

A true believer, one who is truly submitted to God, has many characteristics by which he can be identified. The most obvious of these noble characteristics are honesty of character and truthfulness of speech. Being truthful and adhering to truthfulness, means you will be among the people of the truth and be saved from calamity and that it will make a way out for you from your problems The role model for all humanity in general and Muslims in particular, is Muhammad ﷺ. He was the epitome of all Quranic values. Even before his Prophethood, he had earned the titles of Al Amin (the trustworthy one) and As Sadiq (the truthful). He influenced and inspired all those around him by leading an exemplary life in which honesty and trust were of utmost importance. All those who are interested in leading a life of good moral and ethical moral values should follow in his footsteps.

'Good fortune awaits in this world all who persevere in doing good, but their ultimate state shall be far better; for how excellent indeed will be the state of the Allah-conscious. Gardens of perpetual bliss will they enter through which running waters flow having therein all that they may desire' (16:30,31)

19 HOPEFUL AND OPTIMISTIC

'Those of you who have hope in Allah and the Last Day have certainly a good example in them; but whoever turns away, then surely Allah is above concern, worthy of praise' (60:6)

Few things in the world are more powerful than a positive push, A smile, a word of optimism and hope. A 'you can do it' when things are tough. (R. Devos)

HOPE

You are hopeful if you aspire for success and desire something to happen. You show this quality in your attitude and behaviour. Hope is a belief in a positive outcome of events and circumstances in life even when conditions are not encouraging. When nothing in life seems to be going right, it can be really tough to find a way out. However, it is during these difficult times that your ability to see the good in even the worst situations is tested. A hopeful approach is good not only for your mind, but your body as well. That is why it does not pay to be hopeless or gloomy. Keeping busy and making optimism and hope a way of life can restore your faith in yourself. A famous scientist once said that young people have more optimism and imagination and less bias.

OPTIMISM

Optimism is the feeling of being hopeful about the future and looking at the bright and happy side of everything. It is also your belief that there is good in everything including ugly things. Optimism does not have a scientific explanation; it is simply expecting that good things rather than bad things will happen. Pessimism , on the other hand, refers to its opposite. 'Good expectations are a feature of belief, and nothing can be achieved without belief and hope' said Muhammad ﷺ. Islam calls for optimism and trust. Optimism can do miracles and cannot only save us from troubles, but also give us the chance to learn from them. Qualities; like perseverance, patience and not giving up are all related to this noble attitude of optimism. Optimism is not ignoring problems but simply the best way to deal with it and learning from it for the future. Both the optimist and the pessimist encounter the same problem, but it is the mind set and perception which takes over and decides the solution. One must also not ignore the fact that there are troubles spread all over in our lives, but those who are true believers and have faith in Allah face these troubles with confidence and hope and ultimately resolve them.

'With every hardship comes ease' (94:5).

Remember, 'Whosoever puts his trust in Allah, then He will suffice him' (65:3)

In Islam hope and optimism are encouraged as they re-affirm man's unflinching beliefs in the Most Compassionate, Most Merciful and Most-Glorious Allah. Those whose faith is weak lose hope in the Almighty and ultimately tread the wrong path. The story of Prophet Joseph (Yusuf) and his cruel treatment by his brothers has been related in the Quran. They had left him behind after throwing him in a well thinking that he had died. Prophet Jacob (Yaqoob) never lost hope of seeing his son Joseph (Yusuf) alive. In the Quran we see him addressing his sons:

'(Turning towards his sons he said) O my sons !Go back and try to obtain some tidings of Joseph (Yusuf) and his brother; and do not lose hope of Allah's life-giving mercy; verily none but people who deny the truth can ever lose hope of Allah's life-giving mercy' (12:87)

PESSIMISM

The opposite of optimism is pessimism, doubt, despair and gloom. A common complaint heard from those who are pessimistic and have no hope, is that life has not been fair to them. When something bad befalls them, they feel hopeless and sad. It is quite possible that they may be right that the world is not fair, but it has to be remembered that the world was not created for their benefit alone or that all others are there only to serve them or to make them happy. The Quran refers to those who lose hope when some Divine favours are withdrawn. Such people not only lose hope, but they also indulge in blasphemy. When these favours are restored they become arrogant:

'And thus it is: If We let man taste some of Our Grace and then take it away from him – behold, he abandons all hope, forgetting all gratitude for Our past favours. And thus it is, if We let him taste ease and plenty after hardship has visited him, he is sure to say:'All my problems have left me' And he indulges in over- and becomes arrogant' (11:9,10)

QURANIC VALUES AND LIFE

The fundamental trend of Islamic thought is that the earthly life is worthwhile and that it has meaning and purpose. It encourages man to strive and then be optimistic of attaining dignity, high vocation and freedom. The Divinely ordained Quranic values insist that thought and conduct should be determined with reference not only to celestial bliss and beatitude, but also to the present life and social well being.

'Those who, when calamity befalls them say."Surely we are for Allah and to Him shall we return", on such men are the blessing of Allah and His Mercy for such people are on the right path' (2:156, 157)

Living a good life means recognizing that the world will continue as it does. Making ourselves miserable and sad will get us nowhere except leading us to resentment, anger and jealousy. Remember the old saying that 'he who loses wealth loses much, he who loses a friend loses more; but he who loses hope loses all.' If you are an optimist, you will search out people, circumstances and situations that will be of assistance to you in your life. You should not feel that somebody's success is your failure. Another person's success has to be admired and not resented. True optimism is a source of strength. It makes you confident enough to say, "I can do something to change this situation for the better".

Once you have done all the thinking and planning and praying; get on with it. You have the example of Henry Ford who created a market for cars when everybody else said horses would never go out of fashion.

POWERFUL TOOL

Hope is a powerful tool in giving boost to our physical capabilities. It is also an important ingredient in the healing process. Doctors in most hospitals will tell you that when two patients have similar diseases, the hopeful patient recovers faster as compared to one without hope. Hope can overcome any stumbling block into a stepping stone. It is a real force you can count on.

Never give up on your efforts because one of them failed. It is like giving up your

THE HOPEFUL DONKEY

One day a farmer's donkey fell down into a well. The animal cried piteously for hours as the farmer tried to figure out what to do. Finally he decided the animal was old, and the well needed to be covered up anyway; it just wasn't worth it to retrieve the donkey. He invited all his neighbours to come over and help him. They each grabbed a shovel and began to shovel dirt into the well. At first, the donkey realized what was happening and cried horribly. Then, to everyone's amazement, he quieted down. A few shovel loads later, the farmer looked down the well, and was astonished at what he saw. As every shovel of dirt hit his back, the donkey did something amazing. He would shake it off and take a step up. As the farmer's neighbours continued to shovel dirt on top of the animal, he would shake it off and take a step up. Pretty soon, everyone was amazed, as the donkey stepped up over the edge of the well and trotted off.

The Moral: Life is going to shovel dirt on you, all kinds of dirt. The trick to getting out of the well is to shake it off and take a step up. Each of our troubles is a stepping stone. We can get out of the deepest wells just by not stopping, never giving up! Shake it off and take a step up! Never lose hope when the winds blow.

dreams because one did not come true.

'Man never gets weary of praying for things in life; but when evil befalls him, he loses all hope and becomes disheartened' (41:49)

It does not matter how long you have been stuck in your difficulties. Hope is the light that you switch on in a room that has been dark for a long time. You turn on the light and everything becomes bright and the darkness disappears. Once you use your spirit of hope and optimism, the light has been turned on.

Be kind to yourself if you have done something wrong like not achieving good results in the examination. Tell yourself, "I made a mistake, but that does not make me a bad person. I can always improve." Only you can change your way of thinking and there is nothing better than being hopeful and optimistic. If you want to enjoy the glory of sunrise, you must live through the darkness of the night.

MISPLACED OPTIMISM AND HOPE

While the entire city was in the grip of the examination fever, there was one student who seemed totally unmoved and unaffected. His name was Khalid and while most students were at home studying, he wasted his time on the playground with other boys who were not bothered about passing their examinations. At home, Khalid spent his time watching television and playing computer games. Khalid's parents were uneducated and did not realize that their son was wasting his time when he should be studying. His friends were also surprised by his behaviour and could not understand his careless attitude. His friend Nomi asked him," Khalid everyone is working so hard for the examinations and you are not even worried. Why?" Khalid smiled and said," I'm not worried because I have made all arrangements. I met an astrologer who has assured me that I would be placed amongst the top three positions in the upcoming exams. He also gave me an amulet which would bring me good luck. For this I had to pay him a hundred rupees out of my pocket money." Nomi was shocked at the absurd optimism of his friend.

On the day of the results, Khalid was disappointed as his name was not even amongst those who had passed the examinations.

Khalid's hope and optimism were based on hollow foundations. Everyone has to strive first and then hope for help from Allah because His system is based on justice:

'If anyone acts righteously, he does so for his own benefit, and if anyone commits evil deeds, he will himself bear the burden of its consequences' (45:15).

POSITIVE ATTITUDE

Attitude is a choice. You could be faced with a thousand problems, many or most over which you have absolutely no control. However, there is always one thing you are in complete and absolute control of and that is your own attitude.

When you surrender control of your attitude to what appears to be a hopeless situation, you will react to that situation negatively. On the other hand, if you were to remain objective, you would respond to the situation appropriately, thereby creating a winning situation.

'If We let man taste some of Our Grace and then take it away from him – behold he abandons all hope forgetting all gratitude for Our past favours. And thus it is : If We let him taste ease and plenty after hardship has visited him, he is sure to say, "Gone is all affliction from me" – for he is given to vain exaltation and glories only in himself' (11:9,10)

Remember that the Sun that melts ice also hardens the clay.

CREATIVE CYCLE

Attitude is the composite of your thoughts, feelings and actions. Your conscious mind controls feeling and ultimately dictates whether your feelings will be positive or negative by your choice of thoughts; then your body displays those choices through action and behaviour.

Attitude is actually a creative cycle that begins with your choice of thoughts. You do choose your thoughts and that choice is where your attitude originates. As you internalize ideas or become emotionally involved with your thoughts, you create the second stage in forming an attitude. Your conscious awareness of this vibration is referred to as "feeling". Your feelings are then expressed in actions or behaviours that produce the various results in your life.

Positive results are always the effect of a positive attitude. Attitude and results are inseparable. They follow one another like night follows day; one is the cause, the other, the result. It is a "cause and effect" relationship, it is called The Law of Cause and Effect. Simply stated, if you think in negative terms, you will get negative results; if you think in positive terms you will achieve positive results.

There is the parable of a baby mosquito that had come back from a flight. His mother asked, "How do you feel?" The baby mosquito replied, "It was wonderful, everyone was clapping for me." That is a positive attitude.

When we wake up in the morning, we have two simple choices: go back to sleep or wake up and strive to realize our dreams. The results you achieve in life are nothing more than an expression of your thoughts, feelings, and actions. Take a close look at your life and evaluate the results you are achieving in various areas. See if you are able to relate your attitude to your results.

WINNING AND LOSING

Winning and losing are opposite sides of the same coin—and that coin is attitude. There are many things wrong in this world; unfortunately that is all some people are able to see. Those who view the world in this light are often unhappy and somewhat cynical. It would appear as if they were born with a streak of bad luck and it has followed them around their whole life. These individuals are quick to blame circumstances or other people for their problems, rather than accepting responsibility for their life and their attitude. Do not blame others for your failures. If others are to blame then you have given them control of your life and actions.

Conversely, there are others who are forever winning and living the good life. They are the real movers and shakers who make things happen. They seem to go from one major accomplishment to another. They are in control of their life; they know where they are going and know they will get there.

You can experience that kind of life as well, you only need to decide. Making that simple decision is the first step to a better life. The moral and ethical values described in this book will help you in building and strengthening your positive attitude.

'O men pay heed to Allah's messages for it is He who has endowed you with hearing and sight, and minds to think, yet how seldom you are grateful' (23:78)

YOUR CHOICE

By simply becoming aware that you can choose your thoughts each and every day, you will change your entire outlook. You have the power to choose an abundant life no matter what your circumstances are. That active choice will allow other positive people and opportunities to be attracted into your life. A positive attitude does much more than turn on the lights in the world; what it does is that it connects us magically to all sorts of serendipitous opportunities that were somehow absent before. Don't wait to experience all the wonderful things the universe has in store for you. Start today by working on your attitude, and welcome the abundant life that you were meant to lead. The Islamic way of life encourages positive attitude as it is a reflection of hope and optimism. We are all prone to weaknesses and knowingly and unknowingly tread the wrong path. The important thing is realization. One who realizes his mistakes and decides to make amends has nothing to fear from Allah as He is Merciful and has promised to be merciful to such people:

'Those who have transgressed against their souls ! Despair not of the Mercy of Allah' (39:53)

Verses like these discourage despair and hopelessness; falsify the misconception that by laying great emphasis on punishment and retribution, religion tends to create an atmosphere of fear instead of hope for Allah's munificence and kindness.

Hope and contentment flow from faith in Allah and equally firm belief in future reward for the right things done in this world. The hope in Allah in moments of acute crisis, which only a believer can entertain, makes all the difference. The believer is likely to face anxiety, uneasiness and apprehension in circumstances of impending hazard as any other human being; but as the latter becomes demoralized, and, resultantly, loses determination; the former faces the situation with patience and steadfastness in the hope that Allah's help will ultimately strengthen his position .

'Allah is with those who are patient and who persevere' (2:249)

'Allah is with those who are determined' (8:66)

'Expectations are a feature of belief, and nothing can be achieved without belief and hope', said Messenger Muhammad ﷺ. He also said," Be optimistic and good shall be found." Islamic teachings stress optimism and trust.

Optimism can do miracles and can save us from many troubles. Qualities like perseverance, patience and not giving up are all related with this noble quality. All great leaders owe their success to optimism. As Dale Carnegie once wrote,'Two people looked out of a window from prison; one saw mud and the other stars'.

At times we have felt disappointed about things not going our way. We must have wondered and said something along the lines of," Why did this happen to me ? I worked so hard , I had prayed so much !...why me ?" As believers, we must trust that whatever happens to us comes from the Decree of Allah patient in adversity and having repelled evil with good comes from the Decree of Allah:

'These will be given twofold reward for having been patient in adversity and having repelled evil with good' (28:54)

20 HUMBLE AND MODEST

'I shall turn them away from My signs who behave unjustly with pride and arrogance in the land so that even though they see all the signs, they will not believe in them' (7"146)

Pride kills thanksgiving, but a humble mind is the soil out of which modesty naturally grows. A proud man is seldom a grateful man, for he never thinks he gets as much as he deserves. (H.W. Beecher)

HUMBLE

Humble means to be modest, decent and respectful. A humble person is not proud, or arrogant in his attitude, but is unassuming and mild in his behaviour and manners. Those who are humble, appreciate and recognize the virtues, talents and abilities others possess.

'O you who have attained to faith !No man shall ridicule others, as the latter may be better than themselves; and no woman shall ridicule other women, it may be that those women they ridicule are better than themselves. And neither shall you defame one another, nor insult one another by nick names. It is an evil habit to call a person by an undesirable name, when such a person has attained faith, and those who do not repent are indeed wrongdoers' (49:11).

MODEST

Modesty nourishes virtue. Even dangerous and difficult tasks can be undertaken when attended to directly and simply. One's inner nature is reflected in outward modesty. One must firm, but within the limits of modesty. Care should be taken not to use false modesty as an excuse. Humbleness and modesty is expressed in self-disciplined. We should act only to assert what is right in the light of the Quranic standards of right and wrong.

TWO CATEGORIES OF HUMBLENESS

Humbleness can be divided into two basic categories. The first kind is humbleness before Allah, which implies faith in Him and total submission to His will and commands without feeling haughty.

The second category is humbleness with people, usually defined in dictionaries as the quality of being humble or modest and lacking pride, boastfulness or excessive self-assertiveness. These definitions also reflect Islam's view of humbleness.

According to the Quran, the only basis for varying degrees of honour among people is their piety:

(O humankind! Lo! We have created you male and female, and we have made you nations and

tribes that you may know one another. Lo! the noblest of you, in the sight of Allah, is the best in conduct) (49:13)

Since piety and Allah consciousness are internal and only Allah is able to know whether a person is pious or just pretending, it follows that believers should observe modesty and humbleness as one of their basic traits.

Modesty is mentioned in the Qur'an as one of the characteristics of the people who are loved most by Allah and who themselves love Allah:

'(O you who believe! If any from among you turn back from his Faith, soon will Allah produce a people whom He will love as they will love Him,— lowly with the believers, mighty against the rejecters) (Al-Ma'idah 5:54)

A verse in the Quran instructs Messenger Muhammad ﷺ to show humbleness towards the believers, where it makes a similitude between the modesty of Prophet Muhammad and his message towards all believers, and a bird that lowers its wings in kindness and humbleness to protect its offspring:

'And lower your wing (in kindness) unto those believers who follow you' (26:215)

The Quran also extends its instruction to all Muslims and advises them not to over-praise themselves, where it says what means:

'Therefore justify not yourselves: He knows best who it is that guards against evil' (53:32)

This attitude of over-praising one's self is the cause of many of the malaise in today's civilization. People make a lot of effort to appear different from what they really are, while they could spend much less effort just being themselves. In order to solve this problem, people must try to be humble and have a sense of simplicity in their attitudes and their relationships with others. Whenever he came to a place where the people were sitting, he didn't rush himself to put himself in the forefront, he just sat wherever there was an available place.

A BALANCED PERSONALITY

A modest person is moderate and simple in speech, behaviour and dressing. The opposite of humble is grand, showy, luxurious, assertive, mean and boastful. The opposite of modest is unashamed, proud, immodest, coarse, bold and arrogant. Such a person has excessive pride and has superiority complex.

Those who always boast of their power and riches are not humble but proud and insolent and nobody respects or likes them.

We have the example of Muhammad SAW entering Makkah after its conquest — a victorious event for Islam — he lowered his forehead on his camel, prostrating himself in humility and thanking God that He had finally given victory to the believers.

DISTINGUISHING FACTORS

What distinguishes a human from the devil is arrogance and the absence of humbleness and modesty. It shows one's insolence and pride. If a mistake is committed by a decent and humble human being, he repents and begs Allah's forgiveness and mercy with the promise to refrain from doing it in future. On the contrary, those who are prone to evil deeds show arrogance, self-conceit and proudly persist with disobedience. In this context the Quran repeatedly discusses the story of Adam, the Angels and Satan.

Humility can guide us to Paradise, just as its opposite, arrogance (kibr), can only lead us into Hell. It was Satan's arrogance that caused his expulsion from Paradise; when he refused to humbly obey Allah's command and prostrate before Adam, the father of mankind, he condemned himself and his followers to Hell. Satan's lack of submission, or humility, resulted in one of the most pious of God's creatures falling into the abyss

'Indeed, We created you and gave you form and shape and commanded the Angels to bow before Adam in homage, and they all bowed except 'Iblees' (Satan) who refused to be of those who prostrated. Allah said, '(O Satan) What prevented you from bowing before Adam whom I specifically commanded you to bow ? He replied 'I am better than him. You created me from fire and created Adam from clay'. Thereupon Allah said, 'Descend from this place. You cannot be arrogant and insolent here. Get down because you are one of those who are damned and degraded' (7:11,12,13).

'Except Satan, who refused to be among the prostrators. God said, 'O Satan! What is your reason for not being among the prostrators? 'Satan said: 'I am not the one to prostrate myself to a human being, whom You created from sounding clay..." (15:30-35)

The moral here is that to err is human and Allah is kind to those who repent and ask for His forgiveness. Arrogance and false pride are evil traits that lead to destruction; that is why humbleness and modesty are regarded as positive values in Islam.

HUMBLENESS AND HUMILITY

In our daily lives very little is said about humbleness and humility. Many confuse it with humiliation. Some consider humbleness and modesty a weakness. This is enough to mislead young people away from this great quality or people who possess it. Those who are modest and humble are aware of their limitations and are unassuming, respectful, reasonable and open-minded.

This beautiful poem expresses these qualities aptly.

Down in a green and shady bed
A modest rose grew
Its stem was bent, it hung its head,
As if to hide from view.
And yet it was a lovely flower,
Its colour bright and fair;
It might have graced a rosy flower
Instead of hiding there.
Yet there it was content to bloom;
In modest colours arrayed
And there diffused a sweet perfume
Within the silent shade.
Then let me to the valley go
This pretty flower to see
That I may also learn to grow
In sweet humility.

THE RIGHT APPROACH

Life seems to have a way of happening to us. However, we know that life does not just happen, but rather it is a series of choices that we make daily. A modest and humble approach is always helpful in making the right choices. It brings us closer to people around us. If you lack this quality then you are also ungrateful which is a weakness. Such a person can never really be happy.

Your modesty and humbleness is also seen when you greet people. In Japan, a bow is the traditional way of greeting. Humility is shown when everyone tries to bow lower than the other person. Another way of showing your humbleness and respect is when you stand up in the classroom as soon as your teacher enters or leaves.

If you are humble then you will be popular and worthy of praise. You would be able to work in all situations without fear of failure. You would also be able to diffuse someone's anger with just a few words.

Muhammad ﷺ was a perfect model of modesty and humbleness. He never spoke loudly or in an unseemly manner. In the market, he always passed by the people quietly with a smile. Whenever he heard anything undesirable in an assembly, he did not say anything out of respect for the people, but the colour of his face showed his feelings and the Companions became cautious.

He lived a simple and modest life, both in Makkah as a trader and the Messenger of Allah, and in Madinah as the head of the state and Messenger of Allah. The change in his social status from that of a trader in Makkah to the head of the state in Madinah did not bring any change in his modest living. He did not behave towards others as if he was better than them, nor did he spurn manual work. He used to tidy up his house, tether the camels, feed the animals, take food with his servants, and help them in kneading dough and bringing provisions from the market. He also used to visit the sick, attend funerals, ride a donkey and accept a slave's invitation for a meal and slowed down his pace for the sake of the weak and also prayed for them.

No doubt, at times, it is hard to be humble and modest, especially when you live in a society that is so competitive. But this does not mean that these values should be ignored. It is all up to you; understand your limitations, recognize your faults, avoid comparing, and do not be afraid to make mistakes, seek guidance and help others.

Some pretend to be humble in order to seek praise. Others soon recognize this and such persons are always at a loss. Make it a point that you will not change after achieving a high position or wealth or fame. This is the key to all other forms of goodness.

'If We let him taste Our favours after adversity, he says. "Misfortune has left me", and begins to brag and exalt' (11:10)

'Allah does not love any of those who out of self-conceit and ego, act in a boastful manner' (57:23)

HUMBLE AND MODEST

A young lady was waiting for her flight in the boarding room of a big airport. As she had to wait for quite some time, she bought a book to spend her time. She also bought a packet of biscuit. She sat down in the waiting lounge of the airport. Beside her armchair, where the packet of biscuit lay, a man also sat down in the next seat. He opened his magazine and started reading it. When the lady took out the first biscuit, the man also took one. She felt irritated , but said nothing.

She just thought, "What a nerve ! If I was in the mood I would punch him for this daring act ."

For each biscuit that she took, the man took one too. This was infuriating for the lady. But she did not want to cause a scene. When only one biscuit remained, she thought, "What this ill-mannered would do now ?".To her surprise the man divided the biscuit into half, giving her one half.

"Ah ! That was too much." She was angry now. In a huff she took her book, her things and stormed to the boarding room.

When she sat down in her seat, she opened her purse to take her eye-glasses and to her surprise she found her packet of biscuit in there untouched and unopened.

She felt so ashamed. She realized that she had been wrong all along. She had forgotten that her biscuits were in the purse. The man had shared his biscuits with her without feeling angry or bitter; while she had been angry thinking that the man was eating her biscuits and that too without her permission.. But now there was no chance for her to go back and explain her attitude to the man and apologize for her behavior.

This incident shows that there are things that cannot be recovered once they are gone or the time has passed. To be specific there are four things that can never be recovered:

1. The stone, after it has been thrown
2. The word, after it has been said.
3. The time, after it is gone.
4. The wrong, after it has been done.

'Know that the true servants of Allah are those who never bear witness to what is false, and who, whenever they pass by people engaged in frivolity, pass on with dignity' (25:72)

So, there is a way that we call assess our true worth on the scale of humbleness and humility. Here are accepted standards of being humble and modest :

a) Conduct an honest evaluation of yourself.

Honesty with yourself is the best policy. If you know you are weak in a certain area, your enemies will not be able to have that power over you. Accept yourself as you are.

b) Understand your limitations.

No matter how talented you are, there is almost always somebody who can do something better than you. Look to those who are better and consider the potential for improvement. Even if you are the best in the world at doing one thing, there are always other things that you cannot do, and may never be able to do. Add to this the fact that there are a great many things that no person can do, and you can get some idea of your limitations. Recognizing your limitations does not mean abandoning your dreams, and it does not mean giving up on learning new things or improving your existing abilities.

c) **Recognize your own faults.**

We judge others because it's a lot easier than looking at ourselves. Unfortunately, it's also completely unproductive and, in many cases, harmful. Judging others causes strife in relationships, and it prevents new relationships from forming. Perhaps even worse, it prevents us from trying to improve ourselves. We make judgments about others all the time, usually without even realizing it. As a practical exercise, try to catch yourself in the act of judging another person or group of people, and whenever you do, judge yourself instead. Consider how you can improve yourself.

d) **Think about yourself under different circumstances.**

Much of what we give ourselves credit for is actually a product of luck. Suppose you graduate from a reputed university with honours.. You definitely deserve a lot of credit for the many hours of studying and for your perseverance. Consider though, that there is someone just as intelligent and hardworking as you who had less supportive parents, grew up in a different place, or just had the bad luck to make one wrong choice in life and that person might be shivering in the entryway of a darkened storefront or clinging to life in a hospital bed. Or they may already have died, far from a hospital, from the very same illness for which your doctor treated you with a one-week course of antibiotics.

Always remember that with a little bad luck yesterday, your whole life could be different today and, furthermore, that today could be the day your luck changes.

e) **Appreciate the talents and qualities of others.**

Challenge yourself to look at others and appreciate the things they can do and, more generally, to appreciate people for who they are. Understand that everybody is different and relish the chance you have to experience different people. You will still have your personal tastes, your likes and dislikes, but train yourself to separate your opinions from your fears and you will appreciate others more—you will be humbler.

f) **Stop comparing.**

It's nearly impossible to be humble when we're striving to be the "best" or trying to be better than others. Instead, try describing things more objectively. Rather than saying that so and so is the best guitarist ever, say what exactly it is that you appreciate about his skills, or simply say that you like his playing style. Let go of meaningless, simplistic comparisons, and you'll be able to enjoy doing things without worrying about whether you're better or worse at them than others.

g) **Don't be afraid to make mistakes.**

Part of being humble is understanding that you will make mistakes. Understand this, and understand that everyone else makes mistakes, and you will have a heavy burden lifted off of you. Any one person can know only the smallest bits and pieces of the tremendous knowledge that has accumulated over the past. What's more, each person experiences only a sliver of the present, and knows little to nothing of the future.

h) **Don't be afraid to defer to others' judgment.**

It's easy to acknowledge that you make mistakes and that you're not always right. Somewhat more difficult however, is the ability to acknowledge that in many cases other people—even people who disagree with you—may be right.

i) **Seek guidance.**

Contemplate moral texts and seek proper guidance. It requires that you let go of your preconceived notions and judgments and understand that you don't know as much as you think you do.

j) **Remain teachable.**

Find people you aspire to be like in certain areas, and ask them to mentor you. Under mentorship; good boundary setting, confidentiality and discernment is required. As soon as you cross the line of being 'unteachable', bring yourself back down to earth again.

k) **Help others.**

A big part of being humble is respecting others, and part of respecting others is helping them. Treat other people as equal and help them because it is the right thing to do. It's been said that when you can help others who cannot possibly help you in return, you have learned humility.

l) **Practice gentleness.**

Gentleness of spirit is the sure path to humility.. Absorb the venom from other's attacks and react with gentleness and respect.

m) **Appreciate your talents**

Being humble doesn't mean you can't feel good about yourself. Self-esteem is not the same as pride. Both come from a recognition of your own talents and qualities, but pride, the kind of pride that leans toward arrogance, is rooted in insecurity about yourself.

Think about the abilities you have, and be thankful for them.

- Keep in mind that being humble has many benefits. Humility can help you be more content with your life, and it can also help you endure bad times and improve your relationships with others. It's also essential to being an effective learner. If you think you know it all, you won't be open-minded enough to seek out new knowledge. Humility is also, somewhat counter-intuitively, an excellent tool for self-development in general. After all, if you feel superior, you have no incentive to improve. Most of all, being humble allows you to be honest with yourself.
- Seek trusted and wise counsel and obtain accountability partners if you find this to be a weakness in your life. Pride comes before the fall and prevention is definitely better than cure.
- It is fine to talk about yourself a little, but make a conscious effort to ask people about themselves too.
- Pretending to be humble isn't the same as being humble, and often people who pretend to be humble do it in order to seek out praise. Other people will recognize this, and even if you fool some, you won't derive the same benefits as you would through actually developing humility.
- Similarly, don't confuse being humble with being sycophantic (being overly- praiseful of someone for your own profit). This is a common misconception, but the two attitudes are completely different.
- While a bit of humility is a good thing, don't take it too far, thus becoming a doormat. Remember, everything in moderation.

The Islamic standard of humbleness and modesty negated egoistic pride by which a man wrongly considers himself superior to others. Such an attitude is totally unacceptable in the context Quranic values:

'Nor walk on earth stiffly with insolence and self-conceit ,for you can neither split the earth asunder, nor can you stretch to the heights of mountains' (17:37).

Such people should realize that the Divine Guidance tells them so distinctly:

'The true devotees of the Merciful are those who walk humbly on earth and respond by saying "Peace unto you" when the ignorant address them insolently' (25:63).

21 JEALOUSY AND ENVY

'Are they so envious and jeolous of others for what Allah has given them of His bounty ?' (4:54)

Envy, jealousy and pride are the leading lines to all the misery that mankind has suffered from the beginning of the world to this day. (J. Marrant)

JEALOUSY

Jealousy is a feeling of resentment, suspicion, fear and intolerance against someone because of that person's success. The one who has this bad habit is jealous. For example, a person may be jealous of his rich friend. The opposite of jealousy is satisfied, unconcerned and confident.

Jealousy is an attitude condemned in the Quran. Allah reveals in the Quran that He created people's inner selves as prone to jealousy but that believers have to avoid this:

"...But people are prone to selfish greed. If you do good and have faith, Allah is aware of what you do." (4: 128)

When you are not confident about your capabilities, you become suspicious or fearful of being displaced by someone else. This is a feeling of jealousy and leads you to nowhere except failure. Envy is also another form of jealousy, with a slight difference. An envious person resentfully or painfully desires another's advantages. You must have heard someone saying "Whenever a friend succeeds, a little something in me dies." Jealousy and envy eat your heart out. If your neighbour, friend, relative or colleague succeeds, you should be happy and you should make it a point to work hard for similar or better achievements.

Be aware of any feelings of envy that arise, and counter them by developing your own self-worth.

ENVY

Just like red is associated with danger, envy is associated with the green colour and is called the 'green-eyed monster'. This is so because the monster destroys the one who is jealous and envious. It also leads to sorrow, anger and finally violence.

The Quran relates the example of those who become jealous when others are blessed by Allah; such people also feel happy when misfortune befalls others. Both these attitudes reflect a mind set that Quran rejects and condemns:

'If you are blessed with some goods it grieves them; but if some misfortune overtakes you, they rejoice at it; yet ,if you are patient and guard yourselves against their craftiness, their cunningness will never harm you in the least, for whatsoever they do, is well within the reach of Allah'(3:120).

'And do not covet the thing in which Allah has made some of you excel others. Unto men is a fortune from that which they have earned, and unto women is a fortune from that which they have earned. [Envy not one another] but ask Allah of His bounty. Behold! Allah knows all things'. (4:32)

In the referred verse, Allah reminds us to avoid being jealous, envious, or covetous of another person's blessings and favours when they exceed our own. The life of this world serves as a test, wherein humans shall face both prosperity and adversity. Not only do our tests differ in type, but they also differ in degree. Thus, some humans experience more prosperity than others, and some humans experience more adversity than others. The appropriate response in tests of prosperity is gratitude to Allah and the correct response in tests of adversity is patience, steadfastness, and perseverance in the way of Allah. If a person is bestowed with many more favours and blessings than those around him, he must not allow his blessing to induce hubristic behaviour because with the additional blessing comes the additional responsibility to use his blessing in the way of Allah. Similarly, if a person is bestowed with less favours and blessings than those around him, he must not allow his apparent lack of blessing to induce jealousy, covetousness, or hopelessness because he is faced with a test, an opportunity, which if completed with sincere effort and taken advantage of, shall entail its own satisfying reward with the Ever Merciful. Thus, the verse goes on to imply, rather than envying one another for a discrepancy in favours, we should remain grateful for whatever blessings we possess, irrespective of whether or not they exceed others' blessings, yet we may earnestly request divine favours at any time. The following supplication is an example of how to express this desire:

'Our Sustainer (Rab)! Grant us that which is good in the life of this world and that which is good in the Hereafter, and save us from the terrible doom of the Fire (2:201)

Allah gives as much as He wishes, to whom so ever He wishes, and no one can prevent this.

Finally, we must never forget that all the material blessings we enjoy in this life are only temporary. A believer should always be far more concerned about securing blessings in the Hereafter by cleansing his/her heart, mind and soul.

The overlapping use of jealousy and envy can occur because people can experience both at the same time. A person may envy the qualities or possessions of someone who also happens to be a rival.

Some say that there is a positive side to envy. For example, if a soldier envies another for his wounds and wishes that he too had a wound and a gallantry medal, this is a case of envy leading to a fruitful desire, but such feelings are very rare. In today's world you come across people who are mostly jealous of your success and prosperity.

The Quran directs us to pray and seek refuge with our Sustainer (Rab) against the evil of envious ones, as they practise evil (113:5). It means that we should be watchful in our relationship with envious and jealous people.

INSECURITY AND JEALOUSY

Jealousy is a kind of feeling which develops when you feel insecure. It is more in the mind and thinking than the body. At times you do not even know that you are jealous. It is common to everyone. At some stages of life everyone has felt this emotion, some of us are a little stronger than others. It can be found in a five-month-old child and also in a seventy-five-year-old grown up.

It is normal for us to want more as most of us are not satisfied with what we have. This dissatisfaction leads to jealousy and the desire to have more. It can lead to depression as our lives are lost in envy and jealousy. It is an extreme of selfishness and injustice.

The exalted Messenger Muhammad ﷺ is reported to have said:

'Keep yourselves from envy, because it eats up and takes away good action as fire consumes and burns the wood'

OVERCOMING JEALOUSY AND ENVY

In order to overcome these monsters we need to learn to be happy, satisfied and grateful for all that we already have. Instead of striving for bigger goals in life, a jealous person is more involved in hatred and grumbling, which is very distracting and fogs your focus in life. Observing successful people, their lives and accomplishments is meant to spur you on to find new ways of raising your standards in life. When you come across people who are jealous and envious you must have noticed that they never smile or enjoy the company of friends. They are always irritating and rude in their behaviour. Eventually even their presence at any social function or gathering is looked upon with dislike, disdain, and suspicion and they are usually avoided.

By being jealous you cannot be the person you are jealous of without going through the struggles, efforts and endeavours he had to.

REPENTENCE

Repenting and correcting one's behaviour will allow a person to develop the recommended positive, pious frame of mind. Also, we may learn an important lesson from the story of Iblees. After disobeying Allah, Iblees refused to repent for jealous and envious behaviour toward Adam (A.S.). Iblees allowed his jealousy for man to accumulate so much that he became depraved enough to vow that he would lead man astray into the path of wrongdoing until the Day of Judgment. Of course, Iblees' case is extreme, but this story should remind us to be on guard against jealousy, envy, and all other destructive emotions. It is often by continuously indulging in small sins that we unfortunately become more inclined toward bigger sins.

When you are sincerely appreciative of what you have and where you are, you will greatly expand your own possibilities of being better.

THE JEALOUS PRISONER

There were two prisoners who were chained to their respective places in a common prison cell. One was chained adjacent to the only window in the room and the other was chained to the far end from where he could see nothing out of the window.

It so happened that the prisoner nearer to the window used to describe the beautiful scene outside comprising that of little children playing in the lush green grass, people talking, sunrise and sunset to his fellow partner. He worded the scene so beautifully that the other prisoner felt irresistible desire to be next to the window and felt jealous of the prisoner who had all the time to enjoy the scenes outside his window.

One night, the prisoner next to the window suffered an heart attack and couldn't call for help. The other prisoner watched him fidgeting but due to his jealousy didn't raise an alarm resulting in the death of the first prisoner. After his body was removed, the left over prisoner requested to be shifted to the place near to the window. He wanted to enjoy the beautiful scene described earlier by his cell-mate; but his happiness was very short lived when he discovered that there was nothing of that sort out side the window but a dumb black-grey wall. Now, the prisoner was left alone in the cell with no one to talk to.

The second prisoner was jealous of the prisoner near the window and did not help him when he was in need as he had his mind on the place near the window. Due to his jealousy he suffered a dual blow of having no beautiful scene to enjoy and, he also lost his only partner who he could talk to. He suffered badly at the hands of jealousy.

One should also remember not to say or do things that may create feelings of deprivation in others. This also leads to jealousy and envy.

'O you who believe! Men should not laugh at other men, for it may be that they are better than them; and women should not laugh at other women, for they may perhaps be better than them Do not slander one another , nor give one another nick-names. After believing, it is bad to give another a bad name. Those who do not repent behave wickedly' (49:11)

22 KIND AND HELPFUL

'It was thorough Allah's Mercy that you (Muhammad) dealt with them gently, for had you been harsh and hard of heart, they would have surely broken away from you' (3:159)

Have you had a kindness shown?
Pass it on.
It was not given for thee alone,
Pass it on.
Let it travel down the years,
Let it wipe another's tears'
Till in Heaven the deed appears-
Pass it on. (H. Burton)

KINDNESS

Kindness is seen in a person who is gentle, caring, loving and helpful. You are helpful when you assist others in making things easier either by sharing their responsibilities and workload, or by providing aid and relief. Society also comprises those people who are poor and deprived. They do not even possess the basic necessities to sustain life. Those who have these resources are directed to help their brethren as a religious duty.

Zakat is one of the cornerstones of the Islamic economic and financial system. Its importance can be judged from the fact that at various places in the Quran, the command to perform prayers is followed by the injunctions to pay Zakat:

'Be constant in prayer and practice regular (compulsory) poor-due (Zakat) and bow down in submission with those who bow' (2:43).

During the days of the exalted Messenger Muhammad ﷺ virtually all those who might be in acute need had a valid claim on the beneficence of the entire Muslim community. Zakat is not a charity, nor voluntary alms-giving. It is a right of the poor and needy in the wealth of the rich. In making it a right, Islam has upheld human dignity.

TEAM SPIRIT

In the Seattle Special Olympics, nine athletes, mentally and physically handicapped, were standing on the start line for a race. The gun fired and the race started. Not everyone was running, but everyone wanted to participate and win.

A boy tripped and fell and started crying. The other athletes heard him crying. They slowed down and looked behind them. They stopped and came back... all of them. They hugged the boy and all walked shoulder to shoulder to the finish line. The whole crowd stood up and applauded. The applause lasted for a very long time. People who witnessed this still talk about it. Why? Because deep down we all know that helping others to win in life is much more than winning ourselves. The main thing is to help others to win. Even if that means slowing down and changing our own race.

A candle loses nothing if it helps another candle to light up.

HELPING ATTITUDE

Everybody recognizes a kind gesture and a helping attitude. It shows thoughtful attention when others need it. Tasks become more enjoyable and less tiresome when there is someone at hand to help. This is especially true when you receive or give help in everyday tasks at school, at home, and in your neighbourhood. When you give help, you reduce the amount of time needed to complete a job.

On a larger scale we all contribute to the well being of all. In an ideal society, Islam emphasizes mutual help. No doubt, the work and effort of one person may be more remunerative than that of another. The Quran takes the position that a person who earns more should not keep it all to himself, but should give the surplus to those who through lack of ability or opportunity cannot earn enough to satisfy their needs:

'And Allah has blessed some of you above others in respect of others in respect of capacity to earn livelihood, yet those who are blessed (with abundance) do not part with their wealth to those insubordinate to them so that they might become equal in this respect. Do they still deny the blessings of Allah' (16:71).

Thus we see that the Divine Guidance regards wealth as a gift of Allah and all those who are blessed with this gift should be kind and helpful to others who are needy.

The Quran does not look favourably upon those who help others and then keep on reminding them of their help:

'Those who spend their wealth in the way of Allah, and do not follow their charity by reminders of your generosity or by unjust the feelings of the recipients shall get their reward from Allah' (2:262)

'Those who spend their wealth to show off and do not believe in Allah and the Last Day, take Satan as companion, and Satan is an evil companion' (4:38)

EXAMPLES TO FOLLOW

Kindness breeds kindness. I remember a kind, young man on my way from Lahore to Islamabad, who refused to be paid for the tea and cake he had bought for us during a stopover on the motorway. We shall never meet again, but the kindness and courtesy shown is forever part of my memory and makes it more likely that I will help someone along the way. This can be cultivated as a habit.

Teachers in schools tell their students to say and do at least one nice thing everyday. This is also shared by the brothers and sisters of these students at home. Teachers at some school nominate students for doing a good deed like random acts of kindness or doing some volunteer work.

THE CONSIDERATE FRIENDS

This is a story from a classroom of a small school in a city. Joseph, a student was not feeling well for some time and was growing weak day by day. He was absent from the class for weeks and nothing was heard from him. He was missed because there always existed a special comradeship among all his friends.

One day Robert, his friend, decided to visit Joseph. He went to his house where Joseph's mother, who greeted him, informed him that Joseph was ill. Very reluctantly she told him that Joseph was diagnosed with Leukaemia, a cancer of the blood. He was undergoing Chemotherapy treatment and his disease was under control. As a result of this treatment Joseph had lost all the hair on his head. He was depressed and was also seeing a psychiatrist. This was even more distressful.

The classmates were saddened as they could feel the pain and anguish of their friend. They wanted to share his suffering and decided on a novel idea. They all went to see Joseph at his house. This time they all looked like him. All of them had their heads shaved and the accompanying teacher had also sacrificed his hair. There was no shame of baldness amongst the friends. Joseph forgot all his suffering and promised to attend school regularly.

It took Joseph four weeks to get his hair back and he did not need any psychiatric help after that. He had the help and consideration of his friends.

We should see if we measure up to the qualities of a good friend, a friend everyone would like to have:

- See if you are much fun to be.
- See if you make others happy and they enjoy your company
- See if you touch other peoples' heart with kindness.
- See if you have the wonderful activity to know when to offer advice and when to sit in quiet support.
- See if you have been able to come to the rescue of your friends when they were in trouble and brightened so many of their dark days.
- See if your friends consider themselves fortunate to have a friend like you.
- See if you feel in being considerate and helpful to those around you.
- The Quran points out that:

'Kind words and forgiveness are better than charity, which is followed by insult and injury' (2:263)

BLESSINGS OF GIVING

We all live in this world with certain rules and regulations. It is a basic law of nature– give and you shall receive. The Quran points out that Allah loves those who are kind, helpful and generous:

'Those who spend their wealth generously in the way of Allah, whether in prosperity or in adversity; who restrain their rage and forgive their fellowmen, Allah loves those who do well' (3:134)

Whatever help or consideration you give to others ultimately comes back to you. So, make it a habit of asking, "How can I be of help?"

You can be considerate enough to help your mother at home and your classmates in assignments given by teachers. This will also boost your confidence and self-respect. When you know that you have decided to help someone, you become more responsible, efficient and punctual. It is a very good feeling to know that you have contributed towards the completion of a project or a job.

GREED AND SELFISHNESS

The opposite of kindness, helpfulness and consideration is greediness, meanness, selfishness and rudeness. This negative approach breeds the desire to hoard and exploit the poor. This is outrightly condemned by the Quran:

'Those who hoard up gold and silver and spend it not for the cause set forth by Allah, announce to them the tiding of grievous suffering in the life to come' (9:34).

The Quran gives great importance to the spirit of being kind and helpful. It points out that even nations which devoted their wealth and turned their backs on high ideals, had to face the wrath of Allah.:

'And how many a people that dealt unjustly have We shattered and raised another people in their place' (21:11).

The tendency directly opposed to kindness, helpfulness and generosity is covetousness and greed. It is acquisitive, possessive and egoistic. The unkind and unhelpful man wants to appropriate all the good things within his reach and is callously indifferent to the needs of others. Suppose a number of men are gathered at a water tap. They know that the flow of water will cease in an hour. Each is eager to fill his pitcher. The covetous man elbows his way through the crowd, rudely pushes the pitcher of another from underneath the tap and places his own in its place. He does not care if others have to go without water. All he cares for is to have plentiful supply of water for himself. His unkind attitude deadens the human self and the Quran admonishes us to be on guard against this insidious disease of the self. It exhorts us to help all men and not only our kith and kin. The Quran is objective and universal in its outlook. It seeks the welfare of all humanity and not only of a particular sect, group or community.

LEARN FROM ANIMALS

We can even learn from animals how to treat others. Gorillas avoid conflicts and child discrimination, while a dolphin helps another dolphin to keep afloat if it is hurt. Dog is said to be man's best friend. Elephants are known never to abandon their elders and a lion never uses his strength to humiliate others.

GOOD DEEDS NEVER DIE

It is said that a good deed is never lost. He who sows courtesy reaps friendship and he who plants kindness gathers love. So, never lose a chance to be kind, helpful and considerate.

There is a famous poem by an anonymous poet:

Once and only once I pass,
If a kindness, I may show,
If a good deed, I may do,
To a suffering fellow man
Let me do it now while I can
No delay, for it is plain
I shall not pass this way again.

It is said that a good deed is never lost. He who sows courtesy reaps friendship and he who plants kindness gathers love. So, never lose a chance to be kind, helpful and considerate.

You have to review your life now and focus on how to move ahead. At this young age you have to think and decide that you will not be one of those who simply push and move. While marching ahead you should be considerate enough to take along all those who look up to you or depend upon you whether in school, college, home or your neighbourhood. Being successful is not enough. You have to lead your life according to values. It is excellence that leads to success.

Day in and day out you are probably giving all you have and taking good care of those who rely on you. The trouble begins when you do not receive love and affection in return from the ones who receive your care. As time passes, it is only natural for you to feel resentful. Does that mean that you should stop giving because you are not receiving? Of course not, instead you need to make it known that you need the same love and compassion that you give to others every day. You too need love. When you receive love, your giving effort becomes effortless and easy.

'And be of those who believe, and urge upon one another to persevere, and urge upon one another to be kind' (90:17)

A simple act of kindness gives rise to a chain of good and noble acts.

GLASS OF MILK

One day, a poor boy, who was selling goods from door to door to pay his way through school, found he had only one single dime left and he was hungry. He decided he would ask for a meal at the next house. However he lost his nerve when a lovely young woman opened the door. Instead of a meal he asked for a drink of water.

The young women thought that he looked hungry so she brought him a large glass of milk.

He drank it slowly, and then asked in a low and humble tone, "How much do I owe you?"

"You don't owe me anything," she replied. "Mother has taught us never to accept any thing in return for a kindness."

He said..."Then I thank you from my heart." As Howard Kelly left that house, he not only felt stronger physically, but his faith in God and man was strong also. He was so desperate and had been ready to give up and quit.

Year's later that young woman became critically ill. The local doctors were baffled with her illness. They finally sent her to the big city, where they called in specialists to study her rare disease.

Dr. Howard Kelly was called in for the consultation. When he heard the name of the town where she came from, a strange glow of light filled his eyes. Immediately he rose and went down the hall of the hospital to her room.

Dressed in his doctor's gown he went in to see her. He recognized her at once. He went back to the consultation room and made a resolve and determination to do his best to save her life. From that day he gave special attention to the case.

After a long struggle, the battle against the disease was won. Dr. Kelly requested the business office to pass the final bill to him for approval.

He looked at it and then wrote something on the edge and the bill was sent to her room. She feared to open it, for she was sure it would take the rest of her life to pay for it all. Finally she looked and something caught her attention on the side of the bill a few words were scribbled

She read these words..... "Paid in full with one glass of milk"

Dr. Howard Kelly

Tears of joy flooded her eyes as her happy heart prayed:

"Thank You, God, that Your love has spread everywhere through human hearts, minds and soul."

Please make it a point to remember people who are kind to you and to repay this kindness in whatever way you can.

Just by a kind word this world can be a better place to live.

'The blessings of Allah are at hand for those who do good' (7:56)

23 KNOWLEDGE AND WISDOM

'This is a Message for mankind that they may take a warning from it, and may know that He is the only Allah and that men of wisdom may reflect' (14:52)

We can be knowledgeable with other men's knowledge, but we cannot be wise with other men's wisdom.
(Montaigne)

KNOWLEDGE

Knowledge is what you know and understand. It is the skill acquired through education training and experience. This ability can be applied to a specific purpose whenever required. Knowledge from the word 'know' is also the sum of what has been thought, discovered and learned. The opposite of knowledge is ignorance.

EDUCATION

Education is the process of learning a programme of instruction and teaching of a specified kind. For example, you receive education under a specific plan in your school. Education is what gives you knowledge and scholarship. There is another kind of education which children learn from their environment, family, friends and neighbourhood. This is also called 'informal education'. Both types add up to groom young people into useful citizens of their country.

QURANIC CONCEPT

There is an impression in some quarters that the knowledge contemplated in the Quran means religious or spiritual knowledge only and that the holy book does not advocate the acquisition of any other kind of knowledge or learning. Let us see what the Quran has to say in this regard:

'Read- for your Sustainer (Rab) is the most Bountiful One Who has taught man the use of the pen and taught man what he did not know' (96:3,4,5)

Knowledge in the above verse means knowing that which one does not know. This fact is evident from another verse, which says,:

'My Sustainer (Rab) cause me to grow in knowledge' (20:114)

This process of acquiring knowledge is limitless. One has to continuously strive for it. That is why Muhammad ﷺ emphasized the acquisition of knowledge from the cradle to the grave.

Knowledge can be of different kinds and may be acquired for several purposes. Muhammad ﷺ laid emphasis on the kind of knowledge that benefits humanity. He said. 'Knowledge which does not yield any benefit to the people is like the wealth that is not spent in the way of Allah'. Thus knowledge that is acquired must have the potential of being used for the benefit of all.

During the apogee of Muslim civilization there was no distinction between religious and secular education. The mosque was the university of Islam in its golden era, and it was held in high esteem for it welcomed to its precincts all sciences and knowledge of the Age. It was this amalgam of all learning which made the Muslims shining stars in the firmament of science and technology.

TECHNOLOGY AND EDUCATION

Technology has become an increasingly influential factor in education. Computers and mobile phones are being widely used in developed and developing countries both to complement normal education practices, and develop new ways of learning such as 'online education'. This gives students the opportunity to choose what they are interested in learning. They must be aware of the use of multimedia and powerpoint presentations.

ROLE OF TEACHERS

Your teachers are the ones who help you build your knowledge and intelligence; but its quality will depend entirely upon your efforts. It cannot be spoon-fed. Education begins at the mother's knee and every word spoken within the hearing limits of children tends to formulate their character. One object of school education is to make an individual capable of thinking and differentiating between right and wrong, justice and injustice. It does not merely make you do right things, but enjoy them as well. When you work hard and achieve good grades in the examination, you do the right thing and at the same time enjoy it. You not only learn but also love knowledge.

WISDOM

The migration (Hijrah) of the exalted Messenger ﷺ to Medina marked the advent of a new phase in the history of Islam. It ushered in an era of tolerance and revitalized a decadent social order. As a result the Muslim community welcomed wisdom, knowledge and skills to what it had at its command. It realized how much it had to learn and how much it needed to enhance its knowledge. The same spirit is needed now by Muslims all over the world.

"Then He gave Adam knowledge of the nature and reality of all things' (2:31)

Wisdom is linked to both education and knowledge. While knowledge is a collection of facts, wisdom comes by relating these facts with one another in a positive way. It is the deep, thorough and mature understanding that enables you to make individual sensible decisions and judgements. Young people gain wisdom as they grow up. You can either benefit from the experience and wisdom of your elders or repeat their mistakes, suffer and then become wise. The choice is yours to make. One thing which you should know is that wisdom is not taught, but is developed through experience.

Knowledge can be communicated, but not wisdom. One can find wisdom, live it, be fortified by it, do wonders through it; but one cannot communicate and teach wisdom.

Many times we want to say, "Just a little more... more... more." Human desires often measure with the means of their gratification. Wisdom teaches us when to say, "Enough".

It is a mature integration of appropriate knowledge, you must discover it yourself during the journey through life.

NOT ENOUGH

A poor old beggar, who crept from house to house, wondered why folks who had so much money were never satisfied, but were always wanting more. He said to himself, "If I had enough to eat and to wear I would not want anything more."

Just at that moment fortune came down the street and told the beggar, "Hold your wallet and I will pour this gold into it. But I will pour only on the condition that all gold that falls upon the ground shall become dust. Your wallet is old, so do not load it too heavily."

The beggar agreed and his hands began to tremble. Fortune told him, "You are the richest man in the world now!" "Just a little more, "said the beggar. "Add just a handful or two."

"There, its full. The wallet will burst." said fortune "But it will hold a little more, just a little more!" said the Beggar with greed written all over his face.

Another piece was added and the wallet split. The treasure of gold fell upon the ground and turned to dust. Fortune had vanished. The beggar had now nothing but his empty torn wallet. He was as poor as before.

All the messengers of God including Abraham, Moses, Jesus, Solomon and Muhammad ﷺ were models of knowledge and wisdom. There is a verse in the Holy Quran in which Prophet Muhammad ﷺ prays to Allah to increase his knowledge.

Knowledge without wisdom is dangerous as it may lead to destruction. For example, the use of scientific knowledge in creating atomic weapons. Children are intelligent enough to realize that we all have values and express them through our behaviour, thinking and feeling.

'Those who listen closely to all that is said and follow the best it contains are the ones who have been guided by Allah and are men of wisdom' (39:18)

GETTING RID OF BAD HABITS

A wealthy man requested an old scholar to wean his son away from his bad habits. The scholar took the youth for a stroll through a garden. Stopping suddenly he asked the boy to pull out a tiny plant growing there. The youth held the plant between his thumb and fore finger and pulled it out. The old man then asked him to pull out a slightly bigger plant. The youth pulled hard and the plant came out with its roots. "Now pull that one." said the old man, pointing to a guava tree. The youth grasped the trunk and tried to pull it out. But it would not budge. "It is impossible."said the boy panting with effort. "So it is with bad habits." Said the old scholar, "When they are young it is easy to pull them out, but when they take hold they cannot be uprooted.

This changed the boy's life.

VALUES

Values are the ideals or standards that people use to direct their behaviour, make judgements about what is important in life and what is right or wrong.

'Allah has indeed appointed measure for everything' (65:3)

We judge ourselves and others in terms of our values. Our good qualities or virtues are values that define our character. True happiness depends upon how you exercise and develop these values.

All youngsters should know that underlying the educational process is a set of values and virtues that defines and determines its general goals, purpose and standard of behaviour. The teaching and embracing of these values enhances their overall character and personality development. Becoming an educated person means living these virtuous values throughout one's life.

Knowledge should not be mistaken for wisdom. While knowledge helps you make a living, wisdom helps you make a life.

'And certainly you will be questioned as to what you did' 14:93)

Someone once observed that we have two ears and one mouth and should learn to use them in that proportion

WISE OLD OWL

A wise old owl sat in an oak.
The more he heard the less he spoke;
The less he spoke the more he heard.
Why aren't we all like that wise old bird.

INFORMATION TECHNOLOGY AND KNOWLEDGE

The rapid growth of information technology is taking us towards a time when all human knowledge will be instantly available to anyone on the planet, in any medium. This will be a fully functional global brain in which the technology of television, telephone and Internet will be easily accessible as books are available today. As young people who will be leaders of tomorrow, you have to prepare yourself for this revolution of knowledge. At present, humanity has vast accounts of knowledge, but still very little wisdom. You have to change this scenario for peace, prosperity and progress.

It is necessary for all those who submit to the teachings, directives and guidance of Quran to have good knowledge and insight. Quran discourages blind following.

'It is a Revelation from the Most-Benevolent, ever Merciful. A book whose verses have been distinguished and explained, a lucid discourse for people who understand (41:2,3)

Some of these Principles reflect knowledge and wisdom. In your practical and professional life they will help and guide you to make your life goal oriented, objective, hopeful and worthy of living.

- Winning isn't everything. But wanting to win is.
- You would achieve more, if you don't mind who gets the credit.

- When everything else is lost, the future still remains.
- If you don't stand for something, you'll fall for everything.
- If you do little things well, you'll do big ones better.
- Only thing that comes to you without effort is old age.
- You won't get a second chance to make the first impression .
- Only those who do nothing do not make mistakes.
- Never take a problem to your boss unless you have a solution.
- If you are not failing you're not taking enough risks.
- Don't try to get rid of bad temper by losing it.
- Those who don't make mistakes usually don't make anything
- There are two kinds of failures. Those who think and never do, and those who do and never think.
- All progress has resulted from unpopular decisions.
- Change your thoughts and you change your world.
- Understanding proves intelligence, not the speed of the learning.
- The best way to kill an idea is to take it to a meeting.
- Friendship founded on business is always better than business founded on friendship.
- Don't waste your precious energy on gossip, energy vampires, issues of the past, negative thoughts or things you cannot control. Instead invest your energy in the positive present moment.
- Realize that life is a school and you are here to learn. Problems are simply part of the curriculum that appear and fade away but the lessons you learn will last a lifetime.

'You cannot make the dead listen or the deaf to hear the call, when they have turned their backs. Nor can you lead the blind when they have gone astray. You can make none hear except those who believe in Our signs and have come to peace and submission' (27:80, 81)

24 PATIENCE, TOLERANCE AND FORBEARANCE

'O you who believe ! Seek assistance through patience and prayer, surely Allah is with those who are patient' (2:153)

Toleration is the greatest gift of the mind. The highest result of education is tolerance. It is the first principle of community; it is the spirit which conserves the best that all men think. (Helen Keller)

PATIENCE

You have the quality of patience if you remain calm, do not get annoyed or angry. It means that you have the ability to endure hardship, difficulty or inconvenience without complaint. Patience and forbearance need tolerance and emphasize calmness, self-control and the willingness to withstand delay. The opposite of patience and tolerance is impatience and intolerance. Intolerance can grow only in the soil of ignorance and from its branches grow all manner of obstacles to human progress.

Remember that Thomas Edison who invented the light bulb, failed more than 2000 times. Finally, his patience paid off and he succeeded in giving us the light bulb.

IMPATIENCE

Impatience is one of the most difficult obstacles to overcome. We never bother about cultivating the virtue of patience. We want everything fast. We hate to wait. Patience requires of us to accept ourselves, just as we are, at any moment. It helps keep our expectations to a realistic level. If we do not practise patience, we quickly lose hope and risk failure in whatever way or manner we are practising. However, patience does not mean to accept all situations and avoid facing the difficulties of life

'If We allow men to enjoin Our favours, and then take them away from them, they become despondent and ungrateful. If We let him him taste Our favours after adversity, he says, " Misfortune has left me", and begins to brag and exalt. Only those who endure with patience and do right things will have pardon and a great reward' (11:9, 10, 11)

SHORT TEMPERED

Character of a person involves dispositions that relate to what, in different circumstances, they would feel, how they would think, how they would react and the sort of choices they would make and actions they would perform. So someone is short tempered if they are disposed to feel angry quickly, and often.

RIGHT APPROACH

In our everyday life, we need changes for the better. Only patience and a tolerant attitude can bring us close to these changes, and help maintain them for a long period of time.

The Quran addresses those who believe in its immutable message to persevere and be patient in adversity because Allah has promised His help to such people:

'O you who believe ! Endure the sufferings with patience and courage and show consistency in your behaviour. Observe your duty towards Allah so that you may prosper' (3:200)

'And We shall certainly test you with something of fear and hunger and loss of property and lives and fruits of your toil, but give glad tidings to those who patiently persevere' (2:155).

REACHING THE TOP

"I cannot walk up the hill," said the little boy, "I cannot possibly do it. What will become of me? I must stay here all my life, at the foot of the hill. It is terrible!"

"This is a pity!" said his sister. "But look, dear brother! I have found such a pleasant and interesting game to play. Take a step and see how clear a footstep you can make in the dust. Look at mine! Every single line in my foot is printed clear on the mountain sand. Now, you try; and see if you can do as well!"

The little boy took a step and with delight said," Mine is just as clear!"

His sister was happy and said, "Do you think so? See my footprint again. I tried harder than you. I am also heavier than you and that is why my footprints deeper and clearer."

The little boy patiently tried again and happily exclaimed," Now mine is just as deep! See here, and here, and here, they are just as deep and clear as can be."

"Yes, that is very well," said the sister," but now it is my turn, let me try again, and we shall see."

They kept on moving upwards step by step, matching their footprints and laughing to see the gray dust puff up between their bare toes. By and by the little boy looked up.

"Why," he said, "We are at the top of the hill!"

"Dear me!" said the sister," So we are!"

Tolerance is important because it leads to peaceful coexistence between different people. This leads to social, economic and emotional prosperity for everyone. With tolerance, everyone in society feels valued and respected.

Lack of tolerance leads to fighting, violence, and finally it destroys the peace and security of society. When people fail in their arguments they become intolerant, and then they use force and aggression to support their point of view.

Once, when the Messenger Muhammad ﷺ was sitting at a place in Madinah, along with his companions, a funeral procession passed by. On seeing this, he stood up. One of his companions remarked that the funeral was that of a Jew. The Messenger SAW replied:

"Was he not a human being?"

The younger generation should also understand that it is not right to constantly follow their desires, feelings and ambitions. Allah-conscious people keep away from things that are harmful to their character and they do this by following the path shown by their Creator. The worst form of intolerance is shown when people react harshly and violently against those who do not subscribe to their faith and belief. The Quran clearly asserts that no one has the right to force his religious on others. Those who accept and embrace Islam under compulsion is not acceptable to Allah. Islamic values have to be accepted with conviction and wholeheartedly. We should emulate the example set by Muhammad ﷺ and the clear directives of the Quran regarding tolerance of faiths,religions and the religious views of others:

'There shall be no compulsion in religion'(2:256).

Muhammad ﷺ never forced his faith and belief on anyone and he always respected other religions. In this respect he followed the Quranic directive in letter and spirit:

'Revile not those deities whom the unbelievers call upon and worship' (6:109).

It is pertinent to note that . During the course of their meeting with a delegation of Christians, who had come from Najran, had an extensive discussion in the mosque with Muhammad ﷺ. During the course of their meeting the Christians expressed their desire for an interlude so that they might pray. Muhammad ﷺ invited them to hold their service in his mosque which has always been regarded as one of the holiest places of Islam. Later he granted concessions to Christians that no conqueror had given to its subjects in the following words:

'To the Christians of Najran and the surrounding territories, the security of God and the pledge of from his bishopric, nor any monk from his monastery, nor any priest His Messenger are extended to their lives, their religion and their property to those present as well as those absent, and other besides; there shall be no interference with their faith or their observances; nor any change in their rights or privileges; no bishop shall be removed from his bishopric, nor any monk from his monastery, nor any priest from his his priesthood; no image or cross shall be destroyed; they shall oppress nor be oppressed; nor shall they be required to furnish provision for troops' .

THE BEST EXAMPLE

In the ten years following the migration (Hijrah), Muhammad ﷺ had to face about eighty battles that were mainly defensive in nature. The total number of men killed in these battles was less than three hundred. He set an example of avoiding unnecessary bloodshed. Even Makkah was conquered without any bloodshed. He epitomized tolerance, goodwill, compassion and peace in a world sunk in frequent fratricidal wars, hatred, violence and fanaticism.

CHARTER OF MADINAH

After the establishment of the city state of Madinah, Muhammad ﷺ gave the Charter of Madinah (Meesaq-e-Madinah), which is regarded as the first constitution in history. The full text of the Charter has 52 clauses. Its salient features included the freedom of conscience for each community and also mutual tolerance. The Jews were free to practise their religion and so were the Christians and Muslims. The implication of mutual tolerance allowed everyone not only to have faith in the religion of his choice and observe its ritual norms, but also to follow the laws of the community to which they belonged.

Tolerance is the outcome of patience and breeds justice. All these are Quranic values and are inter-linked:

'Stand firmly for Allah as witnesses to fair dealing, and let not the hatred of others to you make you deviate to injustice and depart from justice. Be just, that is next to piety' (5:8).

The teachings of the Quran radiated a new ray of knowledge and brought the message of equality, fraternity, freedom, benevolence, human rights, dignity of labour, elevation of status of woman, justice, cooperation, economic welfare and toleration.

PEOPLE'S REACTION

It is fair to say that people for the most part tolerate and even forgive others in good-hearted manner, provided others do not treat you too badly too frequently. When people are offended, they are happy to forget that your offence could be due to a simple misunderstanding. For example, burping is exceptionally rude in Italy. Your first offence may well be forgiven, but when you observe the reactions of those around with a keen eye, you will realize not to do it again.

TOLERANCE AND CULTURE

An international code of council based on simple respect and common sense can be easily conceived, recognized and adhered to by anyone. Our personality is greatly influenced by the place we grow up. It becomes difficult for us to change our acquired habits, tastes, perceptions and even morals. Our mother tongue dictates that we think in a certain way within the framework laid out by thousands of years of our own culture's evolution. We base our concept of tolerance on this very basis. As young people acquiring good education, you have to change this attitude and base your tolerance on good common sense and values that are positive. Really great people are courteous, considerate, benevolent and generous not just to some people in some circumstances— but to everyone all the time.

GREAT MEN

Not gold, but only man can make
A people great and strong,
Men who, for truth and honour's sake,
Stand fast and suffer long.
Brave men who work while others sleep
Who dare while others fly__
They build a nation's pillars deep
And lift them to the sky

Islam is a religion of continuity and universality since Adam. The rays of the teachings of the Quran spread the light of tolerance and human rights for the guidance of mankind in the matter of religious affairs of the state and our daily lives.

'Allah is with those who are patient and persevere' (2:249)

'Be patient and steadfast, for surely Allah does not let the reward of those who are upright and do good to go waste' (11:115)

25 RELIABLE AND TRUSTWORTHY

'And be true to your bond with Allah whenever you bind yourself by a promise, and do not break your oaths after having confirmed them' (16:91)

"People of character have the integrity to do what is right even when it is likely to cost them more than they want to pay and more than they think is fair. (Anonymous)

RELIABILITY, TRUST AND INTEGRITY

We lament the increasing lack of trust, reliability and integrity in people. Without exonerating such people, we need to ask ourselves a question: Do we possess these qualities?

Integrity and trust are reflected in our actions when no one is watching. The generally accepted ethical code defines it as a system of principles governing morality and acceptable conduct. The moral code is based on the quality of being in accordance with standards of right and wrong. The absolute Quranic Values openly declare how we can actually measure the difference between right and wrong, good and bad and positive and negative actions

In the Islamic context reliability is based on true belief and trust in Allah's supreme authority and guidance. Those who believe in Him and act according to His guidance have nothing to fear and they do not need any help or protection from anyone else:

'Sufficient is Allah as your Protector and Helper' (4:45).

At the same time , believers are required to honour the trust that the system of Islamic values and guidance places in them:

O you who believe ! Do not betray Allah and His Messenger; nor violate knowingly the trust that has been reposed in you' (8:27).

This is the beginning of a relationship between man and Allah. The response by the Almighty is:

'O you who believe ! If you follow the path shown by Allah, He will give you the faculty of moral evaluation to judge between right and wrong and will cleanse you of your evil thoughts and deeds, and will forgive your shortcomings, and Allah's plans are the best' (8:29) .

A dependable person is considered reliable, as he can be trusted in all matters. The opposite of this is irresponsible, unreliable and untrustworthy.

The term reliability is often used, but what does it really mean? If you think about its use in everyday life, you might get some hint. For instance, we often speak about a machine being reliable such as a car, camera, bicycle or computer. In all these cases reliable means 'dependable' or 'trustworthy' to give us the same result over and over again.

TRUSTWORTHY

The test of being reliable and trustworthy comes up when something is posited to us in trust of being returned when required. The Quran commands Muslims to return whatever is reposed to them as a trust:

'Allah commands you to give to the owners what is held in trust with you' (4:58)

'Honour every promise made for and undoubtedly on the Day of Judgment you shall be made to account for every promise which you may have made'(17:34).

Reliability is not something you are born with. It has to be developed and earned through your attitude, behaviour and actions. Teachers in schools are in constant touch with students who spend a major part of early life under their watchful eyes. The consistent performance and behaviour of students is what makes them dependable in the eyes of their teachers, and they are given more responsibilities because they can be relied upon to fulfil those responsibilities with confident certainty.

PERSONAL INTEGRITY

Young people need to be honest with themselves and others. Personal integrity is a must that is demonstrated by honesty. The ability of others to trust you hinges upon your honesty and integrity. This also means that you should keep your promises and live up to your commitments.

The Quran is critical of those who do not keep their promises:

'Is it not so that every time they made a promise, some of them set it aside? The truth is that most of them do not, in fact, believe' (2:100)

Honouring your promises is the basis of all trust and reliability. It reflects commitment and strength of character. This should also be reflected in your professional life.

THE LOYAL SLAVE

Once a King was told that his servant had no visible qualities of beauty, strength or courage. The King pointed out that he valued his servant more for his virtues than his form and stature.

Once, in a narrow pass, a camel had fallen and a chest of pearls was broken. The King gave the signal for plunder. All the soldiers got busy in gathering the pearls leaving the King behind. None of them remained with the King except his loyal servant. "What have you gained?" asked the King of his slave.

"Nothing", he replied, "I always walk behind you. I do not occupy myself with riches away from my service."

Trustworthiness is another dimension of honesty . In Arabic it is called, "amanah". The meaning of amanah is something someone left for another person to protect or keep in his custody. The opposite of trustworthiness is betrayal or even treason. That is, to fail to keep the trust in the way the person who left it expected or wanted.

Trustworthiness further enhances the integrity and sound moral conduct that is inherent in the notion of honesty. Being trustworthy implies being honest, fair in dealings and punctual (in terms of both regularity and timeliness) as well as honouring trusts and keeping promises and commitments. An important part of the noble Islamic character is being trustworthy. Muhammad ﷺ was known, even before his Prophethood to be Al-Amin (the trustworthy one).

While the qualities of honesty and trustworthiness are inextricably entwined, there are slight differences. Honesty implies a lack of deceit while trustworthiness entails honouring and fulfilling commitments, promises, trusts and covenants. It covers moral, social, legal and religious obligations. Being truthful in promises and covenants is one of the characteristics by which the believers are known. Both promises and covenants involve saying something about an issue to confirm that you will uphold the trust. This is especially so with regard to one's duties towards Allah. Allah praises the believers by promising them Paradise:

(Those who are faithfully true to their amanah (all the duties which God has ordained, honesty, moral responsibility and trusts, etc.) and to their covenants...these indeed are the inheritors. Who shall inherit Paradise. And dwell therein forever) (23: 8-11)

DIVINE GUIDANCE

Trust, and being worthy of another's trust, is inherent in being one who has submitted to the will of Allah. When Allah created us as individuals it became a trust incumbent upon us to nourish ourselves and our families in a way that enables trust and total submission to His commands.

The commands and rules from Allah are designed for our benefit and Islam holds people's rights in high esteem. The systematic arrangement of guidelines and regulations is intended to uphold the rights Islam gives to the believers and to minimize vice and corruption. Islam strongly condemns the violation of Allah-given rights. When Allah commands us to keep the trust, to be trustworthy, it is not a matter to be taken lightly.

In the past Allah dealt severely with people who were dishonest and did not honour their trusts. Reliability, honesty and trustworthiness are characteristics that must be present in anyone who claims to be a believer. Muhammad ﷺ said that "A hypocrite is known by three traits: When he speaks, he lies; when he promises, he reneges; when he is entrusted, he cheats (or embezzles)."

TRUST AS A DUTY AND OBLIGATION

When Abu Ubaydah was the commander of the Muslim armies in Syria, the Emperor of Byzantium set out with a large army to recapture Hims. Abu 'Ubaidah decided to evacuate the city because he had only a handful of soldiers. He gathered the people of Hims in the middle of the city and announced: "We collected the protection tax from you because we planned to defend you. Now we are too weak. In this case, we return the tax we collected."

All the taxes collected were returned to the non-Muslim people of Hims. Such was the depth of feeling and understanding displayed by the early Muslims. They were constantly aware of their obligations towards God, their brothers and sisters and those who were under the protection of the Muslim armies.

Trustworthiness is a quality that is essential if a society is to function as one unit, bearing in mind the needs and aspirations of all its citizens. The Quran directs us to choose those persons as rulers who are trustworthy (4:158)

CONSTANTLY IMPROVE YOUR RELIABILITY

Reliability fosters trust. An important part of this process of improving your level of trustworthiness is never to take advantage of those that are at a disadvantage. This breaks the trust they have in you. Treat others as you would prefer to be treated yourself. Take genuine interest in the problems of others. This caring attitude increases your personal character as someone who can be relied upon. Faithfulness and loyalty to your friends, neighbours, family members, teachers and relatives will help you earn their trust.

You are considered reliable if you are considerate enough to recognize that others have faults and can make mistakes. Trust forms an integral part of friendship. So build all your friendships and relationships on trust. Trust is established by understanding the other person, their wants and needs, likes and dislikes. Let your friends know that they can depend on you and that you will be there for them through good and bad times. Also let them know that their well-being means a lot to you.

"But certainly whoever keeps his promise follows the right path, will be blessed by Allah. Allah loves those who shun evil and follow the right cause' (3:76)

KEEPING SECRETS AS TRUST

You can prove that you are reliable by keeping secrets of your near and dear ones and not gossiping and discussing them with others. If you are loose-lipped with someone else's private information, you can never gain their trust. Stand up for your friends to prove that you can be trusted. When you have a reputation of a fair-weather friend or the kind of person who stabs his friends in the back, you will never be able to recover from it or be trusted. Reliability is earned as an ongoing process and is not granted as a gift.

THE PARROT'S ADVICE

A man had a parrot of which he was excessively fond. He kept it in a silver cage and fed it fruits and nuts and anything else the bird asked for, for the parrot was so clever it could engage in conversation.

The parrot longed for freedom and often asked for it but the merchant would always reply: "Ask for anything else."

One day the parrot said to him: "Give me freedom and I'll give you three pieces of advice that could be of great benefit to you." The merchant loved the parrot but he loved money more. He thought: "If his advice helps me amass wealth, it would be worth it."

"Go," he said, opening the cage.

The parrot hopped out onto his hand.

"Never grieve over loss of wealth," he said. The merchant thought it was tame advice but said nothing.

The parrot flew to the roof of the merchant's house.

"This is my second advice," he said. "Never believe everything that is told to you."

"Tell me something that I don't know," said the man, sounding annoyed.

"What you don't know is that I've two priceless gems in my stomach," said the bird.

"Two priceless gems," echoed the merchant. "Oh, what a fool I was to set you free! I'll regret this for the rest of my life!"

"Don't you want to hear my third advice?" asked the parrot. "Tell me," said the merchant, bitterly.

"I advised you never to grieve over losses but here you are grieving over losing me," said the parrot. "I advised you never to believe everything you hear but you immediately believed me when I told you I had two gems in my stomach. Could I have survived if I really had two gems in my stomach? My third advice is: "Learn to listen with your mind instead of just with your ears."

And with that, the parrot flew away, leaving the merchant gaping.

'Piety lies in observing your devotional obligations, and paying the Zakat and fulfilling a pledge you have given. And being patient in hardship, adversity and times of peril' (2:177)

26 RESPECTFUL AND COURTEOUS

'O you who believe ! Do not laugh at others, for it may be that they are better then them' (49:11)

"You can demand courtesy but you have to earn respect." — Lawrence Goldstone
"Respect was invented to cover the empty place where love should be." — Leo Tolstoy, Anna Karenina

Courtesy and respect are two eminent values that are essential to Islam. Along with courage and bravery, a person needs the quality of being courteous and respectful to strengthen his character. Allama Iqbal in his poem 'Bal-e-Jibrail' (Wings of Gabriel) writes:

'What is humanity ? Respect for man !
Learn to understand the dignity of man,
The man of love learns the ways of God
And as benevolent alike to the believer and the unbeliever'

RESPECTFUL

You are respectful when you care for others and love them as you love yourself. This is because everyone deserves to be treated, as you would like them to treat you. It also means showing regard for the worth of someone or something. It includes respect for yourself, the rights and dignity of everyone and also respect for the environment that sustains all life. Make sure that you treat everyone with dignity and respect.

Foremost of all values is the respect for other human beings. Quran treats all humanity as one nation and ordains respect for all human beings (17:70). At the human level, even gender, nationality or even religion does not matter. You cannot abuse or harm anyone for who they are or their beliefs and faith. Quran treats human life as extremely valuable. That is why it tells us that if 'You take one life without valid reason, it is like taking the life of the whole humanity; and if if you save one life, it is like saving the life of whole humanity' (5:32). That is why taking one's own life or suicide is not allowed in Islam (4:29, 2:195)

SIMPLE ISLAMIC TEACHINGS

One of the distinctive features of Islam is its simplicity. Its teachings is not shrouded in myths and stories and has nothing mysterious, nothing irrational, nothing unpractical, nothing unattainable in it. It lays the foundation of universalism in all walks of life. A Muslim under the categorical injunctions of the Quran can make no distinction between one medium of light and another. He has to respect and believe in all the Messengers and Scriptures sent by Allah from time to time:

'Say,'We believe in Allah and the revelation given to us, and to Abraham,Ishmael, Isaac, Jacob and to descendants, and that given to Moses and Jesus and that given to all Messengers from their Nourisher (Rab); we make no distinction between any of them, and we bow to Allah (in Islam)' (2:136)

'He has ordained to you (Muhammad) the same Faith (way of life) which He enjoined on Noah and which We have ordained to you, as well as to Abraham, Moses and Jesus, advising them to observe the faith and not get disunited into various factions' (42:13).

'Tell them bluntly (Muhammad) 'O you people of the Scriptures! You have no valid ground to stand upon, unless you follow the Torah and the Gospel, and all that have been revealed to you from your Rab (5:68).

REPAYING KINDNESS

His name was Fleming, and he was a poor Scottish farmer. One day while working in the farm, he heard a cry for help coming from a nearby wet and muddy land. There mired to his waist in black muck, was a terrified boy, screaming and struggling to free himself. Farmer Fleming saved the lad from what could have been a slow and terrifying death. The next day a fancy carriage pulled up at the poor Scotsman's house. An elegantly dressed nobleman stepped out and introduced himself as the father of the boy Farmer Fleming had saved.

Sir Alexander Fleming

"I want to repay you," said the nobleman. "You saved my son's life."

"No. I cannot accept payment for what I did." Fleming replied, waving off the offer. At that moment the farmer's own son came to the door.

"Is that your son?" The nobleman asked. "Yes," the farmer replied proudly.

"I'll make you a deal. Let me take him and give him a good education. If the lad is anything like his father, he'll grow to be a man you can be proud of."

And that he did. In time Farmer Fleming's son Alexander Fleming graduated from St. Mary's Hospital Medical School in London, and went on to become known throughout the world as the noted Sir Alexander Fleming, the discoverer of penicillin.

Years afterwards, the nobleman's son was stricken with pneumonia and was saved by the use of penicillin.

The name of the nobleman was Lord Randolph Churchill and his son was the famous prime minister and war hero of Britain, Sir Winston Churchill.

A simple act of courtesy helped create a chain of good and noble deeds which ultimately benefited the whole of humanity. This is the true worth of virtuous deeds.

Sir Winston Churchill

Respect is the restraining side of morality and keeps you from hurting others. Mutual respect is the way to create a harmonious life with each other. The opposite of respectful is disrespectful, unmannerly and mean.

COURTESY

Courtesy is your willingness to be generous in providing something needed by others and reflects your good manners, polite behaviour, and a friendly gesture. Courtesy as etiquette is shown when you greet relatives and friends and others with warmth and respect, comfort the sad and bereaved and do not insult anyone and eat neatly and quietly. Courtesy as a habit is built by constancy and begins with our own behaviour. The opposite of courteous is discourteous, impolite and rude.

In the Quran we have the example of Prophets Moses (Musa) and his brother Aaron (Haroon) who were asked by Allah to be courteous, kind and gentle to Pharoah:

'Go both of you to Pharoah, as he has transgressed all bounds. Talk to him gently, may be he takes heed and becomes conscious of Us' (20:43,44)

How many of us are truly well-mannered? It is very rarely seen that mothers instruct their children to hold open a door when several people are approaching. Courtesy and good manners remind us of others around. Our actions affect all those who come in contact with us. It is a matter of give and take.

27 SELF-IMPROVEMENT AND GROWTH

"Do you enjoin others to do good deeds and forget your own selves. You also read the book (Quran), why do you then not understand ? (2:44)

If you travel on a road made by your own hands each day, you will arrive at the place where you would want to be. (Egyptian saying)

Self-improvement is a process of self-growth which everyone, especially youngsters should adopt. It is not enough to read, you have to practise what you read and this needs your time and effort. There is no such thing as instant self-improvement. Any inner change takes time, and there must be motivation, desire, perseverance and dedication. Usually old habits do not allow us to bring about this change. There is also resistance and opposition from the people around us. The will to change has to overcome this opposition. One way of bringing a change in attitude and behaviour is to observe how people behave and act in different situations and then looking inside to find out if you would have behaved in the same way under similar circumstances. The positive traits of character in such situations should be adopted. In this way you learn and benefit a lot from the behaviour and actions of the people around you, in school, at home, in the street and everywhere else. It is not a matter of judging others, but learning how to act, react and behave in a better way. It will also increase your knowledge about how the mind and thoughts influence behaviour and action. If you do not like what you are, analyze what and why you dislike and then analyze your own behaviour in the same way. Similarly adopt this norm in character traits of others you like. Always practise what you preach or say.

'O you who believe ! Why do you say what you do not practice. It is most hateful in the sight of Allah that you say that which you do not' (61:2, 3)

BORN TO WIN-CONDITIONED TO LOSE

An eagle's egg was placed in the nest of a prairie chicken. The egg hatched and the little eagle grew up thinking it was a prairie chicken. It did what the other prairie chickens did. It scratched in the dirt for seeds. It clicked and crackled, but it never flew more than a few feet because that is what the prairie chickens do.

One day it saw an eagle flying gracefully and majestically in the open sky. It asked a prairie chicken, 'What is that beautiful bird ?' The chicken replied,'That is an eagle. It is an outstanding bird that flies so majestically'. 'Can I fly like that eagle?', asked the young eagle. 'No you cannot fly like the eagle because you are a prairie chicken', replied the chicken.

So the eagle never gave it a second thought believing to be the truth. It lived the life of a prairie chicken and died a prairie chicken, depriving itself of the potential capabilities mainly due to a lack of vision to improve.

The eagle was born to win, but conditioned to lose.

In the story we have a lesson that people and situations should not stop us from visualizing a better future and the chances to improve our position. Some people go through life pleased that a glass is half-full . Others spend a lifetime lamenting that it is half-empty. The truth is that there is a glass with a certain volume of water in it. From there, it is up to us to improve the situation and achieve positive results. A forward looking bent of mind and attitude is needed for improvement.

'Repel evil with good' (23:96)

PUT THE GLASS DOWN!

A professor began his class by holding up a glass with some water in it. He held it up for all to see and asked the students, "How much do you think this glass weighs?"

"50 grams... 100 grams... 125 grams..." the students answered. "I really don't know unless I weigh it," said the professor, but, my question is, "What would happen if I held it up like this for a few minutes?"

"Nothing!" the students replied. "Okay! What would happen if I held it up like this for an hour?" the professor asked. ""Your arm would begin to ache," said one of the students. "You're right! Now what would happen if I held it for a day?"

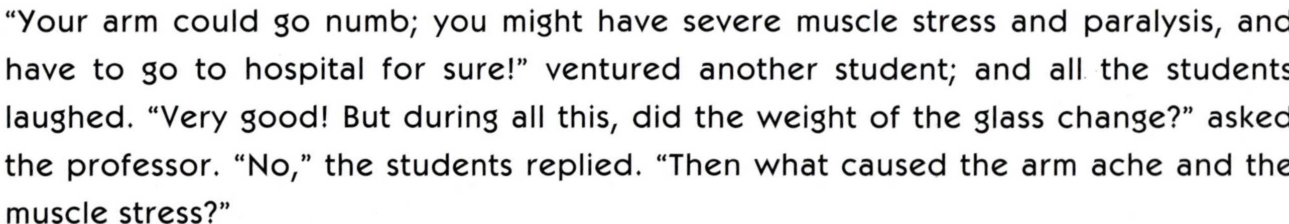

"Your arm could go numb; you might have severe muscle stress and paralysis, and have to go to hospital for sure!" ventured another student; and all the students laughed. "Very good! But during all this, did the weight of the glass change?" asked the professor. "No," the students replied. "Then what caused the arm ache and the muscle stress?"

The students were puzzled. "Put the glass down," said one of the students. "Exactly!" said the professor, "Life's problems are something like this. Hold it for a few minutes in your head and they seem okay. Think of them for a long time and they begin to ache. Hold it even longer and they begin to paralyse you. You will not be able to do anything."

The Moral: My dear friends, it's important to think of the challenges (problems) in our life, but even more important is to 'put them down' at the end of every day before we go to sleep. That way, we are not stressed and wake up every day fresh and strong and can handle any issue, any challenge that comes our way. Remember to 'PUT THE GLASS DOWN' and have tranquillity by putting trust in your abilities and finding solutions to problems that come your way. It is no use wasting your time in lingering over problems that can only go away when a proper solution is worked out.

CHANGING HABITS

You can also decide to change some of your habits and behaviour patterns, and develop new ones because you believe they are necessary and beneficial, even without seeing them in others first. In this case you will become the role model yourself to be followed by others.

'O you who believe! On you rests the responsibility for your own selves. If you follow the right path , those who have gone astray will not be able to harm you' (5:105)

FAILURE

Failure in these efforts should not discourage you. It does not matter how many times you fail or forget to behave as you desired. Persevere with your efforts and never give up. Ultimately you will experience a positive self-improvement and growth.

Ambition and the will to improve is the spur that makes man struggle with destiny. It is nature's own incentive to make a purpose great and its achievement greater. Acceptance and practicing of truth is an essential part of Islam that leads to a growth of the personality:

'Do not yield to those who reject the truth' (68:8).

'Those who are steadfast in adversity and prosperity and work to improve human potential, there is the protection of forgiveness and a great reward' (11:11)

GROWTH AND IMPROVEMENT

Growth is also a process of experimentation, a series of trials and errors and occasional victories. The failed experiments are as much a part of the process as the experiments that work. This process of life means becoming more of what we already are, not what others want us to be. Growth means evolving, waking up and not remaining asleep to the realities of life.

'He is indeed successful who causes his self to grow, and he is indeed a failure who stunts (Stops) it' (91:9,10)

If you put a buzzard in a pen six or eight feet square and entirely open at the top, the bird, in spite of its ability to fly, will be an absolute prisoner. The reason is that a buzzard always begins a flight from the ground with a run of ten or twelve feet. Without space to run, as is its habit, it will not even attempt to fly, but will remain a prisoner for life in a jail with no top.

The ordinary bat you see flying after sunset, a remarkable nimble creature in the air, cannot take off from a level place. If it is placed on the floor or a flat ground, all it can do is shuffle about helplessly, and no doubt, painfully, until it reaches some slight elevation from where it can throw itself into the air. Then, at once, it takes off in a flash.

A bumble bee if dropped into an open tumbler will be there until it dies, unless it is taken out. It never sees the means of escape at the top, but persists in trying to find some way out through the sides near the bottom. It will seek a way where none exists, until it completely destroys itself.

In many ways, there are lots of people like the buzzard, the bat and the bee. They are struggling about with all their problems and frustrations, not realizing that the answer is right above them. Look for solutions to your problems through your intelligence. That is how you will improve your personality.

TOXIC PERSONALITIES

In life one has to proceed ahead and be a party of the improving and growing process. This positive approach is often retarded by personality traits that are negatively poised. They impede growth and can be avoided. Here are some examples of these toxic personalities that you will find in people around you. They should be avoided and so too their personality traits:

MANIPULATIVE:

They are experts in manipulative tactics. In fact, we realize that we have been manipulated when t is too late. Those who are manipulative know what our operative buttons are and push them to get what they want.

NARCISSIST:

They have extreme sense of self-improvement and believe that the world revolves around them. They tend to be a bit overt against getting their needs met. They are toxic because they are solely focused on their need saving your needs in the dust. They zap your energy by getting you to focus so much on them that you have nothing left for yourself.

DOWNERS:

They cannot appreciate the positive in life. They are toxic because they take the joy out of everything. Before you become aware, the negativity of such people consumes you and you start looking at things with grey coloured glasses.

JUDGMENTAL:

They are much like the 'Downers', spending a lot of time with them can inadvertently convert you into a judgmental person as well.

DREAM KILLERS:

Every time you have an idea, these 'dream killers' will tell you that it cannot be done and you shall not be able to do it. As you improve and achieve, they will try to pull you down. They are stuck in the mould of 'what is' instead of 'what you could be'.

INSINCERE:

They are not sincere or genuine in anything. They build their relationship on superficial criteria, leading to shallow and meaningless relationships. When you need a friend, they will not be there. They would rather see you fail or make a fool of yourself.

DISRESPECTFUL:

They are grown up bullies. They have no sense of boundaries and do not respect your feelings. They will cause you to feel frustrated and disrespectful.

NEVER-ENOUGHERS:

You can never give enough to these people to make them happy. They take you for granted. You spend so much time trying to please them that you will end up losing yourself in the process. They will wear you out.

The Quran also identifies such personalities as mischief mongers who never accept the truth and are always selfish hypocritical and mean.

The Quran refers to such people and says:

'And when they are told, 'Do not spend mischief on earth', they say 'We are only trying to make peace'.(2:11)

'These are those who purchase error at the price of guidance; but their bargain brings them no gain, nor have they found guidance elsewhere' (2:16).

'Do not urge other people to be pious and forget yourself to practise it' (2:44).

The toxic persons do not believe in the Divine Guidance. They have their own standard of right and wrong and always try to mislead others. The Quran terms such people as followers of Satan. They influence only liars and sinners (26:211)

Our good sense demands that we should not only understand such people, but also to try and counsel them in convincing terms or leave them alone.:

'Only Allah knows what is their hearts. it is better to leave them alone, and speak to them and counsel them with eloquent words that would touch their hearts'(4:63).

Such persons do not grow or improve in life. Their weakness provides Satan ample opportunities to influence them. The Quran is very explicit in this respect and points out:

'And (O Muhammad) relate to them the story of the person whom We had given knowledge of Our Revelation, but he turned away from their observance, and Satan pursued him, and he strayed like many others into grievous error' (7:175).

SELF IMPROVEMENT

There was a young painter who had just completed his painting under the guidance of a master painter. He decided to assess his skills. He took his painting and displayed it on a busy street crossing. Below the painting he placed a board which read: 'I have painted this piece. Since I am new to this profession I might have some mistakes in my strokes etc. Please put a cross wherever you see a mistake'

When he came back in the evening, he was completely shattered to see that the whole canvas was filled with crosses. The painter returned to his Master and said that he could never become a painter and that people had totally rejected him.

The master smiled and assured his student that he was a great painter. The young painter said, "I have lost faith in my abilities and don't think I am good enough. Don't give me false hopes." The Master asked him to paint an exactly similar painting. The young painter reluctantly agreed and after three days presented a replica of his earlier painting. The Master took him and the painting to the same street corner and placed it with another board that read: 'I have painted this piece. Since I am new to this profession, I might have committed some mistakes in my strokes etc. I have put a box with colours and brushes just below. Please do me a favor, if you see a mistake kindly pick up the brush and correct it.'

They both came back in the evening and were surprised that not a single correction

had been done on the painting. The painting was there for a month but no corrections came in.

It is easier to criticize, but difficult to improve. Your improvement lies in your own hard work, proper guidance and belief in yourself.

Choose rightness and justice over ease and convenience. It will give you pride and peace. Listen to the little voice inside you. It will guide and tell you to do the right thing. Start each day with a commitment to do what is right. With every sunrise comes new opportunities. Make the most of it.

'That man can have nothing but what he strives for' (53:39)

THE WINDOW THROUGH WHICH WE LOOK

A young couple moved into a new neighbourhood. The next morning, while they were having their breakfast, the young woman saw her neighbour hanging out the washing." The laundry is not very clean", she said." She doesn't know how to wash properly; perhaps she needs a better laundry soap." Her husband looked on but remained silent.

Every time her neighbour would hang her wash to dry, the young woman would make the same comments. About a month later, the woman was surprised to see a nice, clean wash on the line and said, to her husband," Look she has learned how to wash properly, wonder who taught her this.?"

The husband said," I got up early this morning and cleaned our windows."

The story makes the point that we are always looking for faults in others and never bother to look at our own shortcomings. Such an attitude will never yield positive results.

WHAT DOES SUCCESS MEAN ?

Most of us believe that success equals some form of achievement in the world. For many it's not the achievement but the recognition and the applause that they crave. For others it's not the arrival but the journey that generates the satisfaction of success.

At some stage in all our lives there's a good chance we will each stop and consider the question, "What does success mean to me?", even if it's only for a few fleeting minutes!

However, if we don't contemplate this question deeply then it's likely we will blindly follow others ideas and measures of success, usually learned in childhood, craved in youth and pursued into our adult years.

How do you define success? Is it simply the completion of the next task, another job well done, a promise kept, an exam passed, a medal won, a mountain climbed, a target hit, a happy family raised or the leaving of a legacy that ensures you will be remembered long after you have gone? If you were to follow the predominant mindset in the world today then success would likely be measured by acquisition. The more you have the more successful you are.

More can be almost any quantity – objects, money, properties, trophies, celebrity, fame, fans. And in terms of position, it simply means higher.

So what does it mean to be successful? At what level, in what context and by whose standards?

If you were to give yourself some time to live in this question you would likely arrive at the fairly obvious insight that, at the deepest level, success in life is not a material thing, it is not something that can be possessed, or won, or even attracted! It is a state of being. Some call it contentment, or happiness, or even peace.

ACADEMIC Success:

Intellectual prowess tends to be the way this kind of success is achieved, coupled with rather a good memory, naturally! It can easily result in an 'I know the most and the best' attitude; a closed and narrow mindset that tends to characterize the 'specialist' and the 'expert'

SCIENTIFIC Success:

New theories, new dimensions of old theories, inventions of new technologies, the creation of new procedures, making fresh discoveries, all carry the 'success kitemark' in the scientific arena. Scientific success certainly dominates our world today, but at what price we now ask, as we live increasingly isolated and technologically dependent lives.

POLITICAL Success:

It tends to be measured by the acquisition of position and power, though much 'lip service' is given to the notion of public service. And while the intentions towards the upliftment of society are authentic and worthy we now know success in this arena is fragile and crumbles easily and can often be easily corrupted.

MATERIAL Success:

It tends to be the main objective of most of us. It is measured in terms of wealth that includes money, property, gold, salary and other material objects that we come across in our daily lives. Like matter, this kind of success is not permanent and is responsible for the many ills that we see around us.

That's not to say that success in any of the above arenas is not worth pursuing. But there is value in considering how success is both viewed, defined and achieved in each context.

INNER Success

When we do take some time out and reflect on what exactly is personal success is we may notice a deepening of our awareness. We may realize that personal success comes in ways that we seldom recognize as signs of success!

Inner success looks and feels more like the capability:

- To act with total honesty and integrity thus generating a clear conscience without which the authentic happiness that we call contentment is impossible
- To remain peaceful and stable when all around you are in crisis or chaos
- To value what you are more than what you have
- To accept full responsibility for all thoughts, feelings, words and actions
- To be able to see past the weaknesses/mistakes of others and focus on their inherent goodness/strengths
- To be able to let go of the past
- To give without the desire for anything in return

    1. Any success that is dependent on public recognition and acclaim will inevitably lead to insecurity and eventual depression, as do all forms of dependency.
    2. When success is defined by an end product, an outcome, or some final achievement, then life tends to be a continuous struggling and striving to 'get there'. Our happiness is continuously delayed. In other words, not such a joy filled journey!
    3. If success is defined by the acquisition or accumulation of anything then fear will always be lurking in the background. Fear of failure which is the same as the fear of loss. Stress will be our companion.

- No matter which way you look at it success is a very personal issue. It tends to be shrouded in many illusions and delusions, depending on our upbringing.

'Time and age are witness. Man is certainly in loss except those who believe and do good and enjoin truth on one another to bear with fortitude' (103:1,2,3,)

IMPORTANCE OF TIME UTILIZATION:

If you had a bank that credited your account each morning with a large sum of money—with no balance carried from day to day—what would you do? Well, you do have such a bank...time.

Every morning it credits you with 86,400 seconds. Every night it rules off as "lost" whatever you have failed to use toward good purposes. It carries over no balances and allows no overdrafts. You can't hoard it, save it, store it, loan it or invest it. You can only use it—time.

Here's a story that drives the point home.

American Arthur Berry was described by Time of USA, as "the slickest second-story man in the East," truly one of the most famous jewel thieves of all times. In his years of crime, he committed as many as 150 burglaries and stole jewels valued between $5 and $10 million. He seldom robbed from anyone not listed in the Social Register and often did his work in a tuxedo. On an occasion or two, when caught in the act of a crime by a victim, he charmed his way out of being reported to the police.

Like most people who engage in a life of crime, he was eventually caught, convicted and served 25 years in prison for his crimes. Following his release, he worked as a counterman in a roadside restaurant on the East Coast for $50 a week.

A newspaper reporter found him and interviewed him about his life. After telling about the thrilling episodes of his life he came to the conclusion of the interview saying, "I am not good at morals. But early in my life I was intelligent and clever, and I got along well with people. I think I could have made something of my life, but I didn't. So when you write the story of my life, when you tell people about all the burglaries, don't leave out the biggest one of all... Don't just tell them I robbed Jesse Livermore, the Wall Street baron or the cousin of the king of England. You tell them Arthur Berry robbed Arthur Berry."

Here are six terrific truths about time:

First: Nobody can manage time. But you can manage those things that take up your time.

Second: Time is expensive. As a matter of fact, 80 percent of our day is spent on those things or those people that only bring us two percent of our results.

Third: Time is perishable. It cannot be saved for later use.

Fourth: Time is measurable. Everybody has the same amount of time...pauper or king. It is not how much time you have; it is how much you use.

Fifth: Time is irreplaceable. We never make back time once it is gone.

Sixth: Time is a priority. You have enough time for anything in the world, so long as it ranks high enough among your priorities.

Ten Proven Time Management Skills Everyone Should Learn

How well do you manage your time? If you are like many of us, your answer may be "Not too well." You may often feel like there is not enough time in a day. Perhaps you even find you constantly have to work late hours to hit your deadlines. Maybe you even feel too busy that you miss meals and sleep. These are all classic signs that you may not be managing your time effectively.

Benjamin Franklin once said that time is money. Just like money, time must be managed properly. If you manage time properly you find the right balance between your work, leisure and rest time. You effectively accomplish the things that matter most in your life. On top of that, you reduce your stress level and feel a lot happier. To help you manage time more effectively, here are ten proven time management skills you should learn today.

1) Set Goals

Goals give you a vision, focus and destination to work towards. They help you have a clear mind on where you want to go and how best to manage your time and resources to get there. By setting goals, you are able to identify what's worth spending your time on and what's a distraction to avoid.

Start by asking yourself where you want to be in six months time. You can go further and look at where you want to be in the next year or even decade from now. Set personal and professional goals that are realistic and achievable. This is a crucial step toward ensure you manage your time better.

2) Prioritize

Prioritizing cannot be overemphasized when it comes to effective time management. It can be difficult to know what tasks to tackle first, especially when a flood of tasks all seem urgent. It is, however, relatively easy to prioritize activities if you have clear goals already set. Ask yourself three basic questions to know what tasks should take first priority:

- Why am I doing this task or activity?
- How does this task help me achieve my goals?
- To what extent does this task I'm doing help me achieve my goals?

Do the most important things first.

3) Keep a Task List

A task list (or "to-do list") is a reminder system that tells you when you need to do what. Keeping a to-do list helps you remain organized and on top of things. It helps break things down into small, manageable tasks or steps so that you never forget to do the important stuff. Don't try to remember everything you need to do in your head. In most cases, trying to remember everything won't work. Instead, keep a to-do list. A simple daily, weekly or monthly planner on a note pad or diary can do.

Write down the things you need to do, including meetings, appointments and deadlines. Prioritize items on your list by listing items in order of importance from high priority to low priority items or highlighting urgent or important tasks on your list with an asterisk. Cross out completed tasks as often as you add new tasks on your task list to ensure you keep moving forward.

4) Schedule Tasks

"A schedule defends from chaos and whim," says author Annie Dillard. If you are a morning person and find you are at your most creative and productive early in the morning, schedule high-value tasks in the morning at your peak creative/productive time. If your creativity and energy picks up when the sun is setting, schedule high priority tasks then. Your "down" time can be scheduled for less important tasks like checking e-mail or returning phone calls.

Understand your rhythm of peak and dead times and schedule tasks appropriately to make the most of peak times. Remember you don't find time for important things; you make time for important things best by scheduling.

5) Focus on One Task at a Time

You get more done in the least time possible when you toggle between talking on your cell phone, browsing the internet and jotting down notes, right? Wrong! According to a study published by the American Psychological Association, you actually spend between 20 and 40 percent more time when you multitask. Besides costing you time and efficiency, multitasking can also reduce the quality of your work.

Forget multitasking. You don't get on top of your workload by multitasking. Focus more on completing one task at a time. Completing tasks in sequence one at a time leads to better use of time, says the study researchers. Switching from one task to another does not usually lend itself to good use of time.

6) Minimize Distractions

Whether it's client e-mail alerts, phone calls from friends or IM chats with prospects while working, distractions are a hindrance to effective use of time. Distractions break your concentration, lower your productivity and often prevent you from completing important tasks on time. They can also cause stress.

Identify what is distracting you from doing core tasks and put a stop to it. Kill that television and turn off your Internet connection and IM chat. Put up a "Do not disturb" or similar sign at the entrance of your dedicated work space to prevent interruptions. Just do whatever it takes to minimize distractions. This ensures you take control of your days and maximizes your productivity.

7) Overcome Procrastination

Edward Young, the English poet best remembered for Night Thoughts, once said procrastination is the thief of time. Don't put off tasks that you should be focusing on right now and let procrastination steal your time. Remind yourself that the best time to do something is usually NOW. Push yourself a little harder to beat procrastination and get what needs to be done DONE.

An effective strategy to beat procrastination is to tell yourself you are only going to embark on a project for a few minutes, say ten minutes. Once you start the project, your creative juices will start flowing. You will then find you want to continue with the task and quite possibly take it to the end. The trick to beat procrastination can be as simple as devoting a small amount of time to start. Just that!

8) Take Breaks

Unless you are Superman, you can't sustain working long hours on end without burning out and sacrificing on quality. However tempting it may be to work to a deadline for 8-10 hours straight, take breaks in between work. This way you give your brain valuable time to rest and recharge. Taking breaks from work is not time wasting. It is smart time management. You produce top quality work when you are well rested.

Squeeze short breaks in between work for down-time. Ideally, take a five minute break every hour or two to rest and think creatively. You may set an alarm to remind you when your break is due. Stop working and just sit and meditate at your desk or go out for a cup of coffee or short walk. Don't forget to give yourself ample time for lunch too. You can't work optimally on an empty stomach.

9) Say "No"

One skill that many high achievers like President Obama, Bill Gates and Richard Branson have mastered is the gentle art of saying "no" to things that are not a priority. Saying "no" to things that are not a priority allows you to focus on those things that are really important. You only have exactly 24 hours in a day to do the things that matter. If you don't learn to say "no" to things that are not important, other peoples' priorities will precede your own and you will be swamped with far too many projects and commitments.

Say "no" amicably to everything that doesn't support your values or help you achieve your goals. You have the right to say "no" no matter who you are talking to. When you get better at saying "no," you put you time to good use and defend yourself from rushed work, poor performance and work overload.

10) Delegate Tasks

The old adage by 17th century author John Donne that no one is an island still holds true today. You can't manage everything on your own. Sometimes it is prudent to let other people help you with tasks, especially when you are swamped. You save time, reduce stress and accomplish a lot more when you assign tasks to the right people.

Relinquish your grip on the wheel and grant authority with responsibility to qualified people. Delegating is not dumping. Give tasks with consequences. This way you promote accountability and ensure goals and deadlines are met.

SLOW DEATH:

Life is a living process which comes to a halt with death. There are many ways of living and a person who has no desire to improve his self is actually in the process of dying slowly.

A person dies slowly when:

- He does not travel.
- He does not read.
- He does not listen to music
- He does not enjoy himself
- He destroys his self-esteem.
- He refuses to help others.
- He becomes a slave of his habits, repeating the same trajectory of life every single day.
- He has no friends.
- He does not admire nature.
- He does not keep himself clean
- He refuses to converse with whom he does not know.
- He is afraid of passions and emotions, the kind that will return light to the eyes and a broken heart.
- He does not dream.
- He does not pursue his dreams and goals
- He has no respect for humanity
- He never smiles
- He will not even once take a chance.
- This slow death can be avoided by a positive approach and a strong conviction in self-improvement. If such a person really wants to come out of his shell and grow, he should:
- Strike a balance between seriousness and laughter.
- Should stick to the truth no matter what happens
- Should realize that falsehoods are like wandering ghosts that consume those who give no importance to truth

- Forgive your enemies as part of the price you pay for the privilege of being forgiven
- Spend some time outside enjoying nature. Walk, get lots of fresh air and sunshine and rain.
- Talk over your troubles, mistakes, dreams, suspicions and doubts with someone you trust
- Give time to prayers, read, understand and practically apply the Quran in your life.
- Respect and interact with people around you
- Start loving children, relatives, friends and the life that Allah has given you.
- Love everything except money, power, lust and greed.

The greatest response that we should give is to 'Allah and His Messenger ﷺ for that response gives life'(8:24)

'Those who proclaim the truth and believe in it are indeed the righteous people. They shall have from their Nourisher (Rabb) all that they desire. That is how the righteous shall be compensated for their good deeds' (39:33,34)

Unless you try to do something beyond what you have already mastered, you will never grow. Self-improvement and growth are also the basis of happiness. True happiness is neither virtue nor pleasure, nor this thing nor that; but simply growth. We are happy when we are improving and growing.

28 SELFLESSNESS AND SACRIFICING SPIRIT

'The fire of punishment shall not touch a person who gives his wealth so that his self may develop' (92:18)

Almost every sinful action ever committed can be traced back to a selfish motive. It is a trait we hate in others but justify in ourselves. (G. Rubin)

SELFLESSNESS

Selflessness is the quality in a person that makes him sacrifice his own interest for the greater good. A selfless person gives preference to the needs of others rather than his own.

The Quran praises those who prefer others before themselves although they themselves are poor. This is the Islamic spirit of selflessness and sacrifice. Allah promises prosperity for such people and we know for sure that Allah's promise is always fulfilled.

CHILDREN AND PARENTS

Young people, especially children are more happy with responsibilities lesser than their parents and elders. They grow up in the company of those who guide them on the path of life. Foremost among them are the parents who selflessly sacrifice almost everything they have to ensure that their children lead a good and successful life. While growing up the children need to see, understand and learn the value of selflessness and the spirit of sacrifice. One day they too will become parents and have to contribute positively in the cycle of life. It is also true that everybody does not have this spirit and that is why we see so much suffering in the world.

'Treat kindly your parents, relatives, orphans and those who have been left alone in society' (4:36)

SPIRIT OF SACRIFICE

You need to be large-hearted, helpful, incorruptible and charitable to acquire the virtues of selflessness and sacrifice in your character. There is no limit to the good you can do in this world, if you do not care who gets the credit. Do not be like those who deny others everything, but refuse themselves nothing.

Selflessness and the spirit of sacrifice do not mean that you should forget or ignore yourself or your family. In Islam everything has to be done in moderation:

'Do not chain your hands to your necks (do not be miserly) and render yourself blameworthy, nor spend recklessly as to exhaust your own substance and become a destitute yourself' (17:29).

Islam wants its followers to lead a normal life with all its frequent trials and tribulations. At the same time, it demands that all Divine Commandments be observed in their true spirit. Muhammad ﷺ set a personal example of normal life and urged the followers to do the same. At times he strained the over-zealous followers urging them to be ,moderate in worship and good deeds.

You must have seen a batsman in a cricket match sacrificing his wicket by running himself out so that his partner on the other end may score more runs or complete his century.

Another example of this spirit is seen when some players in hockey or football matches sacrifice their chance of scoring goals by passing the ball to their teammates who have a better chance of putting the ball in the goal. These examples ultimately lead to success, satisfaction and happiness.

DO NOT FEAR SELFLESSNESS

You don't have to be afraid of selflessness. It does not mean that you cannot enjoy the good things in life. It simply makes you aware that 'enough' is better than 'more than enough' and that the world has enough for everyone's need, but not enough for everyone's greed. It is rightly said that you can make friends in two months by becoming genuinely interested in other people than you can in two years by trying to get other people interested in you.

You have a living role model of selflessness and sacrifice before you in the form of Abdul Sattar Edhi, who has devoted more than 50 years of his life in the service of humanity. He has established, more or less single-handedly, a national and international network of humanitarian services helping destitute orphans, handicapped persons, the sick, hungry drug addicts, mentally ill and animals. He displays a remarkable stamina and energy at the advanced age of seventy-four. He travels extensively and conveys a feeling of being there when needed. This spirit of sacrifice he acquired from his parents. It proves that everyone can be a part of the process of serving humanity and that age is no barrier.

'Everyone has a goal towards which he aims' therefore try to surpass others in good deeds' (2:140).

This is what the grand old man's mission of life is. For such persons the Quran says;

'These will be the people who fulfil their vows, and fear the Day of Judgment, the terror of which would be wide-spread. They feed the destitute, the orphans and the captives, purely for te love of Allah, saying 'We feed you for the sake of Allah alone and do not expect any recompense from you' (76:7,8,9).

SELFISHNESS

Those who are not selfless always think and talk about themselves. You will find them using the personal pronoun "I" very often and will listen eagerly to what people say about them. They will always demand agreement with their views and you will always find them to be suspicious and very sensitive. Such people are selfish and they always grudge against everyone. They never trust anyone and are absolutely unaware of the golden rule that the biggest room in the world is the room for improvement. Anyone wishing to improve his character and personality should avoid these negative traits.

'Do not expect a return for your good behaviour, not even thanks' (76:9)

Our experience tells us that people act from a great variety of motives, greed, anger, lust, love and hate, to name only a few. Sometimes people think only of themselves. At other times they do not think of themselves at all but act from a concern for others.

EXCHANGING GIFTS

A boy and a girl were playing. The boy had a collection of marbles. The girl had some sweets with her. The boy told the girl that he will give her all his marbles in exchange for her sweets. The girl agreed. The boy kept his most beautiful marble aside and gave the rest to the girl. The girl gave all her sweets as she had promised. That night the girl slept peacefully, but the boy couldn't sleep as he kept wondering if the girl had hidden some sweets from him the way he had hidden his best marble.

If you do not give your hundred percent in a relationship, you will always keep doubting if the other person has given his or her hundred percent. This is applicable for any relationship like love, friendship, etc.

Give your hundred percent in whatever you are doing and sleep peacefully.

SPIRIT OF RECONCILIATION

You should stop judging yourself and others for what has happened to you in the past. Playing the 'blame game' never serves anyone least of all yourself. People did what they thought was best at that time; the same way you did. Learn to forgive yourself and others for past mistakes. Harbouring old grudges takes a lot of time and energy that you could be using in more productive ways. Learn how to reconcile, resolve and accept what has happened in the past and know that it has made you a much stronger person. Many of your fears are likely to be groundless, but it is the thinking, attitude and beliefs that cause much of the inappropriate fear.

The Quran reminds us that in life we have to face many ups and downs. This is what makes life worth living. Allah points out:

'We do not burden any human being with more than he is well able to bear and with Us is a record that speaks the truth (about what we do and can do) and none shall be wronged' (23:62).

Our sense of responsibility is not immune to procrastination. We need to guard against 'slow compassion' as we tend to our affairs in daily life.

'You can never attain to true piety unless you spend on others out of what you cherish yourselves, and whatever you spend- verily, Allah has full knowledge thereof' (3:92)

THE APPLE TREE

A long time ago there was an apple tree. A little boy loved to come and play around it

everyday. He used to climb to the treetop, eat the apples and take a nap under the shadow of the tree. Time went by. The little boy had grown up and he no longer played around the tree everyday.

One day the boy came back to the tree and it looked sad.

"Come and play with me." The tree asked the boy.

"I am no longer a kid. I do not play around trees anymore." the boy replied." I want to buy toys. I need money to buy them."

"Sorry, I do not have money, but you can pick all my apples and sell them so you will have money." The boy was excited. He grabbed all the apples on the tree and left happily. The boy never came back after he had picked the apples. The tree was sad. One day, the boy who had turned into a young man, returned and the tree was excited." Come and play with me" said the tree.

"I do not have time to play. I have to work for my family. We need a house for shelter. Can you help me?"

"Sorry, but I do not have any house. But you can chop off my branches to build your house."

So the young man cut all the branches of the tree and left happily.. The tree was glad to see the young man happy, but the man never came back since then. The tree felt lonely and sad again..

One hot summer day, the man returned and the tree was delighted. "Come play with me!" the tree said.

"I am getting old. I want to go sailing to relax myself. Can you give me a boat?" asked the man..

"Use my trunk to build your boat. You can sail far away and be happy."

So the man cut the tree trunk to make a boat. He went smiling and never showed up again for a long time. Finally the man returned after many years.

"Sorry, my boy, but I do not have anything for you anymore. No more apples for you," the tree said.

"No problem. I do not have teeth to bite, I am too old for that now," the man said.

"I cannot give you anything. The only thing left are my dying roots," the tree said with tears.

"I do not need much now, just a place to rest. I am tired after all these years," the man replied.

"Good! Old tree roots are the best place to lean on and rest. Come, come sit down with me and rest."

The man sat down and the tree was glad and smiled with tears.

'In your collective social life make room for others' (58:11)

There are many selfless people around who are symbols of the spirit of sacrifice and love. The best example is that of our parents. No matter what, they will always be there and give everything they could just to see us happy. It is up to us to imbibe this spirit of selflessness and sacrifice and treat our parents with respect, care and love.

OMISSION

It isn't the thing you do,
It's the thing you take undone
That gives you a headache
At setting of the Sun.
The tender word forgotten,
The letter you did not write,
The flowers you did not send,
Are your haunting ghosts at night.

The stone you might have lifted
Out of a brother's way;
The bit of heart some counsel
You were hurried too much to say.
Those little acts of kindness
Those chances to be angels
Which we poor mortals find.

'Show affection and kindness to your parents' (4:36). If one of them or both of them, attain old age in your life-time, never show any sign of disgust to them, nor snub them, but always speak to them gently with kind words' (17:23)

29 SELF-RESPECT AND HONOUR

'He who has more integrity has indeed honour with Allah' (49:13)

Without self-respect there can be no genuine success. Success won at the cost of self-respect and honour is not true success.For what shall it profit a man if he gains the whole world and loses his own honour and self-respect ? (Forbes)

SELF-RESPECT

Self-respect is the regard, esteem and worth that you give to yourself. It is your respect in your own eyes and makes an essential contribution to the life process. Stable and balanced self-respect leads to humility, which by itself is a high quality virtue/goodness. Honour is a feeling of pride that you have when you believe that you are behaving in the best way so that others respect and admire you.

'Certainly Allah loves only such honest people who honour their pledge and abstain from evil, for Allah loves those who follow the right course' (3:76).

Some describe self-respect as conducting oneself in a dignified manner that asserts a claim to deference. In Islam it is considered an ethical virtue of a very high order. Devoid of it, any individual, or an entire society is likely to be treated lightly and of little consequence.

Those who come across un-Islamic concepts, belief and deeds ought to realize that real self-respect can only be achieved by following the Divine Guidance in letter and spirit:

'Those who choose disbelievers for their friends, instead of believers, look for respectability and power from them although respectability and power pertains to Allah' (4:139).

CONCRETE REALITY

Self-respect is the basis of honour and affects not only the individual, but everyone around the person as well. According to a famous thinker, many people deserve their self-respect from love of God, support of family, physical attractiveness, academic excellence and outdoing others in various competitions.

Self-respect is a concrete reality which, develops when a person values moral values that the Quran so vehemently affirms:

'Allah is with those who practise self-restraint, are pious and devout, and do that which is good' (16:128)

The notion of self-respect should not be confused with pride and arrogance. In fact, the Quran is highly critical of haughtiness and vanity. It advises the Muslims not to take much notice of vainglorious, self-complacent and conceited persons, as it is better to pass by with dignity, ignoring the display of vanity and senseless display and ostentation.

Even after the demise of Muhammad ﷺ, his companions showed exemplary courage of conviction and held their heads high. Allah's Messenger Muhammad ﷺ accorded the highest place to the person who fears none but Allah while adopting an honourable and respectable stance in all circumstances.

Beggary, which is the anti-thesis of self-respect has been condemned by Muhammad ﷺ as the best and the most degrading case of human dignity. The Quran points out :

'Alms are for those needy who are engrossed in Allah's service and cannot move about in the land to earn their livelihood whom the ignorant consider free of wants due to their modesty and self-respect. You can know from their faces for they do not solicit from people at all. Whatever alms you give them, Allah surely knows well' (2:273)

RESPECT AND OBEDIENCE

Self-respect also means to listen to your mind, body and feelings all the time and then working hard to achieve goals. It refers to whatever good you have in you. It is also true that there is so much of hatred, violence and crime around that makes respect and honour difficult. Young people have to realize that respect is not the same as obedience. Sometimes you obey because of fear; but true respect is what we feel towards someone who has earned respect through worthy achievements and honourable living. This leads to our own way of achieving goals and honours and the result is the elevation of our self-respect.

THE HONOUR CODE

In a school in America each year students sign an honour code. "I will not lie, cheat or steal; I will respect myself and others". The school teachers want the students to be role models for themselves. Serving others in the community is also part of the education programme as it makes students learn about values that determine the type of people they will be for the rest of their lives.

Self-respect, especially among the youth is shaped by your relationships, experiences and thoughts. Healthy self-respect promotes positive thinking and self-determination. It gives you confidence and you tend to do well at school and college or work. It helps you get rid of hopelessness, loneliness, shame and feelings of worthlessness.

Characteristics of Low Self Esteem:

1. Social withdrawal
2. Anxiety and emotional turmoil
3. Lack of social skills and self confidence.
4. Depression and/or bouts of sadness
5. Less social conformity
6. Eating disorders
7. Inability to accept compliments
8. An Inability to see yourself 'squarely' – to be fair to yourself
9. Accentuating the negative
10. Exaggerated concern over what they imagine other people think
11. Self neglect
12. Treating yourself badly but not other people
13. Worrying whether you have treated others badly
14. Reluctance to take on challenges
15. Reluctance to trust your own opinion
16. Expect little out of life for yourself

Steps to Developing Self-Esteem:

Self-esteem does not just appear out of nowhere; it takes conscious determination, spiritual connection with Allah and emotional balance. You should take one step at a time and build gradually on the quota of your worth.

1) Personal Evaluation

Perform a personal 'Strengths' and 'Weaknesses' analysis. There are always 2 sides to a coin; you cannot be 100% good or 100% bad. So jot down all your worthy habits and characteristics, and also the negative ones. If you're running really low in valuing the good bits about you, have a trusted friend or relative help to point out the good things about you. You can also ask them to point out your faults and flaws. The best references for evaluating yourself are the Islamic values. Once you've reviewed your weaknesses try to get rid of them one by one.

2) Develop a Muslim Psychology

When you are made to feel low about yourself, you can keep your guard up by boosting your faith (Imaan). Islam, is a manifestation of truth, optimism, striving for perfection, and is the secret of personal and community success and happiness.

3) Develop Positive Skills and Habits

Positive self-development and activities can give a major boost in self-esteem. Activities like the recitation of the Quran with translation is a positive step. It will help you to have a better understanding of the values that Quran emphasises.

4) Personal Grooming

Modest dressing and etiquette is sometimes misinterpreted and people end up appearing unkempt or unclean. Islamic values enjoin modest Islamic attire, as well as cleanliness and tidiness.

5) Find Birds of a Feather

Since "birds of a feather flock together", find a supportive peer group. If your gatherings are full of folks that ridicule your beliefs and values, then you are bound to feel worthless. Mingle with the righteous who acknowledge your worth, help you identify your weaknesses, and are indulged in productive and wholesome habits. You can evaluate your gatherings by their activities.

6) Grow From Your Experience

It would all be useless if you learn to value yourself and then forget it at the end of the year! Make a note of how your feeling of self-worth has increased; observe and record the changes in your attitude towards others and towards your life, and also the attitude of others towards you. Your achievements and the changes would keep you motivated.

These steps are just the basics. It is up to you to treat yourself well and discover what uplifts your morale and rebuilds your self-esteem. An important point to remember is that very low self-esteem is corrosive to one's existence because it robs you of happiness and a sense of self-worth. At the same time, too much self-esteem is extremely destructive as it leads to pride, arrogance, and narcissism. Islam distinguishes the most successful living strategies; if you measure your self-worth by Islamic values and not by society, and synchronize your life with your faith, you can overcome the self-esteem deficit soon.

And We have certainly honoured the children of Adam and carried them on the land and sea and provided for them of the good things and preferred them over much of what We have created..." (17:70).

SELF-ASSESSMENT

Allah has honoured you. Dignity is your birthright. It's okay if you're not perfect. No one is. You can still love yourself, with all your special gifts and habits, and whatever is lacking, well, you can work on it. Your self-respect can grow if you are honest, positive, trustworthy, fair, polite, reliable and a good listener. Parents and elders also play an important role in this process by their respectful behaviour, obedience of laws and showing concern for people, animals and the environment. They can also help the young by guiding them to set and achieve goals. Their self-respect will skyrocket when they see themselves achieving those goals. Elders should be aware that the young are quite capable of learning, and becoming considerate, kind-hearted and respectful.

The Almighty bestows honour, respect, authority, security and peace to those who lead their lives in accordance with His directives that are available to us in the Quran as principles of guidance:

'Allah has promised those of you who sincerely believe in Him and do acts of righteousness, that He will surely make them masters in the land as He had made their ancestors before them; that He will certainly establish for them the religion that He has chosen for them; and He will grant them security and peace in place of fear. Let them serve Me and not associate anyone with Me' (24:55)

DUTY OF ELDERS

While it is advisable for the young to have positive goals, elders should also limit their restrictive orders and allow the young to have optimum freedom, especially in the selection of the clothes they wear, the food they eat, the places to visit and other small decisions. The goal is to prepare them to lead an independent family life of their own, without parental control, when they grow up.

Mixing up Ego with Great Qualities

We gather from Quran that ego is the one disastrous idol that believers must fight back and defeat. It seems that in most of the time ego is the foundation for idolizing entities beside God :

Have you seen the person who has taken as his god his [own] desire, and Allah has sent him astray due to knowledge and has set a seal upon his hearing and his heart and put over his vision a veil? So who will guide him after Allah ? Then will you not be reminded?(45:23)

Our ego tends to justify most of the arguments offered by Satan to idolize our opinions, get more attached to our culture, cherish our parents' religion, hesitate to choose rightfully, reject the guidance, refuse to increase our knowledge because we already know it all, and so on. In other words, Satan, his descendants, and his allies rely on our egos to carry out their plan of diverting us from the right path.

We often mix up an arrogant individual with another of a high self esteem. We consider those who are assertive in their views as arrogant ones. We also perceive those whom Allah allows to be in positions of authority as people with inflated egos. All three perceptions when not backed up with knowledge, guidance, and fair analysis, lead us to unjustly draw wrong conclusion and cheat our souls by passing crippled judgments on others. High self esteem, certainty and having leadership qualities are three positive traits when humility guards them. They are totally distinct from ego.

'Have you seen the one whose god is his own ego? Will you be his advocate? [25:44]

Ego is one sign of weakness and hesitance and a negative attribute that we all have by default. Depending on how much ego is able to grow within us, we, wrongly and arrogantly, give ourselves a very distinct status or rank that is totally different from and higher than others. In other words, it is a negative, exaggerated feeling of false superiority, undeserved pride, and baseless self recognition. A person with an ego would seek the attention, need the fame, be thirsty to brag, talk much and do little, and demand the respect instead of earning it.. This attitude reflects insecurity, fear, uncertainty, and weakness. We can control our ego by understanding and implementing the Quranic directives.

CHAOS IN SOCIETY

If there is chaos, crime, disorder and confusion around us, it means that our society is out of control. People make societies. The Quran admonishes those who are responsible for creating chaos and anarchy:

'Do not corrupt the land by spreading chaos on earth after it had been reformed and set in order, and pray to Him in awe and expectation of His mercy; Allah is always near to those who do good' (7:56).

Thus, every person is individually responsible for this problem. Self-control that ultimately leads to self-respect is at its lowest position. You can contribute a lot by gradually changing this position through respect, tolerance and compassion for others and maintaining your self-respect with honour and dignity. You do not need to put someone down or have a lot of money for self-respect. Those who respect themselves also see selfishness, cowardice, dishonesty and anger as wrong and unworthy of them. As young people grow up they learn the lessons of responsibility and develop a good conscience to guide them. They are also unwilling to be exploited or used by others. Patience or tolerance does not mean allowing others to mistreat you. They neither exploit others nor do they allow others to exploit them. They are conscious of their role in society and live by the principles of the Quran:

'Always be conscious of Allah as much as you can, listen to Him and obey Him and spend in charity for the good of your own selves. And he, who protects himself from his own greed will surely be successful in life and in the hereafter (64:16).

ROLE OF PARENTS

While you should work hard to achieve high standards, you also need to know that failure is no embarrassment when you have done your best. It is not the speed with which you achieve your objectives, but the will and determination to continue working incessantly. A small gesture of love from elders develops a sense of respect among children. So, the next time a child does something good he should be praised and maybe there will be less bad behaviour to cope with.

One of the greatest gifts parents can give their children is a strong sense of personal values. Helping them develop values such as honesty, truth, self-reliance and dependability is as important a part of their education as teaching them to read.

Parents have also been warned that they should be very careful and cautious in dealing with their children and each other:

'O you who believe ! Some among your spouses and among your children are your enemies, so be careful of them. But if you tolerate, overlook and forgive- then behold Allah is Much-Forgiving and Most Gracious' (64:14).

HONOUR

Among the things which are valued, honour holds a very high place even above wealth and power. It is the highest reward one receives for good deeds. To honour someone means to treat them with special attention and respect. Every year sportsmen, soldiers, teachers, students are honoured for their services to the nation. If you achieve good grades in your class, you are honoured by the teachers. It raises your self-respect to a very high level. When someone finds and returns a purse or wallet, it is an honourable act deserving respect and praise. The opposite of honour is dishonour. Soldiers who do not serve their country properly are discharged dishonourably. A student apprehended using unfair means in the examination has no honour. Similarly, those sportsmen who cheat lose their honour and self-respect.

The Quran refers to such persons and considers their acts disgraceful:

'Let them laugh a while, for they will weep much more in return for what they have earned for themselves' (9:82).

Muslims are expected to believe strongly in Allah, His Messengers and the Divine Revelation. The final Revelation being the Quran. The case of those who deny these will rest with Allah and His will deal with them. Even then Allah gives a period of respite to these deniers to mend their ways:

'Then leave Me to deal with them; those who have denied the Revelation. We shall gradually chastise them in a manner they will perceive not. Yes I will give them respite for a while; but My scheme will be subtle and firm' (68:44,45).

A confident and positive mind is capable of achieving any goal in life.

CONFIDENT & POSITIVE ATTITUDE

Paul applied for a new job. He had a low self-esteem and considered himself as a failure and unworthy of success. He was sure that he was not going to get the job. He had a negative attitude towards himself.

His mind was full of doubts and fears about the job before the interview. He was sure that he would be rejected. On the day of the interview he got up late and found that one of his shirts was dirty and the other one needed ironing. As he was getting late, he had no choice but to wear the wrinkled shirt. During the interview he was tense, displayed a negative attitude and showed lack of confidence. This overall behaviour left a bad impression and consequently he did not get the job.

Jim applied for the same job, but approached the matter in a different way. He had a positive attitude and was sure that he would get the job. The evening before the interview he prepared the clothes he was going to wear and went to sleep a little earlier than usual. On the day of the interview he got up early and had ample time to have a good breakfast, dress properly and then to arrive for the interview before the scheduled time.

He got the job because he made a good impression. He had also, of course, the proper qualifications for the job, but so had Paul.

This shows that confidence and positive attitude leads to more energy, pleasant feelings and constructive approach. Your body language shows the way you feel inside. Those who make everything that leads to happiness depend upon themselves, and not upon other men. They are the ones who have adopted the very best plan for living happily.

If you are a self respecting person, you will take care to maintain your reputation and image. You will also learn not to be dependent on others.

Self-esteem also involves having confidence in one's abilities. This is very important as it leads to progress in life. It makes you aware of your hidden abilities and unlocks many doors of opportunities. If you believe in yourself, the world will believe in you. Everything that happens to us , and every choice we make, is a reflection of what we believe about ourselves. We cannot out-perform our level of self-esteem. We cannot draw to ourselves more than we believe we are worth. The things we believe and say about ourselves come back to us in many ways. Self-motivation comes from self-knowledge. We must inspire ourselves by believing that we have the power to accomplish we set out to do. We must put faith in the ability to use our abilities to the maximum for our benefit and the benefit of those around us.

You need to be aware of the opportunities that you can avail with your confidence. Similarly you need to be aware of the threats that would follow once you lose your self-respect and honour. Once you lose your image and become overly dependent on others, people start taking you for granted. This ultimately affects your social life adversely.

Sometimes compromises have to be made in one's life and this goes for self-esteem as well; for example, a crude remark or comment from an elder may hurt your self-esteem and you may feel a strong urge to fight for it. You have to control yourself in such situations because respect and love of your family member is more important than your angry reaction.

Islam emphasizes control of tongue for there are veils which flow from its uncontrolled use like vain talk, backbiting, flattery, falsehood, name-calling etc. At times, remaining silent is the best option. The other option is to be polite and courteous (2:83). At another place (31:19) we have been asked to keep our voices low as the most repulsive voice is that of the donkey.

'Do not walk in the footsteps of Satan, your acknowledged enemy' (2:168)

30 SENSE OF HUMOUR

'Allah created you, then formed your symmetry, and then gave you right (balanced) proportion' (82:7)
'Indeed the companions of Paradise, that Day, will be amused in joyful occupation' (36:55)

Humour is a great thing, the saving thing after all. The minute it crops up, all our hardnesses yield; all our irritations and resentments flit away, and a sunny spirit takes its place. (Mark Twain)

Humour is the ability to perceive, enjoy or express what is amusing, comical and funny. This quality is an important part of your character and personality. If it is balanced, then it is said that you have a sense of humour. It is the ability in you to amuse others and be amused by them. It is also a source of laughter, happiness and enjoyment.

'The Quran says that the inhabitants of paradise would be joyful and rejoicing in a state of brightness and joy:

Enter Paradise, you and your kinds, delighted.'(43:70)

'Faces, that Day, will show pleasure.'(88:8) 'Enjoying what their Lord has given them, and their Lord protected them from the punishment of Hellfire.'(52:18)

'And as for those who had believed and done righteous deeds, they will be in a garden [of Paradise], delighted.'(30:15).

JOYS OF LIFE

There cannot be any happiness, joy or laughter in life unless we have a sense of humour. In our times the sight of a pleasant and smiling face is somewhat of a rarity. In the mosques, sermonizers rarely look happy or pleased. That is why they fail in uplifting the spirits of those who listen to them.

'Cultivate tolerance, enjoin justice, and avoid the fools' (7:199)

JOKES AND HUMOROUS INCIDENTS

The opposite of humour is depression, sadness and seriousness. Jokes, interesting anecdotes, ironical statements, witty remarks and riddles show a man's sense of humour.

The Internet has many resources where new jokes and humorous incidents are available every day. Internet users visit these sites for their daily dose of humour and enjoyment.

A joke is a short story or ironic depiction of a situation meant to be humorous. Jokes show your sense of humour. The desired response is generally laughter. When this does not happen, the joke is said to have fallen flat or the listeners do not have a sense of humour.

Gentle and angelic qualities of joy, laughter and sweetness, best reflected in the blessed Messenger of Allah ﷺ are in sharp contrast with the severity, heartaches and bitterness that we see around us in religious sermons and congregations. According to a tradition there was no one who smiled more and beautifully than the exalted Messenger ﷺ.

DO NOT MAKE FUN OF OTHERS

'O you who believe ! Men should not laugh at other men, for it may be that they are better than them; and women should not laugh at other women, for they may be better than them. Do not slander anyone, nor give one another nick-names. After believing, it is bad to give another bad name. Those who do not repent behave wickedly' (49:11)

This quality does not permit you to make fun of others or ridicule them. This hurts others and is an undesirable act. Humour is meant to ease uncomfortable situations and not to create an unfavourable and nasty atmosphere.

A good sense of humour also means that you should have the ability to laugh at yourself and situations around you. At times people are afraid to look silly in front of others. They shirk from the fear of giving the impression to be foolish. It is necessary to know that all people make mistakes and it is when you have a pleasant smile that makes these mistakes appear human. Laughter is the shortest distance between two people.

President Abraham Lincoln of USA, who had a great sense of humour, was accused of being two-faced, a kind of person who criticizes someone when that person is absent, but is pleasant to the same person when he is present.

Lincoln said, "If I had two faces, do you think this is the one I'd be wearing?"

THE RIGHT MOMENT

Do not throw away your chances to be happy because you did not succeed on the first attempt. The art of happiness lies in the power of extracting happiness from common things.

Laughter and humorous remarks must wait for the right moment. You can learn to be more humorous than you are. Above all be someone who appreciates humour. Try not to make someone feel bad when you do not find them funny. Creating humour such as jokes and witty remarks is a valuable skill. While humour comes naturally to some people, others must learn to be humorous.

GENTLE HUMOUR

Humour and kindness played a significant role in the spread of Islam. The fourth Caliph Hazrat Ali (RA) said,'Minds get tired, as do bodies, so treat them with humour'.

It is reported that the Muhammad ﷺ was asked by his companions : "You are joking with us." He said, "But I never say anything but the truth."

The companions (Sahabah) took the same approach to humour. There are many delightful reports about the jokes exchanged between the Prophet and the Sahabah.

There are a few reported incidents of the Messenger ﷺ joking or appreciating a humorous incident. 'Usman will enter paradise laughing because he made me laugh', said the Messenger ﷺ. He had seen the third caliph Usman (RA) eating dates while one of his eyes was afflicted and remarked,'What ? Eating dates when your eye is afflicted?' Usman (RA) answered, 'I am eating from the other side'. The Messenger ﷺ laughed heartily.

Those who have this sense are always cheerful. To them each day is sunny. Should dark clouds appear, they depend upon laughter and remain confident that all problems will pass. Those who cannot laugh at themselves, will allow others to laugh at them.

Imam Abu Hanifa advised his student Yusuf Ibn-e-Khalid, 'Show affection to people as much as possible and greet even blameworthy people. Do not rush to disagree. Be friendly with those who disagree with you, joke with them sometimes and chat with them. Love a sense of humour and gentle attitude encourages people' .

THE OLD STUDENT

Henry's first day in college was quite interesting. He was young, enthusiastic and full of hope. In the classroom he met a lady sitting next to him. She was old and wrinkled, but very friendly. She said, "My name is Rose. I am 87 years old." Henry asked, "Why are you in a college at this age?"

"I always dreamed of having a college education and now I am getting one!" she replied. They became good friends. Henry always enjoyed listening to her wisdom and experience. Rose made friends with most of the students and became very popular on the campus. At the end of the semester she delivered a speech about her life's experience, "We do not stop playing because we are old; we grow old because we stop playing". The key to success and staying young is to laugh and find humour every day.

We have so many people walking around who are dead and don't even know it. There is a great difference between getting old and growing up. Anybody can grow old. That does not take any talent or ability. The idea is to grow by always finding opportunity in change. Have no regrets. The elderly don't have regrets for what we did, but rather for things we did not do."

At the year end, Rose finished the college degree she had begun all those years ago. One week after graduation she died peacefully in her sleep. Over 2000 college students attended her funeral in tribute to the wonderful woman who had a good sense of humour and taught by example that it is never too late to be all you can possibly be.

The true story not only speaks about the old lady's sense of humour and wisdom, it also teaches us that we make a living by what we do not have, but we make a life by what we give.

HUMOUR AND GOOD LIFE

If you can take a joke, it will encourage your humility and courage that are needed to take off your mask of insecurity. Humour is a part of the art of leadership of getting along with people and of getting things done. It gives a new meaning to life and human relationships. According to a recent medical survey, ten minutes of laughter resulted in two hours of pain-free sleep for many patients. So, when you feel that you do not laugh as much as you should, associate yourself with happy people and go to pleasant places.

The Quran says, 'Those who are destined for paradise shall on that day have joy in whatever they do' (36:55)

TWO HEADS

A man from Shiraz met a scholar from Damascus at a public bath. Noting that the scholar was balding, the Shirazee upturned a brass vessel and pointing to its rounded shining base said,

'How is it that all of you Damascans have heads like this?"

The Scholar took the vessel from the man, upturned it and pointing its empty cavity said, "How is it that all Shirazees have heads like this?"

Humour acts both as cause and effect of hope. Your cheerful approach will see more humour in everyday life than a sad, serious and gloomy person. You can spot small, fun-filled situations and enjoy them. You can also look at your shortcomings with amusement. Most humour sees old things from unexpected angles.

The careful use of humour can work positively in a relationship where encouragement is required. A mother used it effectively when she found that her son was delaying the repair of the lawn mower. He had promised to fix it. The grass grew taller and thicker while he carelessly delayed repairing the machine. Then one day he came home and found his mother seated on the lawn cutting the grass with a small pair of sewing scissors, one blade at a time. "Mother", he said, "When you finish cutting the grass would you mind sweeping the side walk with a tooth brush?"

They both laughed and more important, the mower was fixed. So, be polite and respectful. It is more about how you say it than what you say. People respond best when they are valued and respected. Do not laugh at them, but with them.

'O you who believe ! Obey the commands of Allah and say straightforward things' (33:70)

It is said that if your friend is without a smile, give him one of yours. You make life more beautiful and liveable by your smile and sense of humour. Use this good quality as a key for making others happy. Moreover, your look will also improve. A smile does not cost anything.

THE WORRY-MAN

The residents of a town decided that there was no point in all of them worrying about their various problems.

"Let us appoint a Worry Man, somebody who will worry for all of us." Said the mayor. Everybody hailed it as a great idea and when one of the elders suggested that Yamin the cobbler, who seemed to have a lot of time on his hands should be given the job, the man was at once sent for. "How much will I be paid?" asked Yamin. "One gold sovereign a week," said the mayor.

"It won't work." said Yamin. "Why not?' asked the Mayor. "Because if you give me one gold sovereign a week, I will have nothing to worry about."

Wit is an important part of humour and reflects your intellectual capacities, your alertness and sense of quick reasoning.

PERFECT REMEDY

We respect a person who has a sense of humour because we feel that such a person can control a difficult situation.

If something goes terribly wrong and you can find humour in it, the inference is that you can handle the situation. You can turn a painful situation around through laughter. So improve upon your sense of humour as it is a tranquillizer without any side effects.

31 SOCIAL AND FRIENDLY

And when you are greeted with a greeting, then greet with one fairer or repeat the same' (4:86)

A friend is one that knows who you are,
Understands where you have been,
Accepts what you have become,
And still gently allows you to grow. (Shakespeare)

SOCIAL VALUES

Man lives in a society among human beings. This means that he cannot live without relationships. Islamic values give top priority to human relationships as it forms the core of an individual's and society's development and progress. These interactions take the shape of traditions, customs and social norms. Unless we are social and friendly it will not be possible to have a happy and satisfied nation.

Islam holds that this world has been created for man and everything in the world has been made subservient to him. Many virtues rest on social values such as kindness, feeding the hungry, keeping promises, helping others and being friendly. The 'best man' according to Muhammad ﷺ 'is the one from whom good accrues to others'. The Quran declares that those who believe in its guidance are protectors of each other:

'The believers, man and women, are protectors of one another, they enjoin what is good and forbid what is evil' (9:71).

The Muslim who truly understands the teachings of his religion is gentle, friendly and likeable. He mixes with people and gets along with them. This is something which should be a characteristic of the Muslim who understands that keeping in touch with people and earning their trust is one of the most important duties of the Muslim. It is an effective means of conveying the message of truth to them, and exposing them to its moral values, because people only listen to those whom they like, trust and accept.

THE BEST EXAMPLE

Muhammad ﷺ set the highest example of good behaviour towards people. He was skilful in softening their hearts and called them to follow him in words and deeds. He demonstrated how to reach people's hearts and win their love and admiration. He was always cheerful and easy-going, never harsh. When he came to any gathering, he would sit wherever there was a free space, and he told others to do likewise. He treated everyone equally, so that no one who was present in a gathering would feel that anyone else was receiving preferential treatment. There are three things that he never did to people: he never criticized anyone, he never said "Shame on you!" to anyone, and he never looked for anyone's faults. He would be patient with a stranger who might be harsh in his requests or questions, and his Companions would ask the stranger to speak gently. He said, "If you see someone in need, then help him." He never accepted praise except from someone who was thanking him for a favour, and he never cut off anyone who was speaking; he would wait until the person indicated that he had finished, or stood up.

'And turn not your cheek away in pride from people and walk not haughtily on earth, for behold Allah does not love anyone, who, out of self-conceit,act in a boastful manner' (31:18)

The concept of being social and friendly is not confined to Muslims alone; it extends to the entire humanity. Islam fully recognizes the fact that the world at large belongs to both Muslims and non-Muslims and also regards the entire creation of Allah as one family :

'All mankind were once but one single community, and only later did they begin to hold divergent views' (10:19) 'Allah has bestowed dignity to all human beings' (17:70).

Muhammad ﷺ once said,' The whole creation is Allah's family and the best of creation is he who is good to his family'.

GOOD FRIEND

Friendly means behaving in a kind way as a friend would behave. True friendship is a gift shared by hearts that care. Some say that the word FRIEND stands for a 'Few Relations in Earth Never Die'.

Not long ago, John answered a telephone call from an old friend he had not heard from for a long time. "Hi! John, I just wanted to see how you were getting along." For whatever reason, their paths had simply not crossed for months. He felt nice to talk to his friend. He wondered why they had not kept in touch.

At the end of the conversation his friend said, "If you need me in any way, I'll be happy to help you out", and he meant it. That call came at the right moment, as John needed those words of encouragement. He hung up the phone feeling a satisfying warmth in his heart. That day he learned that life is primarily about people. To love and to know that we are loved is the greatest happiness in life. Happiness is something that is in short supply for many of us. John's friend reminded him that it is never enough to just love; we must express it as well.

RADIATE LOVE

Do not keep the alabaster box of your love and friendship sealed up until your near and dear ones are dead. Fill their lives with sweetness. Say the kind things you mean to say when they are gone, before they go.

Happiness may be just a phone call away. Life is too short to wake up with regrets. Love the people who treat you right. Forget about the ones who don't. Believe that everything happens for a reason. If you get a second chance, grab it with both hands. If it changes your life, let it.

Whatever we say, the words we use in conversation, always plays a key role in our relationship with others. The right choice of words at the right time shows the love, respect and affection' we have for others.

'And tell My servants that they should speak in the most kindly manner. Surely Satan is always ready to stir up discord between men- for surely Satan is man's open enemy' (4:53)

WORDS ARE WONDERFUL THINGS

Keep a watch on your words,
For words are wonderful things;
They are sweet like the bee's fresh honey,
Like the bees they have terrible stings;
They can bless like the warm, glad sunshine,
And brighten a lonely life;
They can cut, in the strife of anger,
Like an open, two edged knife.

JOYS OF DAILY LIFE

It is not unusual for us to postpone our pleasures and happiness, hoping for a better day to come. Do you place demands on your happiness like I'll be happy when I get the first position in class? Or I'll be happy when I get a new disc player or a pair of jeans? Why put off your happiness for some other day? The real fun in life is the journey and enjoying the present moment. You will be amazed by the joys of daily life.

FAMILY AND FRIENDS

'When you enter the houses, salute the inmates with a greeting in the name of Allah, invoking blessings and good health' (24:61)

'Be good to your parents and relatives and the neighbour from among your own people, and the neighbour who is a stranger, and the friend by your side and the wayfarer, and your servants and subordinates' (4:36)

There is something morally special about family and friends. We do not treat our family and friends as we would treat strangers. We are bound to them by love and affection and we do things for them that we would not for just anybody. But this is not merely a matter of our being nicer to people we like. The nature of our relationship with family and friends is different from our relationship with other people because our duties and responsibilities are different. How could I be your friend and yet not treat you with special consideration? A philosopher once said that no one would choose to live without friends even if he had all other goods. Friendship goes beyond material assistance. We would be lost without friends. Our triumphs would seem hollow unless we have friends to share them, and our failures are made bearable by their understanding. Even our self-esteem depends in large measure on the assurance of friends. By returning our affection they confirm our worthiness as human beings.

TRUE FRIEND

I need to know if you're my true friend
Will you be there by my side until the end ?

Can I tell you my secrets deep ?
And trust them in your heart you will keep

We are neither of us without our flaws
Can you accept mine as I will yours ?

I will be a shoulder to cry on when you are blue
Will you be there for me when I need you ?

No matter how busy, I will make time for you
If you are busy will you make time for me ?

I will take your hand and comfort your tears
Will you hold mine and soothe my fears?

I will give you joy and many warm smiles
Can we share that across many miles ?

I will not forget what is important for you
Will you remember what is important for me too ?

With you, my most favourite things I will share
If only I know do you truly care ?

If you can accept me as I do you
Then I will know you are a friend most true.

RESPECT FRIENDS

Friends should be respected as they can be counted on. Friends stick by one another when the going is hard. They make allowances for one another; they forgive offences and they refrain from harsh judgments. Sometimes a friend will be the only one who can tell hard truths about us.

Good friends are like stars. You do not always see them, but you know they are always there. They overlook your failures and are happy at your success.

'Believing men and women are friends of each other and they do what is right and prohibit what is wrong' (9:71)

POSITIVE QUALITY

People who move around and are active in society are social. It is a positive quality and shows that the person is interested in what is happening around him. He does not lead a lonely life away from people, but actively participates in activities. A social person is also friendly and loving and generally found in the company of friends, relatives and neighbours.

It is very difficult to live in a society and fulfil our needs without social cooperation and association. That is why people are organized in a society as members of associations, groups, institutions, neighbourhoods, and clubs. The study of society is called Sociology.

Islam stresses that all human beings are brethren and parts of the same body. If a part of the body is hurt, the whole body responds to it. Similarly, if a man is subjected to suffering, the entire humanity should rise up to the occasion to relieve him of his sufferings.

HOW TO BE POPULAR

The opposite of social and friendly is unsocial and unfriendly. Such people keep aloof and never mix with friends, relatives and neighbours. Such persons are usually not welcome and ultimately people avoid their company. An unfriendly and unsocial person is not capable of loving anyone. Even his close relatives show no desire to see him around. You must have seen that some of your colleagues are more popular than others. One of the reasons for this popularity is their loving and friendly attitude.

'O you who believe! Avoid suspicion. Some suspicions are indeed sins. So do not pry into others' secrets and do not backbite. Would any of you like to eat a dead brother's flesh ? (49:12)

Young people should be more social and friendly as compared to their elders because they move around a lot and come in contact with people of all ages. This will help them in attaining good manners that provide an effective shield against indiscriminate curiosity, unnecessary intrusiveness and hostile rudeness. This civility has its own rewards.

'Speak unto people in a kindly way' (2:83)

THE DEADLY ENEMIES

The ship was on its way when a severe storm struck the ocean. Despite the best efforts of the ship's crew, it was not possible to save the ship from sinking. Among the passengers were two men who were deadly enemies. They hated each other to the limits. The captain of the ship announced that the ship would soon sink, so everyone should say their prayers and beg for God's forgiveness and mercy. The passengers realizing that their end was near, resorted to prayers. The two passengers were more bothered about each other's fate than their own safety. One of them asked the captain, "It is true that we are all going to drown, but between the two of us, who will drown first?"

Hatred breeds enmity which makes us immeasurably cruel hearted. This is beneficial to no one.

Nobody likes to be ignored. At a get-together or party, a good host welcomes you in a friendly and loving manner. Similarly when someone visits your home, your friendly gestures are admired and valued. Another way of being social is to greet all those whom you come across heartily.

'Devotees of Allah the Most-Gracious are those who walk with humility on earth, and when they are addressed by the foolish, they, reply with words of peace' (25:63)

HATIM'S FRIENDLY NATURE

The rich, social, friendly and generous Hatim had a camel that was very strong and fast. The king was informed that Hatim's generosity was well known and so was the speed and gait of his camel. The king wanted to own the camel and dispatched a messenger to Hatim along with ten courtiers. They alighted at Hatim's house and were openheartedly greeted.

That night Hatim had a feast prepared for them with delicious camel meat.

On the following day, when the messenger explained the purpose of his visit, Hatim became sad and replied, "Why did you not give me the message earlier? That swift paced camel was slaughtered to prepare your meal last night. I had no other means to entertain you and I would not let you go to sleep without a hearty meal."

Hatim gave splendid robes to the courtiers before they returned. When the news of generosity reached the king, he showered a thousand praises upon Hatim's generous and friendly nature.

LOVING NATURE

"Dispel evil with good' (23:96)

If you are social and friendly, it means that you have a loving nature. You are affectionate in your attitude towards others. The opposite of this is cruel, disliking and hateful. Those who are not loving, do not help anyone, neither are they kind and soft. This is of no help to any one.

'You shall never come to true piety unless you spend on others out of what you cherish yourselves' (3:92)

If a person falls, there are others to reach out and help, but those who have never been friendly or loving will always be alone when they face problems and difficulties in life. People in all societies organize themselves in relation to each other for work and other duties, and to establish bonds of relationship. They commonly organize themselves according to family traditions, work duties, social needs, religion and economic position. People who share ties by blood and marriage commonly live together in families. They love, respect and care for each other thereby bringing in happiness and satisfaction.

DIVINE COMMANDS

So much is the stress on being social and friendly in Islam that this value has been equated with service unto Allah. A Muslim is not only forbidden from doing harm to others, but he is also commanded to be positive and social and also to prevent others from causing any harm to the people in general. Removing a stone from the path or a thorn from the shadow of a tree may appear as trifle deeds, but they are good deeds which will be rewarded by Allah

Muhammad ﷺ asserted that no one can be a believer till he wished for his fellow-being what he wishes for himself.

NO PREJUDICES IN ISLAM

Islam does not ignore the differences that exist among human beings,but it disapproves of the prejudices which have arisen among mankind. Islam says that if there is any real difference between man and man it cannot be one of race, colour, country or language, but of ideas, beliefs and principles. Two children of the same mother, though they may be equal from the point of view of a common ancestry, will have to go their different ways in life if their beliefs and moral conduct differ. On the contrary, two people, one in the East and the other in the West, even though geographically and outwardly separated by vast distances, will tread the same path in life if they share the same code of moral behaviour. On the basis of this fundamental tenet, Islam seeks to build a principled and ideological society very different from the racial, nationalistic and parochial societies existing in the world today.

COOPERATIVE EFFORT

The basis of co-operative effort among men in such a society is not the place of one's birth but a creed and a moral principle. Anyone, if he believes in Allah as his Sustainer accepts the guidance of the Quran as the basic principle of his life, can join this community. All those who join this community will have the same rights and social status. They will not be subjected to any racial, national or class distinctions. No one will be regarded as high or low. No one will be looked down upon because of his birth or work. No one will claim any distinctive rights by virtue of his caste, community or ancestry. Man's merit will not depend on his family connections or riches, but only on whether he is better than others in moral conduct or excels others in piety and righteousness.

Such social order, transcending, as it does, geographical boundaries and the barriers of race, colour and language, is appropriate for all parts of the world; on its foundations can be raised the universal brotherhood of man. Those who do not accept this creed, while obviously not being received into the community, are treated with tolerance and humanity and guaranteed all the basic human rights.

It is clear that if two children of the same mother differ in their ideas, their ways of life will be different; but this does not mean that they cease to be brothers. In the same way, if two nations or two groups of people living in the same country differ in their fundamental beliefs, principles and ideology, their societies will also certainly differ; yet they will continue to share the common ties of humanity. Hence, the Islamic society offers to non-Muslims societies and groups the maximum social and cultural rights that can possibly be accorded.

When we care for somebody, we put their interests above our interests and the interest of complete strangers. They may be our relatives or friends. When your attitude reflects love and care, it makes others happy and an atmosphere of peace prevails. Happiness thus achieved shows that all fears and worries have disappeared. This acts in both ways and there is certain improvement in your life.

Being social and friendly does not depend on one's position in society or wealth. Islam makes no distinction between the rich and the poor in this regard. While the rich may be good with the help of their wealth, the poor may be good with the use of their hands and tongues. Under the Islamic system, every person is capable of good deeds. The Quran says that one who does good or evil, does it for his own benefit or loss:

'Whoever works righteousness benefits his own self, whosoever works evil, it is against his own self' (41:46)

Hospitality finds permanent place in Islamic teachings as it reflects our social and friendly nature. Guests should be invited regardless of their social status because, according to a holy tradition, the worst food is that in which the rich are invited and the poor are neglected.

Invitations should be accepted regardless of the social status of the host and the kind of food to be served. In this context the Quran relates the story Messenger Abraham (Ibrahim) (AS) and his guests:

'When they came to him, they said "Peace be to you", and he replied, "Peace be to you as well". They were rather unusual people who he could not recognize. He quickly went to his family in the house, and came back with a roasted calf. And served it to his guests saying 'Will you not eat of this?'(51:25,26,27)

QUALITIES OF FRIENDSHIP

The ancient Greeks considered friendship among the highest of virtues. It was an essential element in the happy or fully flourishing life. There are three kinds of friendship. The ones that are based on pleasure in another's company, or on usefulness in association or on mutual administration. All are essential to the good life. When we honestly ask ourselves which persons in our lives mean the most to us, we often find that they are those who, instead of giving advice, solutions or cures, have chosen rather to share pain and touch our wounds with a warm and tender hand. The friend who can be silent with us in a moment of despair or confusion; who can stay with us in an hour of grief and bereavement; who can tolerate all our misfortunes and face with us the reality of our powerlessness. That is a friend who cares.

BRIDGE OF LOVE

Once upon a time, two brothers who lived on adjoining farms faced a conflict. It was the first serious rift in forty years of farming side by side, sharing machinery and trading labour and goods as needed, without a hitch. Then the long collaboration fell apart. It began with a small misunderstanding and grew into a major difference, and finally it exploded into an exchange of bitter words followed by weeks of silence.

One morning there was a knock on John's (the elder brother) door. He opened it to find a man with a carpenter's toolbox. "I am looking for a few days work" he said. "Perhaps you could have a few small jobs here and there I could help with? Could I help you?" "Yes", said the elder brother, "I do have a job for you. Look across the creek at that farm. That's my neighbour, in fact he's my younger brother. Last week there was a meadow between us and he took his bulldozer to the river bank and now there is a creek between us. Well he may have done this to spite me, but I will do him one better. See the pile of lumber by the barn? I want you to build me a fence...an eight-foot fence...so I won't need to see his place or his face anymore."

The carpenter said, "I think I understand the situation. Give me the nails and wooden logs and I'll be able to do a job that pleases you."

The older brother had to go to the town, so he helped the carpenter get the material needed and then he was off for the day. The carpenter worked hard all that day measuring, sawing, nailing and hammering. About sunset when the farmer returned, the carpenter had finished his job. The farmer's eyes opened wide, his jaws dropped.

There was no fence there at all. It was a bridge—a bridge stretching from one side of the creek to the other. A fine piece of work. The neighbour, his younger brother, was coming across, his hands outstretched. He said, "You are quite a fellow to build this bridge after all that I have said and done!"

The two brothers stood at each end of the bridge, and then they met in the middle, taking each other's hand. They turned to see the carpenter hoist his toolbox on his shoulder. "No, wait! Stay a few days. I have a lot of other projects for you," said the younger brother.

"I'd love to stay on," the carpenter said, "but I have many more bridges to build."

BE A CARING PERSON

A careless word may kindle a strife, a cruel word may wreck a life while a timely word may level stress and a loving word may heal and bless. The happy ones do not necessarily have the best of everything; they just make the most of everything that comes along their way. Your friends, family and community are all situations that allow you to bring yourself together as a caring and giving person. Use that energy to reach out, get involved and serve others. Make yourself available not to control or benefit from a situation but rather to go and put your energy out for a loving, caring, helping and friendly gift.

FRIENDSHIP

Friendship favours no conditions,
Scorns a narrow-minded creed,
Lovingly fulfils its mission
Be it word or be it deed.

Friendship cheers the faint and weary,
Makes the timid spirit brave,
Warns the erring, Lights the dreary,
Smoothes the passage to the grave.

Friendship-pure, unselfish friendship,
All through life's allotted span,
Nurtures, strengthens, widens, lengthens,
Man's relationship with man

'Surely the Angels will come down to those who say, "Our Sustainer is Allah", and then remain steadfast, saying, "You should have neither fear nor regret but rejoice in the happy news of Paradise that has been promised to you. We are your friends in this life and in the Hereafter where you will get whatsoever you desire." (41:30,31)

32 AMBITIOUS AND FOCUSED

'If they cannot give you an answer, know that they are only following their lust and desires, and who can be farther away from truth than he who follows his lust without any guidance from Allah '(28:50)

One very important aspect of motivation is the willingness to stop and to look at things that no one else has bothered to look at. This simple process of focusing on things that are normally taken for granted is a powerful source of creativity. (Edward de Bono)

Ambition has both its negative and positive aspects. Negatively it is a desire for the possession of power, fame and superiority. In a good sense , it is the desire for excellence and to attain something. To lead a good , peaceful and decent life is what we all desire. The problem begins when we cross or exceed the limits of such a life and enter the domain of greed and avarice. Islamic values are very clear about achievements and excellence. Islam encourages a society that is free from the clash of interests among individuals. It declares that man is capable of conquering and subduing nature for his benefit if he holds firmly to the permanent values of life. These values are preserved in the Quran. They are true, trustworthy and reliable.

The personality and character of a person develop as a result of his own reaction to the different situation he faces in life. Every human being possesses infinite capacity for development and progress. Those who desire excellence and strive consistently for achievement are encouraged by Allah:

'For them are good tidings in the worldly life and in the Hereafter. No change is there in the words of Allah . That is what is the great achievement' (10:64).

'And Allah shall deliver those who guard (against evil) with their achievement; evil shall not touch them, nor shall they grieve' (39:61).

MANAGING EMOTIONS

To be true to yourself and those around you, it is a must to learn to manage your emotions. It is a critical step toward living a happy, successful and fulfilled life. This does not mean that you control them by ignoring and repressing them; it simply means listening to what they are telling you and trying to understand.

When you let your emotions control you, you miss the message they carry. When you ignore them for fear of what they might cause you to do or feel, they simply return later as anger. The power to control emotions is within yourself—no external force will control it for you.

Observe what you say as your emotions peak and fall. Identify any judgements you might have about the way you feel. These thoughts translate with what you believe is true about yourself. They can be accurate or untrue and damaging. You decide if change is in order. Yesterday is gone, tomorrow has not come yet. We have only today. Let us begin. If someone asked you how failure can be defined, the answer is simple. Failure is an important part of your success. Every failure provides an opportunity to improve. There are many forms of failures and their use should be avoided, for example:

1. Failing to act on the dreams and visions you have for yourself.
2. Hurting others for personal gain whether on purpose or by accident.
3. Failing to understand why you are here in this world.
4. Failing to understand that you are here to serve and help others and in return your needs will be taken care of.
5. Failing to continually raise your standards every day.

It must be remembered that the smallest deed done is greater than the best of intentions. People do not care how much you know until they know how much you care. Love is a language that can be heard by the deaf and seen by the blind.

'Do not bid others to be pious and do good deeds, while you forget your own selves' (2:44)

RIGHT CHOICE

As you travel through life and grow up, there are times when decisions are hard and have to be made, the solutions are scarce and confusing. There are some situations where all you can do is simply let go and move on. That is the time when you have to gather courage and choose a direction that would lead you to a new beginning.

'And to those among you who choose to move forward in virtue, or prefer to lag behind; every soul will be a hostage to its own deeds' (74:37,38).

Islamic values stand for life fulfilment and not life-denial. They command us to face facts and not to shrink from them. Asceticism, quietism and monasticism are all repugnant to the teachings of Islam. Islam recognizes the needs of the body and encourages all that is good in life.:

'(O Muhammad) Ask them 'who has forbidden the beautiful garment provided by Allah for His creatures? And who has forbidden the good and pure things of life provided by Him for sustenance?' (7:32)

'O children of Adam! Dress well, fully and decently at the time of every prayer. Eat and drink, but do not transgress and waste, for Allah does not like transgressors and those who waste' (7:31)

All you have to do is take a step forward. The process of change can be tough, there might be adventures you never imagined just waiting around the next bend; and wishes and dreams just about to come true in ways you will not understand.

Perhaps you will go places you never expected and see things you have never seen before. Perhaps you will find comfort in knowing that your friends are supportive of all that you do and believe whatever decisions you make. Remember very few people are ambitious in the sense of having a specific image of what they want to achieve. Most people's sights are focused on the next increment of money. Your goals are the maps that guide you to show what is possible in life.

If these goals and objectives are rightly guided and oriented in line with the Quranic values, the results will be positive and encouraging.

'Quran is the book We have sent down to you so that you may lead men out of darkness into light, by their Sustainer's command, to the path that leads to the Al-Mighty. The One to Whom all praise is due' (14:1)

THE 'WIKIPEDIA' MAN

Jimmy Wales, a 39 year old trader set out in 1999 to reinvent the encyclopedia for the Internet-age, free, up to date and available to all. He started by commissioning articles from experts. These articles were reviewed by knowledgeable people. In the first 18 months there were only 12 entries. At that rate it would have taken countless years to even come close to Encyclopedia Britannica. So, Wales created a free-form companion site based on a little-known software programme called Wiki (the Hawain term means quick) that makes it easy with the "edit this page" button—to enter and track changes to Web pages. The result was an overwhelming success. Wikipedia now has more than two million articles in English, nearly 20 times as many in Encyclopedia Britannica. The number doubles every year. Today Wales is celebrated as a champion of Internet enabled knowledge-base for everyone. He believes that amateurs can contribute as much as professionals and that talent can be found anywhere.

The efforts and confidence of Wales has led to what may prove to be the most powerful model of the 21st century.

LOOKING AHEAD

So, keep putting one foot in front of the other and taking your life day by day. There's a brighter tomorrow down the road. Don't look back, you are not going that way. If the circumstance of your life is not yet what you desire, there is a reason. It is because you have not yet become the person you should have been. Circumstances will change for the better to the extent you change for the better from your inside.

Develop the ability to recognize what is before your eyes, and what is hidden will be revealed to you. All great personalities in history understood their inner self and were focused on goals and objectives. This is the positive quality of being ambitious. Ultimately they were able to change the entire complexion of their nation. The important thing to see is what is written on the carpet and what is under it.

The Quran refers to different people and nations who were intelligent and wise, but they followed their evil desires and ambitions and had to pay the penalty.

'The tribes of Aad and Thamud too did We destroy as should have become obvious to you from whatever remains of their dwellings. They perished because Satan had made sinful doings seem attractive to them, and this had turned them away from the path of Allah despite their having been endowed with the ability to perceive the truth' (29:38

You cannot directly control everything in the world around you, but there is no need for that anyway. By controlling yourself and your thoughts feelings and actions, you can bring about the necessary changes that would fulfil your dreams.

We have the example of the 'Father of the Nation' Quaid-e-Azam Muhammad Ali Jinnah; who focused his thoughts and actions towards one goal – the creation of Pakistan. He was never emotional in his approach and always controlled the harsh circumstances around him. This gave him the necessary ability to fulfil his dreams.

WORK

Work is applied effort, it is whatever we put ourselves into. It is not what we do for a living, but what we do with our living. There are no menial jobs, only menial attitudes. The most satisfying work involves directing our efforts towards achieving ends that we ourselves endorse as worthy expressions of our talent and character.

The Quran recognizes those who strive for positive achievements:

'As for those who believe, and do righteous deeds, they are indeed the best of created beings' (98:7).

THE ANT CARRYING A HUGE BURDEN

This is a great lesson of life from one of the smallest creatures of nature—the Ant. One morning a tiny ant was carrying a huge feather on its back. Several times it was confronted by obstacles in its path, and after a momentary pause it would make the necessary detour. At one point the ant had to negotiate a crack in the concrete. After brief contemplation, the ant laid the feather over the crack, walked across it and picked up the feather on the other side then continued on its way. The ingenuity of the ant was fascinating. Here was a minute insect, lacking in size yet equipped with a brain to reason, explore, discover and overcome. But this ant, like the two-legged co-residents of this planet, also shares human failings. After some time, the ant finally reached its destination—a flower bed at the end of the terrace and a small hole that was the entrance to its underground home. And it was here that the ant finally met its match. How could that large feather possibly fit down small hole? Of course it could not. So the ant, after all this trouble and exercising great ingenuity, overcoming problems all along the way, just abandoned the feather and went home. The ant had not thought the problem through before it began its epic journey and in the end the feather was nothing more than a burden.

The Moral: Isn't OUR LIFE like that? We worry too much about our family; we worry about money or the lack of it, we worry about work, about where we live, about all sorts of things. These are all burdens—the things we pick up along life's path and lug them around the obstacles and over the crevasses that life will bring, only to find that at the destination they are useless and we can't take them with us. The focus should be on the essentials of life and our efforts should be well-planned in advance.

BELIEF IN SELF

Success grows from the inside out. Become successful on the inside to the point where superficial tokens of success do not matter. You will surely have more than you could desire.

Mark Twain pointed out, "Keep away from people who try to belittle your ambitions. Small people always do that but the really great make you feel that you too can become great."

Keep the company of those who believe in you. Your life is too important for anything less.

THE CONFIDENT PEASANT

A peasant named Shin lost his crops due to drought. He decided to go to another village and try his luck. He obtained a dozen boiled eggs from a merchant for his journey.

Seven years later Shin returned to his village riding a fine, black horse, followed by a servant and a carriage full of goods. He had become a rich man. The news of his arrival spread in the village and the merchant who had given him the dozen eggs on credit came demanding five hundred pieces of silver in payment of the old debt. Shin, of course, refused to pay such a large sum and the matter was taken before a judge. The merchant said, "I asked Shin for payment of five hundred silver coins, because twelve chickens might have hatched from the eggs he had taken on credit seven years ago. Those chickens would have become hens and cockerels, more eggs would have been laid, these too would have been hatched and so on. After seven years I might have had a great flock of fowls." The judge agreed and asked Shin the reason for his being late in appearing before him. Shin said, "I had a plate of boiled beans in the house and I was planting them in the garden to have a good crop next year!"

"Fool!" exclaimed the judge. "Since when did boiled beans begin to grow?" To which Shin promptly retorted, "And since when did boiled eggs grew into chickens?" The judge understood the point and the case was dismissed.

REALISTIC APPROACH

A simple and realistic approach to a matter solves many problems. It also shows how reasonable you are. Instead of being pessimistic and thinking you can't achieve your goals, be positive and thrive challenges. So keep yourself busy with positive tasks. Worrying too much is harmful. Spend time with your pets and friends and also develop a good creative hobby such as painting, reading good books, and writing short essays and stories. Don't do anything harmful to yourself such as the use of drugs, smoking and hanging around in the company of bad people.

When something goes wrong, people either tend to bounce back or fall apart. Those who have confidence in their capabilities harness inner strength and rebound more quickly from a setback or challenge. The guidance of the Quran in this respect is clear:

'Indeed with every hardship there is relief. Thus when you are relieved of your distress, still continue to work diligently and turn to your Rab (Nourisher) fervently with all your ;love' ((94:6,7,8).

SELF-CONFIDENCE

In contrast, those who are less confident, become overwhelmed and turn to unhealthy coping mechanisms. At times they even develop mental health problems. Self-confidence may not necessarily make your problems go away, but will give you the ability to see past them, find some enjoyment in life and handle future stresses better. Self-confidence is the ability to adapt well to stress, adversity, trauma or tragedy. It enables you to remain calm, stable and maintain healthy levels. It does not mean that you have to ignore feelings of sadness over a loss; nor does it mean that you always have to keep strong and that you cannot ask others for support. In fact, it makes you willing to reach out to others.

In such situations the best recourse is in the Divine Guidance which is the absolute truth and never fails:

'We have set you on the right path, therefore, follow that path, and follow not the whims of ignorant persons who do not know' (45:18).

There is no substitute for hard wok. To achieve success your top priority should be sincere hard work. Allah helps those who help themselves:

'Allah answers the prayers of those who believe and do righteous deeds and gives them more of His Grace' (42:26).

'Allah never changes the condition of the people, unless they themselves exert to change their own characteristics and their inner- selves' (13:11)

THE FATHER & HIS SONS

A farmer, being at death's door, and desiring to impart to his sons a secret, called them round and said, "My sons, I am shortly about to die, I would like you to know that in my farm there lies a hidden treasure; dig and you will find it." As soon as their father died, the sons took spade, fork and shovel and turned up the soil of the farm over and over again in their search for the treasure which they never found. However, the farm, after so thorough a digging produced a crop such as had never before been.

There is no treasure without toil.

'He who believes in his Sustainer need not have fear of loss or injustice' (72:130)

'It is neither your riches nor your children that can bring you nearer to Us; only he who attains to faith and does what is right and just, comes near Us, and it is these whom multiple reward awaits for all that they have done; and it is they who shall dwell secure in peace in the mansions of paradise' (34:37)

33 LOVING BOOKS AND READING

'This book (Quran) is free of doubts and is a guidance for all those who are conscious of Allah' (2:2)

No matter how busy you may think you are, you must find time for reading or surrender yourself to self-chosen ignorance. (Confucius)

There are two kinds of books; those written by men and those that are Divinely revealed. The Divinely revealed Books are the gifts of Allah to humans for their guidance, happiness and peace. All previous Divine Revelations have been updated and preserved in the Quran:

'Follow what is revealed to you by your Sustainer, Surely Allah is All-Knowing and All-Wise.' (33:2)

There is nothing that We have left out from recording (in Quran). (6:38)

Reading, writing, observing, listening and thinking are the main sources through which we acquire knowledge, wisdom and awareness. Books help us to assimilate all these sources and enrich ourselves and our culture and ultimately the whole nation benefits from it.

A book is a set of printed or written pages, fastened along one side and encased between protective covers. From an etymological perspective the word 'book' is synonymous with 'beech'; both branches of the same tree. In the old days the German tribes used strips of beech tree to write on. The Latin word for book is "Liber" from which we have the word 'library'. Nowadays we are lucky to have easy access to libraries and books.

The present century has revolutionized the communication systems. Internet and computer users have the entire world at their fingertips. Consequently we rely less on reference books now. Visits to the libraries have also become redundant. All this is no substitute for a book that will take its readers, of any age, along a steady and enlightening journey. Many people swear that if it were not for books, they would find the world a very dull and bleak place. The famous poet Lord Byron once said, "If I could always read, I should never feel the want of society."

GIFT OF A LIFETIME

Some years ago, at the Kolkata Book Fair, there was an elderly gentleman who visited a bookstall every day. He would inquire about the price of Encyclopedia Britannica, negotiate the discount available and leave. On the last day of the book- fair the salesman felt relieved to see that the elderly gentleman had finally decided to buy the Encyclopedia. He had a bag in his hand which he opened to pay. The bag was full of coins and currency notes of different denominations. As it is unusual for a customer to settle a bill in such a manner, the salesman's curiosity was aroused and he asked the elderly gentleman about the contents of the bag. The elderly gentleman replied that he had been saving money since his daughter was a little child just to give her the Encyclopedia as a wedding gift. As she was getting married it was time for him to fulfil his long cherished dream.

The Encyclopedia Britannica in those days was a prized possession. It was voluminous and expensive. It has always been considered a treasure of information and knowledge.

This episode not only shows a father's love for his daughter, but also his resolve to enrich her with a wonderful set of books when she was embarking on a new journey in her life.

Those who love books consider them to be their never failing friends. Like a good friend books enrich our life and help us in understanding life and humanity. Many people carry these friends around. They feel that they have the company of their favourite volume of whatever suits their fancy. Reading is a basic tool in the living of a good life. Although books are not made for furniture, yet there is nothing else that so beautifully furnishes a house. Unlike a computer you can take a book to bed. Those who love books and reading know that the knowledge of a good book awaits them at the end of a long day.

Reading broadens the mind's horizons and one can learn so much without actually living through the experience one reads about. Reading a variety of books gives one an understanding of the different dimensions of personalities and events, offering the reader a better perspective of the times one is living in. Readers' choice of books also shed light on the intellectual input that has shaped their thinking and thought process.

INTERESTING QUOTES ABOUT BOOKS AND READING

- A good book on your shelf is a friend that turns its back on you and remains a friend. (Anonymous)

- I find television to be very educating. Every time somebody turns on the set, I go in the other room and read a book. (Groucho Marx)
- Let books be your dining table,

  And you shall be full of delights

  Let them be your mattress

  And you shall sleep restful nights. (Anonymous)
- Books are not made for furniture, but there is nothing else that so beautifully furnishes a house. (Henry Ward Beecher)
- A house without books is like a room without windows. (Heinrich Mann)
- To acquire the habit of reading is to construct for yourself a refuge from almost all the miseries of life. (W. Somerset Maugham)
- Reading is to the mind what exercise is to the body. (Richard Steele)
- That place that does contain

  My books, the best companions, is to me

  A glorious court, where hourly I converse

  With the old sages and philosophers;

  And sometimes, for variety, I confer

  With kings and emperors, and weigh their counsels;

  Calling their victories, if unjustly got,

  Unto a strict account, and, in my fancy,

  Deface their ill-placed statues. (Francis Beaumont and John Fletcher)
- Never lend books, for no one ever returns them; the only books I have in my library are books that other folks have lent me. (Anatole France)
- Books are delightful society. If you go into a room and find it full of books—even without taking them from the shelves they seem to speak to you, to bid you welcome. (William Ewart Gladstone)
- If you can read this, thank a teacher. (Anonymous)
- No matter how busy you may think you are, you must find time for reading, or surrender yourself to self-chosen ignorance. (Confucius)
- There are many little ways to enlarge your child's world. Love of books is the best of all. (Jacqueline Kennedy)
- There are worse crimes than burning books. One of them is not reading them. (Joseph Brodsky)
- You don't have to burn books to destroy a culture. Just get people to stop reading them. (Ray Bradbury)

So what is it about books that can create such an immense grip on their readers? The answer lies in the essence of nearly every person's basic desire to satisfy his imagination and curiosity. Most readers relate to the books they are reading and subconsciously identify with certain characters and incidents of the plot. Reading is an active mental process that builds self-esteem through confidence. It also improves one's memory, discipline, and creativity and widens the horizon of life. A book inculcates the qualities of tolerance and forbearance. A book is a living force, yet it never strikes or harms you if you do not agree with it. It is an effective tool against intolerance and ignorance.

WHY READ BOOKS ?

The basic question that comes to mind is, 'Why should I buy a book?' or 'Why should I read a book?' Ask a horticulturist why he loves flowers and he will give you a thousand reasons. Similarly book-lovers, despite the adverse impact of television, cinema and computers, will give you a long list of reasons behind their love of books and reading.

Books and reading will always remain the primary source of knowledge throughout the world. They are also an important part of the Book Culture that contributes to human development and environment which is the sum total of knowledge, beliefs, arts, morals, laws, customs and habits acquired by humans as members of society. Despite the many advancements made in the world, reading still stands as one of the greatest gifts a parent can give to a child. Parents who incorporate the child's life will ensure success for both parent and child.

Our country is in need of a vision for its future. Young people must realize that this vision of progress, welfare, tolerance and peaceful coexistence will also depend upon the type of books they read.

BOOKS AND READING CULTURE

This book points to the importance of culture in the development and achievement of a nation. Culture in Latin means 'to cultivate'. But cultivate what? Generally all agree that it refers to three basic senses:

1. An intelligent pattern of human knowledge, belief and behaviour depending upon the capacity for learning.
2. A set of shared attitudes, values and goals that characterize institutions, organizations and social groups.
3. Excellence of taste in the fine arts and humanities.

All these ingredients of a bright vision can be achieved through our love for books and reading. Books contain the best that has been thought and said in the world. Most of our youth look to the West as model of progress. The least they can do is to be aware of their thoughts and practice. Books are the only medium through which this objective can be achieved

As compared to other means of entertainment that include music, cinema, playing games, watching television etc., reading is the most productive one as it improves vocabulary, knowledge and word power. Scientific research has proved that children and teenagers who love reading have comparatively higher intelligence level as compared to those who watch television and movies a lot. Reading enhances mental development and stimulates the muscles of the eyes thereby improving concentration and observation abilities. It enables you to come up with innovative and creative ideas.

This book reminds young people that man has natural gifts which differentiate him from other creations. Unlike them he is not a figure in the landscape, but he is the shape of the landscape. Books are the companions that will never fail you. They tell us about the code of heredity in the DNA spiral. They are the guide who leads us to the faculties of the human brain and philosophic thoughts of the philosophers and scientists. They tell us about the romantic beauty of the poets, artists and authors. They tell us about the reality of matter.

Young people should resolve to buy at least one or two books in a month and read them too. Remember there is no such thing as a bad book. A book is either good or badly written. It is the life blood of the master spirit.

Books authored by humans are relative and time bound. They do help in enhancing knowledge and understanding of history and concepts, theories and laws. They help in keeping in touch with past and contemporary situations and events. With every passing moment new ideas emerge and new discoveries are made. These should be evaluated and assessed in the light of Quranic values and applied practically for the benefit of humanity. Allah has not left out any facet of life untouched in the Quran. It is up to us to acquire knowledge and wisdom and to understand the guidance of this Book.

'Say," Then should I seek the source of law elsewhere than Allah, when it is He who has revealed the Book (Quran) to you, which distinctly explains everything' (6:114)

The Quran is the last and final Divine Revelation and is the ultimate guidance for the whole humanity. We have to seek guidance from it every moment of our lives. It has the solutions to all our problems and difficulties; but we too have to read it intelligently with rapt attention, imbibe its message, directives and principles with wisdom and then apply the Quranic values practically for a peaceful, happy and contented life.

A list of Quranic values , directives and guidance has been given in the first chapter of this book titled, 'Straight path of life'.

34 UNBIASED AND UNPREJUDICED

'O you who believe ! Be custodians of justice and witnesses for Allah even though your evidence and judgement is against yourselves or against your parents or your relation; whether it be against rich or poor, for Allah is nearer to both than you are to them. So, follow not the lusts of your hearts for you swerve from justice. If you twist and distort your evidence know ot well that Allah is fully aware of what you do' 4:135)

Prejudice is the child of ignorance. That is why opinions founded on prejudices are always sustained with the greatest violence. (K. Jeffrey)

Unbiased and unprejudiced means to be fair and impartial. Any tendency to favour a certain person or action leads to biased, prejudiced or unjustified personal likes and dislikes. The most common bias is to consider yourself superior to others because of your race and the colour of your skin. This is also called racism or racial prejudice. It is the belief that human races have distinctive characteristics that make them superior or inferior. So you should remember that no one is inferior or superior because of the colour of their skin, the language they speak, the country they live in or their position in society. It is only our good or bad deeds that determine our position as a human being. So remember not to be biased or prejudiced in a matter under dispute. Your approach should be fair, and unbiased; only then will you be able to take the right decision.

In his farewell address, Muhammad ﷺ proclaimed:

'O people ! Your Allah is one. An Arab has no preference over a non-Arab. Nor is a white man superior to a black man except by Allah-consciousness. Your lives, your properties and your honour are as sacred as this day (of Hajj)'

The Quran says:

'Those who are unjust to others in their daily lives will fail to balance their own personalities. They will spend their lives in sadness and humiliation as a result of their own actions. They will wander as if the darkness of night had covered their face. They are the ones who have built their Hell and they will inherit it in the Eternity' (10:27).

'We shall set up just balance on the Day of Judgment and no human being shall be wronged in the least, for though there be in him but the weight of a mustard seed of good or evil, We shall bring it forth, and none can take count as We do' (21:47).

HUMAN PREJUDICES

Human prejudice is a very strong and difficult emotion. Often we will want to believe some version of the facts because it supports our preconceptions. This book constantly points to the idea of impartiality. Each individual's interests are equally important. From within the moral point of view, there are no 'privileged' persons. Therefore, each of us must acknowledge other person's welfare as important as our own. No one should be treated as morally inferior. All oral judgments have to be supported by reason and established values.

Some feel that mentioning genders (male/female) also shows bias. Hence, instead of using words like businessman, chairman, forefathers, mailman, husband and policeman they use terms such as business-person, chairperson, ancestors, mail carrier, spouse, and police officer. Even words like aged, old and elderly are no more used. They have been replaced with words such as senior citizens and seniors. This shows that the choice of words in the language you use is very important and at times it shows your likes and dislikes. At times it becomes rude. For example, the word 'Negro' is no more used in the USA. 'African American' is the term now in use.

Parents and teachers are required to be unprejudiced, unbiased and impartial towards their children and students who should be treated fairly and without discrimination. The same is true of the treatment you give to your friends.

UPHOLDING FAIRNESS AND JUSTICE

The opposite of unbiased and unprejudiced is biased, prejudiced, partial and discriminatory. You must have noted that people unnecessarily and unjustly favour their relatives and family members even if they are wrong and have broken the law. This bias leads to corruption in society and the whole nation suffers. Only those countries have progressed that are unbiased and unprejudiced in their system of law and justice.

Prejudices are the basis of injustice. The Quran explicitly directs the Muslims to uphold fairness and justice in all circumstances and with everyone:

'O you who believe! Stand up firmly as witnesses for Allah for all fair dealings, and not let the hatred of a people deviate you from justice. Deal justly as it is next to piety and be conscious of your duty to Allah. Surely Allah is aware of all that you do' (5:8)

Nowadays all important hockey, football and cricket matches are supervised by neutral umpires so that the chances of favouring the host country could be done away with. Earlier there were complaints of biased umpiring in favour of the countries where the matches were played.

Do you know that about one person in every twenty-five is affected by prejudice? The early years of childhood is the time to begin to learn how to get along with people who are different. Prejudices and discrimination of all kinds create serious hurdles in the healthy development of people's personalities. It is also necessary to stop all kinds of prejudices. You should remember that what you do is as important as what you say. You can get a head-start by resisting bias and recognizing the differences between people as much as the similarities.

'Do not follow your desires lest you deviate from justice' (4:135)

'Surely Allah enjoins justice' (16:90)

THE PREJUDICED PASSENGER

The following scene took place on a British Airways flight between Johannesburg and London.

A white woman, about 50 years old, was seated next to a black man. She called the air hostess.

"Madam, what is the matter?" the air hostess asked. "You obviously do not see it then?" the white woman responded. "You placed me next to a black man. I do not agree to sit next to someone from such a repugnant group. Give me an alternative seat."

"Be calm please", the air hostess replied. "Almost all the seats on this flight are taken. I will go to see if another seat is available". The air hostess went away and then came back a few minutes later. "Madam, just as I thought, there are no other available seats in the Economy Class. I spoke to the captain and he informed me that there is also no seat in the Business Class. All the same, we still have one seat in the First Class."

Before the white woman could say anything, the air-hostess continued. "It is not usual for our company to permit someone from the Economy Class to sit in the First Class. However, given the circumstances; the captain feels that it would be scandalous to make someone sit next to someone so disgusting."

The air-hostess turned to the black man, and said. "Therefore, sir, if you would like to, please take your hand luggage because a seat awaits you in the First Class."

At the moment, the other passengers who were shocked by what they had just witnessed stood up and applauded.

Good and bad are properties of situations and people, and right and wrong are properties of actions. We all make mistakes. We should understand what is right and what is wrong. This prepares us to a standard of behaviour that is independent of what we want.

'You should always speak justly even if it involves a near relative' (6:152).

THREE LEVELS OF DEALING WITH PREJUDICES

In Islam the guidance about prejudices and bias are dealt with at three levels. The firsdt and the foremost level is that of the Creator. Muslims in general, and human beings in particular should note how the Quran treats this important facet of life:

Whatever wrong any human being commits, rests upon himself alone, and no bearer of burden shall bear the burden of another person'(6:164)

'Even if every soul who had transgressed and sinned, possessed the wealth of the earth and would willingly give as ransom on the Day of Judgment to redeem himself from the torment that would be in store for it; and they would feel remorseful in seeing the punishment. But the judgment passed against them would be in all fairness and none would be wronged in any manner' (10:54)

The second level is that of the exalted Messengers of Allah. In this context Allah's directives are clear and convincing. Addressing Muhammad ﷺ it says;

'Those who eagerly listen to falsehood, greedily swallowing all that is evil and if they come to you for judgment; you may either judge them or leave them alone; for if you leave them alone, they cannot harm you in any way. But if you judge between them then you should judge with utmost justice for Allah loves those who act justly' (5:42)

'My Nourisher (Rabb) has enjoined just action' (7:29).

The third level is that of all human beings. The Quran is full of verses in which human beings are directed to be unbiased, unprejudiced, just and fair. The Quran says:

'When you judge between people, judge with justice' (4:58).

On all levels we see that Islam discourages bias and prejudice and endorses justice and fairness.

35 PATRIOTISM

'O you who believe ! Stand up as witnesses for Allah in all fairness, and do not let the hatred of a people deviate you from justice' (5:8)

I should like to be able to love my country and still love justice. (Albert Camus)

PATRIOT

A patriot is a person who loves his country and is always ready to stand up and fight for its interests. This loyalty is shown in many ways. For example, the respect which is given to his national anthem and flag. The celebration of independence and republic days is another way people express their patriotic feelings.

PATRIOTISM

Patriotism is the virtue which slows the honour we give to our country. It is also the willingness to defend the country should it find it self under attack.

Patriotism means that the interest of the nation has to be placed above your own. In war time, patriots even sacrifice their lives. Patriotism becomes more evident and common when the country is fighting a war or is on the verge of fighting one. It has a definite function at such times to build national unity and strength through solidarity in the face of a common enemy.

The Quran treats all humanity as one:

'All men were one as community of one faith, but they differed and followed different ways. Had it been for the Word (Allah's Message) proclaimed by your Sustainer before, the differences would have been resolved' (10:19)

The differences mentioned in the above Ayat (Verse) led to enmity among men and lines were drawn to create nations who fought each other. Patriotism for a Muslim means to be justly loyal to the Divine Values that are practiced in letter and spirit in one's country

NATIONAL FLAG

Every country has a flag. It is a piece of cloth, usually rectangular and of distinctive colour and design. It is a symbol of national pride and allegiance. Flags were held high on crowded battlefields by the chiefs and commanders to let the soldiers know where their leader was. It also showed the soldiers that he was still alive and inspired them to keep fighting. Nowadays every country has a flag.

You must have heard and seen national songs honouring the spirit, beauty and historical personage or events of the nation. On the 14th of August (Independence Day) and 23rd March (Republic Day) the national flag of Pakistan is hoisted on buildings and people carry the green and white crescent flags with pride, loyalty and honour to show their love and devotion to the country.

A lot of patriotism is also seen when Pakistan and India play cricket matches. It is not bad to applaud and encourage your team, but the sense of hatred for the other team is against the spirit of the game.

'Whosoever ever kills a human being except as punishment for murder or for speaking corruption in the land, it shall be like killing all humanity; and whosoever saves a life serves the entire human race' (5:32)

Patriotism reflects your love and devotion to your country, but if you do not have an open mind and good nature, there will be extreme enmity, dislikes, aggression and hatred towards others. "My country–right or wrong", is the form of patriotism that has to be avoided. In today's world people of the world have to come closer for universal living and happiness. See what the two World Wars did killing millions and destroying so many cities. This is known as 'Demonic Patriotism' and has to be replaced by 'Healthy and positive patriotism'.

Young people, especially children need to feel a sense of belonging in their family, their classrooms and in their country. They can develop themselves in an atmosphere of respect, compassion, kindness and stability. If parents and teachers teach them to love, honour, be sympathetic and respectful towards their country as well as for their fellow men, they will not only be graced by a sense of patriotism, but will become better citizens and, in turn become role models for the future generations.

Patriots also keep their communities clean, cooperate in all walks of life, educate themselves and stand up for what is right and good about their country. Setting good examples of patriotism teaches them that every person counts no matter where they live, who they might be, or what country they represent.

'Allah loves those who purify themselves and are clean' (9:108)

In the above Ayat (verse) it is clear that those who follow the Divine Guidance are not only physically clean, but their minds are also unbiased and unprejudiced.

TRUE PATRIOTISM

It is now recognized the world over that patriotism today means loyalty not only to one's own country, but to the ideals and goals of a peaceful international community. It is better to be a citizen of the world than of one particular country. Right is right and wrong is wrong, no matter who does or says it. The Quran ordains that no human being, regardless of his position can enslave anyone (3:79)

Patriotism is selfless, but can be selfish when you place your country above all others even if others are equally good. You should love your country and at the same time appreciate others. Patriotism should not be the reason for hate and bias. Patriotism is love and devotion to your country and nationalism is love and devotion to one's government.

Learn about the history of your country. It will give you a better understanding when debating or discussing the merits of your feelings towards your country.

Speak well of your nation when visiting other countries. Involve yourself in activities geared towards the well-being of your country and participate in holiday events in honour of your country and those patriots who serve it.

Here are some heroes of Pakistan who dedicated and sacrificed their lives to serve Pakistan They are models of outstanding achievement and qualities. They did not exceed the limits of patriotism as desired by Islam.

PILOT OFFICER RASHID MINHAS SHAHEED

Born: 17th February 1951

Commissioned: 1971, Pilot, PAF

Pilot Officer Minhas was taxiing for take-off on a routine training flight when an Instructor Pilot forced his way into the rear cockpit, seized control of the aircraft and took off. When Minhas realized that the absconding pilot was heading towards India, he tried to regain control of the plane but was unable to do so. Knowing that it meant certain death, he damaged the controls and forced the aircraft to crash thirty two miles short of the border on 20th August 1971.

MAJOR RAJA AZIZ BHATTI SHAHEED

Major Raja Aziz Bhatti was a Pakistani soldier who received Pakistan's highest award for valour. He was born in Hong Kong in 1928. He moved to Pakistan before it became independent in 1947, living in the village of Ladian, in the district of Gujrat. There he enlisted with the newly formed Pakistani Army and was commissioned to the Punjab Regiment in 1950. Throughout his career, he was a brilliant officer and stood out in his class. He did very well at the academy and was awarded the Sword of Honour-the best in his year's batch of 300 officers, and the Norman Medal. He received his honours from Liaquat Ali Khan, the first Prime Minister of Pakistan, who was later assassinated.

On 6 September, 1965, the Indo-Pak War of 1965 broke out between India and Pakistan. Major Bhatti was posted in the Burki area of Lahore sector. As the company commander, Major Bhatti chose to move his platoon forward under constant firing from Indian tanks and artillery. For three or more days he went without rest. He resisted for five days and nights defending a Pakistani outpost on the strategic BRB canal. On 11 September, he was reorganizing his company and directing the gunners to shell the enemy positions. In order to watch every move of the enemy, he had to place himself in an elevated position, where he was exposed to enemy fire. He led his men from the front under constant attack from Indian Artillery. Although he countered every Indian offensive in his area, he was hit by an enemy tank shell in the chest while watching the enemy's moves, and thus dying instantly. His death struck many hard and he is remembered by many.

A day before his death, the commanding officer had sent to him word that since he had been fighting untiringly for the last six days, he should take a little rest and that another officer was being sent to replace him. Major Aziz, who was filled with a battle spirit and the will for martyrdom replied, "Do not recall me. I don't want to go back. I will shed the last drop of my blood in the defence of my dear homeland." He is buried at his village in Ladian in the Gujrat district.

Each year, Major Bhatti is honoured in Pakistan on 6 September, also known as Defence Day. Bhatti was awarded the Nishan-e-Haider, the nation's highest military award for gallantry for the exemplary courage he displayed till his death.

JAHANGIR KHAN

Jahangir Khan, born on December 10, 1963, is a former World No. 1 professional squash player from Pakistan, who is considered by many to be the greatest player in the history of the game. During his career he won the World Open six times and the British Open a record ten times. Between 1981 and 1986 he was unbeaten in competitive play for five years. During that time he won 555 matches consecutively. This was not only the longest in squash history, but also one of the longest unbeaten runs by any athlete in top-level professional sports. He retired as a player in 1993 and has served as the President of the World Squash Federation since 2002.

PROFESSOR ABDUS SALAM

The name of Abdus Salam is linked forever to the International Centre for Theoretical Physics, Trieste, Italy. Not only did he envisage the Centre as a place where scientists could carry out research of the highest level, but through the ICTP he also managed to set an example for other nations to follow. Professor Salam became a widely known and charismatic figure in international, scientific and political circles. He travelled extensively throughout the world and, in his discussions with heads of states and governments, he was able, in a convincing manner, to put forward his views regarding the paramount importance of supporting science in their own countries for the benefit of humanity. His pursuit of science for peace capable of filling the gap between the North and South of the planet shall remain as an example for those who endeavour to achieve the cultural and social development in poor countries. Thanks to the leadership of Professor Salam, ICTP has been a major forum for the international scientific community and a model for similar establishments both in Trieste and abroad. Professor Salam has been one of the greatest exponents in physics this century. Born in Jhang, Pakistan, in 1926, he was educated at Punjab University, St. John's College, Cambridge and Cavendish Laboratory, Cambridge where he obtained his Ph.D in 1952. He then returned to Pakistan where he served as a Professor at Government College, Lahore and Punjab University. There he suffered the isolation which scientists experience when they are not supported by their home countries. There was no tradition of doing any postgraduate work; there were no journals; there was no possibility of attending any conferences. He returned to Cambridge to take up the position of a lecturer. In 1957 he was appointed as full professor of Theoretical Physics at Imperial College. Fired by his own unhappiness at having had to leave his country, he was determined to find a way of making it possible for those like him to continue working for their own communities while still having opportunities to remain first-rate scientists. It was thus in 1960 that he conceived the idea of setting up an International Centre for Theoretical Physics with funds from the international community. The Centre was setup in 1964 in Trieste, Itlay and has now been renamed The Abdus Salam International Centre for Theoretical Physics.

SOHAIL ABBAS

Sohail Abbas is the highest scorer of goals in International Hockey breaking Paul Litjens of Holland record of 274 goals for the most goal scored in international compitition.

Early life:

Born in karachi on 9th June 1975, Sohail comes from a sporting family. Sohail has often said that his inspiration came from his uncle, Safdar Abbas, a left-winger who scored against Argentina during the 1973 World cup as a 16-year-old boy. As a young hockey player, his potential was not realized for some time.

He had difficulty making an impact on the professional hockey leagues. Like many Pakistani hockey players, he is a product of the Pakistan Junior Squad. He played for Pakistan in the 3rd Junior Asia cup at Singapore in 1996.

He made his debut in 1998 in the national team and has since become arguably hockey's most prolific goalscorer of all time.

He was leading scorer in 8th Pakistan-India (10 goal), 9th Azlan Shah Cup (12 goals) and 5th Asia Cup (16 goals). Of 16 Asia Cup's goals, seven were against Sri Lanka which allowed him a place in a select band of nine players who registered double hat-tricks in international circuits for Pakistan. His 60 goals in 1999 beat the world record of Litjens (58 goals) and national record of Sardar (50 goals) in one calendar year.

He is the highest goal scorer in the history of field hockey with his current goal tally at 348, as of 9 August 2012. Abbas scored his 267th international goal during the Champions Trophy in Amritsar, India to equal the 22 year old record of Dutch penalty corner specialist Paul Litjens on 4 October 2004 and then on 8 October he broke the Dutchman's record while the Pakistan Hockey team was playing in India. He retired in December 2004, just after the Champions Trophy in Lahore along with another Pakistani great Waseem Ahmad, when he was only 27 years of age. In July, 2006, he decided to return to international hockey. Since the summer of 2005 Waseem and he both have played for a Dutch club. He struck his 33rd goal to break Mark Hager's 9-year old record. His 33rd goal emerged from the penalty-mark when he converted a 66th minute penalty-stroke against India in Pakistan's 2-1 win on fourth day of 26th Champions Trophy. The Australian striker had registered 32 goals from 1985 to 1995. He took 11 editions for his 32 goals while Sohail did the needful in his 6th CT and added another on 12 December tie to make his final Champions' Trophy total 34.

Sohail was also leading scorer at the 2000 Olympic Games, Athens, with 11 goals, and of the 9th Indo-Pak series, with seven goals. Mixing his impressive hitting abilities with drag-flicks, Abbas has proved himself to be the world's most consistent drag-flick converter, his success rate being over 65% mark.

Sohail matched the world record on 4 October 2000 during the fifth test against India at the Dhyan Chand Stadium, Amritsar. Sohail was already the holder of three world records in his six-year international career, before Amritsar's landmark. He is the scorer of the highest number of goals (60) in a calendar year as well as the holder of the title of fastest century and double century of goals in international hockey. He reached the double century of goals on 17 August 2003 at Wagener stadium when he struck twice in 6-5 thrilling win over Argentina during 25th CT.

Sohail's extraordinary talent and goal scoring prowess mean that he is a target of hockey clubs all over the world. He gets offers from clubs of numerous countries and represented Dutch club Amsterdam in 1999. In Netherlands, the hockey league, like soccer, runs for as long as six months with a winter break in between. Due to his commitments with the Pakistan team, Sohail only played for nine weeks and that too in two spells. He was provided with free lodging and boarding, offered a car and paid as much as 700 dollars per match.

After serving Pakistan for almost 14 years, Abbas was awarded the captaincy of the national hockey side for the first time in the Azlan Shah Cup and London Olympics 2012.

HANIF MOHAMMAD

Hanif Mohammad (born 21 December 1934 in Junagadh - now in Gujarat, India) is a former Pakistan cricketer. He played for the Pakistani cricket team in 55 Test matches between 1952/53 and 1969/70 and averaged 43.98, with twelve hundreds.

The highest of Hanif's Test centuries was the famous 337 made against West Indies in a six-day test at Bridgetown in 1957/58. After Pakistan found itself following on from a first-innings deficit of 473 runs on the afternoon of the third day, Hanif spent more than sixteen hours at the crease compiling his runs, allowing Pakistan to draw the game. It remains the longest innings in Test history (and stood as the longest in all first-class cricket for over 40 years). It is the only test match instance of a triple century in a team's second innings. Displays such as this earned him the nickname "Little Master".

In 1958/59, he surpassed Don Bradman's record for the highest individual first-class innings. Hanif made 499 before being run out attempting his five hundredth run; this mark stood for more than 35 years before being eclipsed by Brian Lara in 1994. In all he made 55 first-class centuries and finished with a strong first-class career average of 52.32. He could bowl with either arm, and kept wicket on a number of occasions.

Many of Hanif's brothers and son were also cricketers: his brothers Mushtaq, Sadiq and Wazir all played Tests for Pakistan, as did his son Shoaib. Another brother Raees was once twelfth man for Pakistan, and four nephews had first-class careers.

RANA LIAQUAT ALI KHAN

Begum Rana Liaquat Ali Khan was born in a Kumauni family at Almora in the United Provinces of Agra and Oudh. She was educated at the University of Lucknow where she obtained a first class Masters degree with honours in Economics in 1929.

She began her career as a teacher in the Gokhale Memorial School after completing the Teachers Diploma Course from the Diocesan

College, Calcutta. She was later appointed as Professor of Economics in the Indraprastha College, Delhi.

In December 1932, she was married to Nawabzada Liaquat Ali Khan. After the reorganization of Muslim League, Begum Rana devoted herself to the task of creating political consciousness amongst the Muslim women. Her struggle for emancipation continued till the creation of Pakistan for Muslims of India in 1947.

After the assassination of her husband Liaquat Ali Khan in 1951, Begum Rana continued her services for the social and economic benefit of women of Pakistan till her death in 1990.

As wife of the first Prime Minister of Pakistan, Begum Rana took the lead in starting the women's voluntary service in 1948. Women were encouraged to take up responsibilities in administering first aid, organizing food distribution, dealing with health problems, epidemics and clothing, and above all, in providing moral and emotional support. She also took the initiative of introducing defense training for women. On her own initiative, she formed the Pakistan Women's National Guard (PWNG) and the Pakistan Women Naval Reserve (PWNR) in 1949, and was appointed as the Chief Controller of both, with the rank of a Brigadier. Viewed in the perspective of the partition massacres, where helpless women had been brutally treated, the idea was not entirely unrealistic. The PWNG and PWNR could not survive for long and were disbanded soon after Begum Rana went abroad as Pakistan's Ambassador.

Establishment of APWA:

In 1949, Begum Rana arranged a conference of over 100 active women from all over Pakistan. The conference announced the formation of a voluntary and nonpolitical organization for the social, educational and cultural uplift of the women, named as All Pakistan Women's Association (APWA). She was nominated as its first President.

Begum Rana served as Pakistan's ambassador to the Netherlands in the 1950s and as ambassador to Italy in the 1960s. She was the:

First Muslim woman Ambassador and Doyen of the Diplomatic Corps (while in the Netherlands),
First Muslim woman Governor (of Sindh Province in the mid-1970s),
First Muslim woman Chancellor of a university (all the universities in Sindh)
First Muslim woman delegate to the UN, and
First Muslim woman to win the United Nations Human Rights Award,
First Muslim woman to receive the Woman of Achievement Medal, (1950).

Awards and honours:

- Queen Juliana of the Netherlands conferred on her the Grand Cross of Orange-Nassau. Recipient of the International Gimbel Award for service to humanity. (1962)
- United Nations Prize in the Field of Human Rights for her outstanding contribution to the promotion and protection of the human rights embodied in the Universal Declaration of Human Rights and in other United Nations human rights instruments. (1978)

Hakim Mohammed Saeed (1920-1998)

Hakim Mohammed Saeed was a prominent and world acclaimed medical researcher, scholar, philanthropist and a former Governor of Sindh Province from 1993 until 1996. He was one of Pakistan's most renowned medical researchers in the field of Eastern Medicine. He established the Hamdard Foundation in 1948. In a few years time, the herbal medical products of Hamdard Foundation became household names in Pakistan and around the world. He authored and compiled about 200 books in English and Urdu on philosophy, science, health, religion, education, culture, natural medicine, social problems and travelogues. Besides writing travelogues of countries he visited, he also wrote books for youth and children. He also edited some journals such as Hamdard Islamicus, Hamdard Medicus, Journal of the Pakistan Historical Society "Historicus", Hamdard Sehat and Hamdard Naunehal.

He obtained B.Pharm and B.S. in Medicinal Chemistry in 1942 from the University of Delhi and M.Pharm in Pharmacy from the same institution. After partition he came to Pakistan with his wife and daughter. He established the Hamdard Laboratories and served as its first director until his death in 1998. In 1952 the University of Ankara conferred Ph.D in Pharmacy and he returned to Pakistan to devote his life to medicine research. In 1953, after his doctorate, Said joined the Sindh University as the Associate Professor of Pharmacy..

In the fifty years of his active career as a practitioner of Greco-Arab medicine par excellence, Hakim Mohammed Saeed also achieved international recognition as a scholar and researcher in Medicine. In recognition of his meritorious services and scholarly achievements, he was awarded Nishan-e-Imtiaz (Posthumous) by the Government of Pakistan in 2002.

He was a man of vision, a multifaceted personality, a physician, author of books, and editor of journals, bibliophile, an organizer, an idealist, an innovator, an educationist and above all a patriot of the highest order. He sacrificed his life in the service of the nation. In a life span of 78 years he made enormous contributions in the field of health, science, education and culture, which has left an imprint on the course of history for generations to follow.

The crowning activity of his life is the establishment of Madinat-al-Hikmah. It comprises Hamdard University with such institutes as Hamdard College of Medicine and Dentistry, Hamdard Al-Majeed College of Eastern Medicine, Hafiz Muhammad Ilyas Institute of Herbal Sciences, Hamdard Institute of Education & Social Sciences, Hamdard Institute of Management Sciences, Hamdard Institute of Information Technology, Hamdard School of Law, Faculty of Engineering Science & Technology, Hamdard Public School and Hamdard Village School. Bait-al-Hikmah (the Library) is also a constituent part of Madinat-al-Hikmah. This is one of the biggest and well-stocked libraries of Pakistan. The University has city campuses in Karachi, Lahore and Islamabad which are a testament to his vision of a prosperous and progressive Pakistan

Apart from being a great educational leader, he was also one of the finest exponents of Eastern Medicine and had treated millions of patients from all over the world including Pakistan, Europe, Africa and the Middle East by the time of his death in October 1998. He had lent a new dimension to Alternative Medicine having it recognized by the World Health Organization (WHO).

He attended and read papers at numerous conferences all over the world and organized a number of International conferences for promotion of science in Pakistan in collaboration with national and international organizations including UNESCO and WHO. He also held important offices and memberships of dozens of national and international organizations related to education and health care, the fields to which his contributions are universally acknowledged.

On October 17 in 1998, Hakim Saeed was assassinated by a group of unknown assailants while he was on his way to the Hamdard Laboratories.